Modular A-Level

Aiming High

A Flexible Learning Course for the new
AS and A–Level Mathematics Syllabuses

P1

by
Barbara Young

Tarporley Community High School, Cheshire

Cartoons by Jenny Smith and Matthew Staff

This text delivers the P1 syllabuses for OCR, AQA and Edexcel

ACKNOWLEDGEMENTS

Many thanks to all those Y12-13 Tarporley High School students who have borne the brunt of the experimentation which has gone with the development of these texts, over a period of 5-6 years. Their patience, good humour and positive criticism has been excellent, and I cannot thank them enough for the many good ideas that they have given me.

The publishers would like to thank the following examination boards for their kind permission to include questions from past examination papers: OCR, AQA and Edexcel.

© The 'Maths Is ...' Jugglers
2, Millview Close, Bulkeley, Malpas, Cheshire, SY14 8DB

This edition was first published in Great Britain 2000
British Library Cataloguing in Publication Data

ISBN   1 – 874428 – 75 – 1

Printed and bound by PRINTCENTRE WALES, Mold, Flintshire

CONTENTS

Unit 6: Completing the square   (pages 102-110)
Completing the square
Solving quadratic equations by completing the square (derivation of 'the formula')
Quadratics (max/min values, vertex and curve sketching)   COMPETENCE TEST

Unit 7: Integration   (pages 111-122)
Integration as reverse of differentation
Integration of x^n
Solve problems involving constant of integration
Definite integrals
Improper integrals   **[OCR only]**
Area under the curve or between two curves   COMPETENCE TEST

Unit 8: Trigonometry   (pages 123-135)
Sine, cos, tan graphs and sin, cos, tan for any angle
Identities ($\tan x \equiv \sin x \div \cos x$ and $\sin^2 x + \cos^2 x \equiv 1$)
Exact values of sin, cos, tan of $30°$, $45°$, $60°$ **[OCR only]**
Solutions of trig equations (not radians)
Solutions of trig equations (radians) **[Edexcel only]**
Odd, even and periodic functions **[AQA only]**   COMPETENCE TEST

Unit 9: Sequences and Series   (pages 136–152)
Sequences, inc.those given by a formula for the nth term **[Edexcel & AQA only]**
Arithmetic Series **[Edexcel & AQA only]**
Sigma notation **[Edexcel & AQA only]**
Geometric Series **[Edexcel only]**
Σr, Σr^2, Σr^3 **[AQA only]**   COMPETENCE TEST

Unit 10: Functions and Numerical Methods   (pages 153-165)
Function notation **[AQA only]**
Composition of functions **[AQA only]**
Domain, range and inverse **[AQA only]**
Graphs of functions and their inverses **[AQA only]**
Location of roots by change of sign **[AQA only]**   COMPETENCE TEST

Unit 11: Polynomials and the Factor Theorem   (pages 166-174)
Manipulation of polynomials **[Edexcel only]**
Algebraic division **[Edexcel only]**
Factor theorem **[Edexcel only]**
Identities **[Edexcel only]**   COMPETENCE TEST

A-Level Questions : start of revision for P1 modular exam.

ANSWERS

> *If two teachers are taking the same class, suggest:*
> *Teacher A: Units 1, 4, 5, 8   Teacher B: Units 2, 3, 6, 7*
> *[Units 9, 10, 11 are totally independent]*

This book can be used as a standard text book. All topics are developed using a structured approach. However, it was developed as a Flexible Learning course.

Features of the Flexible Learning Course

- The first unit in P1 is a "bridge" between GCSE and AS/A-Level. A diagnostic test is provided and advice given on ways of using this unit.
- Each module is divided into units, lasting 2-5 weeks.
- Students work through each unit on their own, asking for help from the teacher as it is required. This way students get individual tuition as and when they need it. However, the teacher can teach some or all of the material to the whole class or to groups of students, using their experience and expertise to judge what is best for their group of students.
- At the end of each unit, the student does a competence test, using the text for reference, if needed. The competence tests are in the text, at the end of each unit. When the teacher has marked this, the teacher discusses it with the student, looking for weaknesses in understanding and/or explanation, and hands it back to the student for corrections to be done. In extreme cases, the student knows that the teacher may ask to see the student's file of work on this topic. This picks up the cases where a student has not done all of the work ! [The answers to the competence tests are not included, as students need to be able to do this test without access to any answers.]
- Only when all corrections are done to the teacher's satisfaction, can the student sit the end-of-unit test, which is done under standard test conditions. Marks below 70% trigger an investigation into what has gone wrong and, eventually, a re-test.
- Each student is also given a booklet containing study advice, which comes complete with due dates for each competence test, and for the modular exams. As soon as the competence test has been handed to the teacher for marking, the student starts the next unit.
- At the end of each module will be a selection of exam questions for the relevent board, organised into topics.

Advantages of the Flexible Learning Course

- Students take responsibility for organising their own work. Having due dates for the whole module, and the date for the modular exam, they can see that there is little room to get behind.
- University visits, field trips, etc. do not disrupt the course. Since students have dates to work to, they organise their work to fit round these interruptions.
- Individual tuition means that students get help as and when they need it.
- Able students have everything they need here to work on their own. Let them go and watch them fly.

AIMING HIGH

Unit 1
The Bridge between GCSE and AS/A-Level

CONTENTS
Section 1: Equation solving techniques
Section 2: Changing the subject of a formula
Section 3: An important technique (rearranging equations like $px - q = cx + t$)
Section 4: Expansions (including difference of two squares, squaring brackets)
Section 5: Properties of a circle (including brief review of trig and Pythagoras)
Section 6: Cosine Rule and Sine Rule
Section 7: Applications of ratio (dividing lines in a given ratio, similar Δs, areas and volumes of similar shapes)
Section 8: Proportion
Section 9: Miscellaneous Techniques (LCMs and applications to algebraic fractions, HCFs and applications to factorisation, volumes of cones and spheres)

Note to the Teacher:
'The Bridge' is entirely different to all the other units in this course.
Think carefully about how you can best use it, with your students.

Suggestions on how to use 'The Bridge':

- do all of it

- leave it out

- just pick the parts out that you think are necessary for your group, and do those (Section 3 is recommended)

- set students the **DIAGNOSTIC TEST** and devise an individual programme of work for each student. This could be done over a set period of time *or* it could be set to run alongside another unit, with a date by which it should be completed. This is useful for classes where there are both Intermediate and Higher Level GCSE students.

- leave the unit at first, and send students back to a part of it, when you think they need that part

- set it to some students to be done in the summer vacation before they start AS/A-Levels.

Diagnostic Test for Unit 1 ('The Bridge')

Each question in the diagnostic test is related to part of 'The Bridge' (link is in brackets). For each question:
- if you have not met questions like this, or cannot do them, do the whole of the related part of the unit
- if you can do the question only after you have looked at the relevant part of the unit, you need to do some practice on this technique. Do as much practice as you feel you need.
- if you can do it easily, omit the related part of the unit.

1. Solve $3p + 5 = 7p - 15$. Show all working. (D1.1)

2. Solve $5v - 2(3 - v) = 15$. Show all working. (D1.2)

3. Solve $5\sqrt{(x - 2)} = 30$ Show all working. (D1.3)

4. Solve $\dfrac{x-1}{5} + \dfrac{1}{4} = 2$ Show all working. (D1.4)

5. Solve $\dfrac{n+1}{n-1} = \dfrac{7}{9}$ Show all working. (D1.5)

6. Make x the subject of this formula: $mx + ny = p$ (D2.1)

7. Make p the subject of this formula: $\dfrac{h + pn}{m} = v$ (D2.2)

8. Make n the subject of $\sqrt{(2d - n)} = k$ (D2.3)

9. Explain why $n = \dfrac{a-b}{-c}$ and $n = \dfrac{b-a}{c}$ are equivalent formulae (D2.4)

10. Make n the subject of $\dfrac{bn}{a} + c = d$ (D2.5)

11. Make x the subject of $ax + t = d - cx$ (D3.1)

12. Multiply out $(3x + 1)(2x - 5)$ (D4.1 & 4.2)

13. Factorise $25a^2 - 49b^2$ (D4.3)

14. Expand: $(2x - 7)^2$ (D4.4)

15. Copy and complete: $x^2 + 10x + 25 = (\ldots\ldots\ldots)^2$ (D4.5)

16. Work out the sizes of the lettered angles and the length of the chord.

    O is the centre of the circle and XY is a tangent. (D5.1)

17. Work out the sizes of the lettered side and the lettered angle in $\triangle$PQR. (D6.1 & 6.2)

18. Work out the area of $\triangle$ PQR. (D9.4)

19. A is (1,4), B is (11,9). P is on the line AB
    and AP : PB = 2 : 3. Find the coordinates of P. (D7.1)

20. Work out the lengths of
    PT and ST. (D7.2)

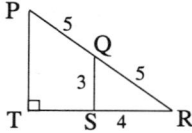

21. Two similar triangles have heights 2 cm and 5 cm. (D7.3)
    The area of the larger triangle is 12.5 cm².
    Calculate the area of the smaller triangle.

22. Two similar prisms have lengths 10 cm and 15 cm. (D7.4)
    The volume of the smaller prism is 24 cm³.
    Work out the volume of the larger prism.

23. V is directly proportional to r and s^2 and inversely proportional to t.
    When $r = 4$, $s = 3$ and $t = 15$, $V = 12$. Work out the value of V when
    $r = 3$, $s = 6$ and $t = 20$. (D8.1 & 8.2)

24. Simplify this expression: (D9.1)
    $$\frac{3}{x(x + 1)} + \frac{4}{x}$$

25. Factorise fully : $4mn^2p^3 + 2m^3np^2$ (D9.2)

26. Work out the volume of a hemisphere with base radius 10 cm (D9.3)

ANSWERS

1. $p = 5$ 2. $v = 3$ 3. $x = 38$ 4. $x = {}^{39}/_4$ 5. $n = -8$

6. $x = \dfrac{p - ny}{m}$ 7. $p = \dfrac{vm - h}{n}$ 8. $n = 2d - k^2$

9. If you multiply numerator and denominator by -1, you get the
   alternative equivalent form of the fraction.

10. $n = \dfrac{a(d - c)}{b}$ 11. $x = \dfrac{d - t}{a + c}$ 12. $6x^2 - 13x - 5$

13. $(5a - 7b)(5a + 7b)$ 14. $4x^2 - 28x + 49$ 15. $(x + 5)^2$

16. $a = 30°$, $b = 60°$, $x = 17.32$ cm   17. $c = 9.42$ cm, $d = 72°$ 18. 22.3

19. (5,6)   20. PT $= 6$, TS $= 4$ 21. 2 cm²   22. 81 cm³

23. 27   24. $\dfrac{7 + 4x}{x(x + 1)}$ 25. $2mnp^2(2np + m^2)$

26. 2093 cm³

Unit 1: The Bridge

Section 1: Equation solving techniques

> In this section you will review techniques for solving linear equations.

DEVELOPMENT

D1.1: Basic linear equations

> **A linear equation** is any equation that can be rearranged into the form
> $y = mx + c$, which is the standard equation of a straight line.

1. Which of these are linear equations ?

    A: $y = 3x$ B: $x + 3y = 7$ C: $xy = 4$

    D: $y = 2x^2 + 4$ E : $x = 5y + 2$ F: $y = x(x + 1)$

<u>Solving linear equations</u>   REMEMBER :

Headbanger

- whatever you do to one side of an equation, you must do the same to the other side
- aim to get all the letters on one side of the equation and all the numbers on the other side
- ALWAYS SHOW ALL THE WORKING OUT.

In all examinations candidates are expected to construct and present clear mathematical arguments, consisting of logical deductions and precise statements involving correct use of symbols and connecting language.

Use the examples as a guide on how to set out solutions.

EXAMPLE   Q: Solve $3x + 1 = x + 7$

A:
$$3x + 1 = x + 7 \quad \big|{-x - 1}$$
$$\Rightarrow \quad 2x = 6 \quad \big|{+2}$$
$$\Rightarrow \quad \boxed{x = 3}$$

Hints:
- start by stating the given equation
- the necessary working is shown in the dotted box
- $\Rightarrow$ is read as 'implies' or 'which gives'
- the explanations to the right of the dotted box, which clarify how the next line is obtained, are useful but not essential

Solve each equation. Show all working.
Give exact answers (integers or fractions).

2. $3v - 7 = v + 6$ 3. $5m + 4 = 2m + 9$

4. $5 + 2c = c + 3$ 5. $4 + 3e = 8 - e$

Integers are ...−2, −1, 0, 1, 2, ...

EXAMPLE   Q: Solve $x - 5 = 3x - 7$

A:
$$x - 5 = 3x - 7 \quad \big|{-x + 7}$$
$$\Rightarrow \quad 2 = 2x \quad \big|{+2}$$
$$\Rightarrow \quad 1 = x$$

Hint: It is easier if the lettered term is positive.
To achieve this, you may sometimes need to put the lettered terms on the right of the equation.

Solve each equation. Show all working. Give exact answers.

6. $5m + 17 = 7m - 3$ 7. $13 - 4p = 2p + 3$ • *Check your answers.*

D1.2: Equations with brackets

EXAMPLE	Q: Solve $9m - 2(m + 3) = m + 7$
A:	$9m - 2(m + 3) \;=\; m + 7$
$\Rightarrow$	$9m - 2m - 6 \;=\; m + 7$
$\Rightarrow$	$7m - 6 \;=\; m + 7$
$\Rightarrow$	$6m \;=\; 13$
$\Rightarrow$	$\boxed{m \;=\; {}^{13}/_6}$

Solve each equation. Show all working. Give exact answers.

1. $4(n - 3) + 7 \;=\; 2n$

2. $7(4 - 2u) \;=\; 3u + 2$

3. $2m + 7 - (m - 2) = \; 5m - 3$

4. $6(p - 3) + 2(3p + 5) \;=\; 9$

5. $7b - 2(4 - 2b\,) \;=\; 3b$

6. $5v - (9 - 2v) \;=\; 5$

7. $3m + 2(4\,m - 3) \;=\; 3 - 5m$

• *Check your answers.*

D1.3: Equations with square roots

Cringo

The trick here is to get the term inside the √ sign on its own, on one side of the equation. Then square both sides of the equation.

EXAMPLE	$\sqrt{x} + 2 = 5$		EXAMPLE	$\sqrt{(x - 1)} = 4$	
$\Rightarrow$	$\sqrt{x} = 3$		$\Rightarrow$	$x - 1 = 16$	*squaring*
$\Rightarrow$	$\boxed{x = 9}$		$\Rightarrow$	$\boxed{x = 17}$	

Note: $\sqrt{x-3} = \sqrt{(x-3)}$ but $\sqrt{x}-3 = \sqrt{(x)}-3$

Solve :

1. $\sqrt{x} - 2 = 9$

2. $\sqrt{(x - 2)} = 9$

3. $3 + \sqrt{x} = 7$

EXAMPLE	*Using a little common sense*	
	$16 - \sqrt{(x - 3)} \;=\; 10$	
$\Rightarrow$	$\sqrt{(x - 3)} \;=\; 6$	[since $16 - 6 = 10$]
$\Rightarrow$	$x - 3 \;=\; 36$	
$\Rightarrow$	$\boxed{x \;=\; 39}$	

Solve :

4. $9 - \sqrt{x} \;= 3$

5. $\sqrt{9 - x} = 3$

6. $3\sqrt{x} + 1 = 10$

7. $12 + \sqrt{(x - 2)} = \; 15$

7. $3\sqrt{(x + 1)} = 15$

8. $15 - \sqrt{x + 1} = 8$

• *Check answers*

D1.4: Working with fractions

Fractions complicate equations, so the best thing to do is to
GET RID OF ANY FRACTIONS.

EXAMPLE   Q: Solve $\frac{1}{2}(3x + 4) = 15$

A: $\frac{1}{2}(3x + 4) = 15$ | x2

$\Rightarrow$ $3x + 4 = 30$ | −4

$\Rightarrow$ $3x = 26$ | +3

$\Rightarrow$ $x = \frac{26}{3}$

$\dfrac{3x + 4}{2}$ is the same as $\frac{1}{2}(3x + 4)$

Solve each equation. Show all working.

1. $\frac{1}{2}(p - 3) = 7$ 2. $\dfrac{5x + 3}{3} = 5$ 3. $\frac{1}{3}(2x - 3) = 4$

EXAMPLE

Q: Solve $\dfrac{x}{3} + \dfrac{1}{4} = 5$

A: $\dfrac{x}{3} + \dfrac{1}{4} = 5$ | x 12

Multiply every term by the lowest common multiple (LCM) of the denominators, which is 12.

$\Rightarrow$ $12 \times \dfrac{x}{3} + 12 \times \dfrac{1}{4} = 60$

$\Rightarrow$ $4x + 3 = 60$ | simplify

$\Rightarrow$ $4x = 57$ | −3

$\Rightarrow$ $x = \frac{57}{4}$ | +4

Driller

Solve each equation. Show all working. Give exact answers.

4. $\dfrac{a}{2} + 5 = 9$ 5. $\dfrac{c}{2} + \dfrac{1}{3} = 3$ 6. $\dfrac{m}{5} + \dfrac{3}{8} = 2$

7. $3x + \frac{2}{3} = 14$ 8. $\dfrac{2x - 5}{4} = \dfrac{2}{3}$ 9. $\dfrac{7p - 2}{6} = \dfrac{4p}{5}$

10. $\dfrac{4(x + 1)}{5} = \dfrac{2x}{3}$ 11. $\frac{1}{4}(3c - 1) = c$ 12. $\frac{1}{3}(8n - 5) = 6$

• *Check your answers.*

In all examinations candidates are expected to construct and present clear mathematical arguments, consisting of logical deductions and precise statements involving correct use of symbols and connecting language.

Insufficient explanation/justification will lose marks.

Use the examples as a guide on how to set out solutions.

D1.5: The cross-multiplication shortcut

LEARN THIS SHORTCUT

$$\frac{a}{b} = \frac{c}{d}$$

is the same as $\quad ad = bc$

This method is called 'cross-multiplication'

Big Edd

EXAMPLE

$$\frac{x-3}{x-5} = \frac{7}{4}$$

$$\Rightarrow \quad 4(x-3) = 7(x-5)$$

$$\Rightarrow \quad 4x - 12 = 7x - 35 \qquad (-4x + 35)$$

$$\Rightarrow \quad 23 = 3x$$

$$\Rightarrow \quad \boxed{x = {}^{23}/_3}$$

Give an exact answer wherever possible, as here.

Solve:

1. $\dfrac{3}{2x-1} = \dfrac{4}{x+1}$

2. $\dfrac{1}{c+1} = \dfrac{3}{c+2}$

3. $\dfrac{u+3}{u-5} = \dfrac{7}{4}$

4. $\dfrac{3n-2}{5n} = \dfrac{4}{3}$

5. $\dfrac{3-p}{1-p} = \dfrac{5}{4}$

• *Check your answers.*

PRACTICE

P1.6 : Solving miscellaneous equations

A-Level students must be good at algebra.
It is an essential computational tool.
If you have got all the questions correct so far,
then you need not do the practice exercises.

Spoton

Solve each equation. Show all working out. GIVE EXACT ANSWERS.
Check your answers at the end of each batch.

Batch A :
1. $2m - 3 = 3 - 4m$
2. $5p - 2(3 + 2p) = 5$
3. $\frac{1}{2}x + 3 = 9$
4. $\dfrac{3n-2}{5} = 7$
5. $\dfrac{5}{3m} = 8$
6. $\dfrac{5n+1}{2n-3} = 4$
7. $\sqrt{x-2} = 5$
8. $17 - 3(2 - p) = 4$

Batch B :
1. $2 - 2x = 4(1 + x)$
2. $\frac{1}{2}(5 - 2n) = 13$
3. $2m - 1 = 3(2 - 4m)$
4. $\dfrac{d+7}{3} = 5$
5. $\dfrac{x}{3} + \dfrac{2x}{5} = 7$
6. $\dfrac{2v-1}{3v} = \dfrac{7}{8}$
7. $\sqrt{(x-5)} = 6$
8. $14 + 3(m - 1) = 2m + 7$

Section 2 : Changing the subject of a formula

(In this section you will rearrange formulae.)

DEVELOPMENT

D2.1: Simple formulae

The technique for changing the subject of a formula is exactly the same technique used for solving equations. *Big Edd*

EXAMPLE

Q: (a) Solve $2x + 3 = 9$

A:
$$2x + 3 = 9$$
$$\Rightarrow \quad 2x = 6 \quad \begin{array}{c} -3 \\ \div 2 \end{array}$$
$$\Rightarrow \quad \boxed{x = 3}$$

(b) Make x the subject of $Ax + B = Q$

$$Ax + B = Q$$
$$\Rightarrow \quad Ax = Q - B \quad \begin{array}{c} -B \\ \div A \end{array}$$
$$\Rightarrow \quad \boxed{x = \dfrac{Q - B}{A}}$$

EXAMPLE

Q: (a) Solve $5(m - 1) = 7$

A:
$$5(m - 1) = 7$$
$$\Rightarrow \quad 5m - 5 = 7 \quad \begin{array}{c} \text{multiply out} \\ +5 \\ \div 5 \end{array}$$
$$\Rightarrow \quad 5m = 12$$
$$\Rightarrow \quad \boxed{m = \dfrac{12}{5}}$$

(b) Make n the subject of $p(n - a) = x$

$$p(n - a) = x$$
$$\Rightarrow \quad pn - pa = x \quad \begin{array}{c} \text{multiply out} \\ +pa \\ \div p \end{array}$$
$$\Rightarrow \quad pn = x + pa$$
$$\Rightarrow \quad \boxed{n = \dfrac{x + pa}{p}}$$

HINT: aim to get all the terms with the required letter onto one side of the formula — and all the rest on the other side.
Headbanger

Make x the subject of each formula:

1. $3x = 11$

2. $mx = n$

3. $px = q^2$

4. $5x = K + L$

5. $Mx = y + nz$

6. $x + v = w$

7. $K + x = 3$

8. $x - m = n$

9. $3x + 5 = k$

10. $5x + v = T^2$

11. $Px + z = 3t$

12. $2(x - 3) = 16$

13. $5(x - n) = p$

14. $N(x + y) = z$

15. $mx - v = 3p$

• *Check answers.*

D2.2: Formulae with fractions

EXAMPLE

Q: (a) Solve $\dfrac{2n + 5}{3} = 7$ (b) Make x the subject of the formula

$$\dfrac{px + q}{n} = u$$

A: $\dfrac{2n + 5}{3} = 7$

$\Rightarrow \quad 2n + 5 = 21$ $\times 3$
$\Rightarrow \quad\quad 2n = 16$ -5
$\Rightarrow \quad\quad \boxed{n = 8}$ $\div 2$

A: $\dfrac{px + q}{n} = u$

$\Rightarrow \quad px + q = nu$ $\times n$
$\Rightarrow \quad\quad px = nu - q$ $-q$
$\Rightarrow \quad\quad \boxed{x = \dfrac{nu - q}{p}}$ $\div p$

Make n the subject:

1. $\dfrac{an + b}{c} = t$ 2. $e = \dfrac{n - 2x}{y}$ 3. $\dfrac{n - a}{b} = k$

4. $\dfrac{4 + 3n}{n + 1} = 5$ 5. $\dfrac{k + pn}{a} = q$ 6. $\dfrac{5 - k}{n} = A$

• *Check answers*

D2.3: Squares and square roots

EXAMPLE   Make x the subject

$\sqrt{(x^2 - a^2)} = b$

$\Rightarrow \quad x^2 - a^2 = b^2$ *squaring*
$\Rightarrow \quad\quad x^2 = b^2 + a^2$ $+a^2$
$\Rightarrow \quad\quad \boxed{x = \sqrt{(b^2 + a^2)}}$ *square root*

EXAMPLE   Make x the subject

$(B - Ax)^2 = k$

$\Rightarrow B - Ax = \sqrt{k}$ *square root*
$\Rightarrow B - \sqrt{k} = Ax$ $+Ax - \sqrt{k}$
$\Rightarrow \quad \boxed{x = \dfrac{B - \sqrt{k}}{A}}$ $+A$

Make x the subject:

1. $\sqrt{x} = a$ 2. $\sqrt{(x + a)} = b$ 3. $\sqrt{(x + 2y)} = z$

4. $\sqrt{x} - k = m$ 5. $\sqrt{(a - x)} = b$ 6. $\sqrt{a - x} = c$

7. $x^2 = 5t$ 8. $n = d - x^2$ 9. $2\sqrt{x} = c^2$ 10. $x^2 = 3c + p$

• *Check answers.*

D2.4: Equivalent formulae

EXAMPLE

Q : Make n the subject of $p - qn = r$

Method 1

$$p - qn = r$$
$$\Rightarrow \quad -qn = r - p \quad |-p$$
$$\Rightarrow \quad n = \frac{r-p}{-q} \quad |\div -q$$

Method 2

$$p - qn = r$$
$$\Rightarrow \quad p = r + qn \quad |+qn$$
$$\Rightarrow \quad p - r = qn \quad |-r$$
$$n = \frac{p-r}{q} \quad |\div q$$

equivalent formulae

Make n the subject : (use either method)

1. $6 - n = 3$

2. $a - n = b$

3. $19 - 5n = 4$

4. $x - 2n = y$

5. $3A - Bn = C$

6. $f = s - mn$

7. $\dfrac{5 - 3n}{2} = 1$

8. $\dfrac{x - n}{5} = r$

9. $\dfrac{m(x - n)}{c} = t$

• *Check answers*

D2.5: Using cross–multiplication

EXAMPLE

Q: Make x the subject of $\dfrac{n}{x} = a$

A: $\quad \dfrac{n}{x} = a$

$$\Rightarrow \quad n = ax$$
$$\Rightarrow \quad x = \frac{n}{a}$$

EXAMPLE

Q: Make x the subject of $\dfrac{x}{m} + n = y$

A: $\quad \dfrac{x}{m} + n = y$

$$\Rightarrow \quad \frac{x}{m} = y - n$$
$$\Rightarrow \quad x = m(y - n)$$

Aim to get the term in x on its own, with the x on top.

Frizzbang

Make x the subject :

1. $\dfrac{6}{x} = 5$

2. $\dfrac{m}{x} = q$

3. $\dfrac{c}{x} = a + b$

4. $\dfrac{a}{2x} = 5t$

5. $\dfrac{2x + 1}{3} = 7$

6. $\dfrac{nx + 1}{3} = 11$

7. $\dfrac{ax + n}{5} = 11$

8. $\dfrac{hx - g}{5} = 7$

9. $\dfrac{3x - p}{t} = q$

10. $\dfrac{4x}{e} = a$

11. $\dfrac{7x - t}{c} = s$

12. $\dfrac{xn - p}{g} = m$

• *Check answers*

Section 3: An important technique

> In this section you will work with a very useful technique.

DEVELOPMENT

D3.1 : You must master this

Get all the terms in x onto one side and all the other terms on the other side.

Factorise $\Rightarrow$ $x(\quad) =$ $---$

Then divide $\Rightarrow$ $x =$ $\dfrac{---}{(\quad)}$

Apul

EXAMPLE : Make x the subject :

(a)
$$px - q = cx + t$$
$$\Rightarrow px - cx = q + t$$
$$\Rightarrow x(p - c) = q + t$$
$$\Rightarrow \boxed{x = \frac{q + t}{p - c}}$$

Get all the terms in x onto one side.

Take out x

Divide to give x = ...

(b)
$$x + t = \frac{x + v}{a}$$
$$\Rightarrow a(x + t) = x + v$$
$$\Rightarrow ax + at = x + v$$
$$\Rightarrow ax - x = v - at$$
$$\Rightarrow x(a - 1) = v - at$$
$$\Rightarrow \boxed{x = \frac{v - at}{a - 1}}$$

Yusu Al

Make x the subject :

1. $5(x + 2) = 3(x - 1)$ 2. $5px + q = px + 2q$ 3. $mx + p = q - mx$

4. $tx - u = v - 2tx$ 5. $ax + p = q - bx$ 6. $3ax + y = bx + 3z$

7. $xy - z = w + x$ 8. $ax + b = cx - 2b$ 9. $rx - t = d - ex$

10. $\dfrac{1 - x}{1 + x} = a$ 11. $2x + p = \dfrac{cx + d}{c}$ 12. $\dfrac{x + t}{x - t} = 4$

• *Check answers.*

PRACTICE

P3.2: Miscellaneous rearrangement exercise

Make x the subject :

1. $3x + y = k$ 2. $a - 2x = 3b$ 3. $a - mx = 5b$

4. $\dfrac{16}{x} = 3a$ 5. $\dfrac{6}{x} + u = y$ 6. $(n + x)^2 = m$

7. $\dfrac{a - m}{x} = 2a$ 8. $a(x + b) = x + 2$ 9. $2(x - d) = ax$

Make n the subject :

10. $an^2 = 36$ 11. $e = p - n^2$ 12. $\dfrac{t}{cn} - u = 3u$

13. $7k = p - 2n^2$ 14. $6p - xn = 3q$ 15. $\dfrac{n - 5}{3} = 4$

• *Check answers.*

Section 4: Expansions

In this section you will:
- multiply out brackets to get quadratic expansions;
- learn the expansions of some special pairs of brackets.

DEVELOPMENT

D4.1: Multiplying out brackets

Note that $\Rightarrow$ is <u>not</u> used here.
This is not a sequence of linked statements. Here, each subsequent expression is <u>equal</u> to the previous expression.

EXAMPLE

$$(x + 3)(x + 7) = x(x + 7) + 3(x + 7)$$
$$= x^2 + 7x + 3x + 21$$
$$= \boxed{x^2 + 10x + 21}$$

Expand and simplify:

1. $(x + 5)(x + 2)$ 2. $(x - 3)(x + 2)$ 3. $(x - 1)(x - 4)$
4. $(x + 6)(x - 2)$ 5. $(2x + 1)(x + 3)$ 6. $(3x + 2)(x - 4)$

• *Check your answers*

D4.2 : Writing out expansions directly

You need to be able to write down expansions like these, without doing any working out on paper.

$$(x + 3)(x + 2) = x^2 + 5x + 6$$

$$(x - 3)(x + 2) = x^2 - x - 6$$

Write down the expansions of each of these.
Write down both question and answer – but no working.

1. $(x + 1)(x + 5)$ 2. $(x - 2)(x + 7)$ 3. $(x + 4)(x - 3)$ 4. $(x - 10)(x - 2)$
5. $(x - 3)(x + 5)$ 6. $(x + 11)(x - 3)$ 7. $(2x + 1)(x + 5)$ 8. $(x + 7)(2x - 1)$
9. $(3x - 4)(2x + 1)$ 10. $(7x - 2)(x + 5)$ • *Check your answers*

D4.3: The difference of two squares

Expand and simplify:

1. $(x - 3)(x + 3)$ 2. $(a - 1)(a + 1)$ 3. $(c - 7)(c + 7)$ 4. $(2x - 3)(2x + 3)$

$a^2 - b^2$ *factorises to give*

$$a^2 - b^2 = (a - b)(a + b)$$

LEARN this factorisation.

Write down the factorisation of each of these. Write down both question and answer.

5. $p^2 - q^2$ 6. $x^2 - 4$ 7. $m^2 - 25$ 8. $4p^2 - q^2$
9. $49x^2 - 9y^2$ 10. $36y^2 - 100$ 11. $u^2 - 4v^2$ 12. $m^2n^2 - p^2$

• *Check your answers*

D4.4: Squaring brackets

EXAMPLE	Q: *Expand and simplify* $(x-5)^2$
	A: $(x-5)^2 = (x-5)(x-5)$
	$= \boxed{x^2 - 10x + 25}$

Remember: always start by writing down the expression that you are working from.

Driller

Expand and simplify:

1. $(x+3)^2$ 2. $(x-6)^2$ 3. $(x-1)^2$ 4. $(x+y)^2$ 5. $(a-b)^2$

A short cut: you need to be able to write down, <u>without any working</u>, the expansion of any expression like $(a+b)^2$

$$(a+b)^2 = a^2 + b^2 + 2ab$$

the sum of the squares   *plus*   twice the product

LEARN THIS TECHNIQUE

EXAMPLE	Q: *Write down the expansion of* $(5m-3)^2$
	A: $(5m-3)^2 = \boxed{25m^2 + 9 - 30m}$

Write down the expansion of:

6. $(x+7)^2$ 7. $(2x+1)^2$ 8. $(n-3)^2$ 9. $(2x+3y)^2$ 10. $(2t+5u)^2$

11. $(x-4)^2$ 12. $(m+8)^2$ 13. $(2x-5)^2$ 14. $(4x-y)^2$ 15. $(3a-b)^2$

• *Check your answers.*

D4.5: Perfect squares

Copy and complete:

1. $x^2 + 2x + 1 = (x + ...)^2$ 2. $x^2 + 10x + 25 = (x + ...)^2$

3. $x^2 - 8x + 16 = (x - ......)^2$ 4. $x^2 - 20x + 100 = (x - ......)^2$

5. $x^2 + 6x + 9 = (............)^2$ 6. $x^2 - 14x + 49 = (............)^2$

7. $x^2 - 4x + ... = (............)^2$ 8. $x^2 + 24x + ... = (............)^2$

9. $x^2 + 30x + ... = (............)^2$ 10. $x^2 - 12x + ... = (............)^2$

• *Check your answers.*

Section 5: Properties of a circle

In this section you will:
- meet/review three important properties of circles
- briefly review trig ratios and Pythagoras' Theorem

DEVELOPMENT

D5.1: Working with circles

The material in Section 5 is part of the **background knowledge** that all students are expected to be able to use in A-Level questions. Questions will not be set on this material. However, it may be assessed within questions focused on other material within the A-Level syllabus.

Students are advised to do as much as they need to develop/recall sufficient expertise with each technique.

Reminders:

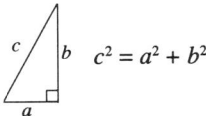 $c^2 = a^2 + b^2$

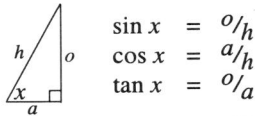

$\sin x = {}^o/_h$
$\cos x = {}^a/_h$
$\tan x = {}^o/_a$

The angle in a semicircle is a right angle	The perpendicular from the centre of the circle to a chord bisects the chord	A tangent to the circle is perpendicular to the radius at the point of contact.
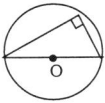	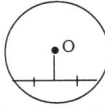	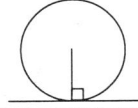

Work out the size of each lettered angle and the length of each lettered line:

1.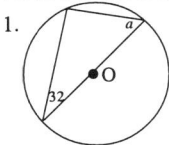

2.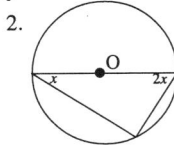

3.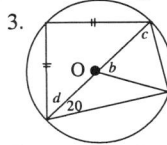

4.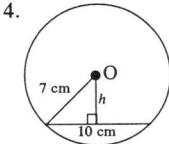

5.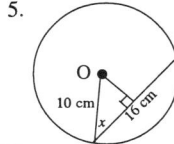

6.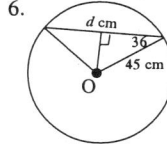

7.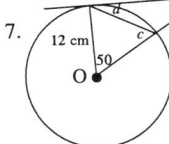

8.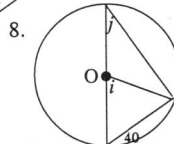

9.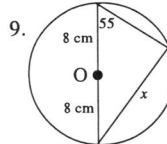

Headbanger

Hints:
- copy each diagram and do your working out on the diagram
- mark the radii of a circle as lines of equal length
- look for isosceles triangles
- use Pythagoras' Theorem and trigonometry, where necessary.
- *Check answers.*

Section 6: Cosine Rule and Sine Rule

In this section you will:
- meet and use the Sine and Cosine Rules;
- calculate sides and angles in non–right–angled triangles;
- work with triangles that have an angle greater than 90°

DEVELOPMENT

The material in Section 6 is part of the **background knowledge** that all students are expected to be able to use in A-Level questions. Questions will not be set on this material. However, it may be assessed within questions focused on other material within the A-Level syllabus.

Students are advised to do as much as they need to develop/recall sufficient expertise with each technique.

Standard notation for triangles

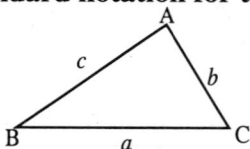

Note:
The trig ratios sin, cos, tan can only be used in right–angled Δs. When you need to find angles or sides in Δs that do not have a right–angle, then you should use the Cosine Rule or the Sine Rule.

Capital letters are used for vertices.
Lower case letters are used for sides.
Side b is always opposite angle B, side t is opposite angle T…

D6.1: The Cosine Rule

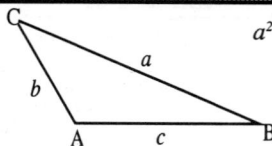

$$a^2 = b^2 + c^2 - 2bc \cos A$$

Use this form of the rule to find one side given the other two sides and the included angle.

or

$$\cos A = \frac{b^2 + c^2 - a^2}{2bc}$$

Use this form of the rule to find any angle given all three sides.

EXAMPLE   Find the largest angle in ΔPQR
where p = 14.1 cm, q = 10 cm, r = 7.5 cm

The largest angle is opposite the longest side.
We need to find ∠ P

sides next to angle ⟶   side opposite to angle

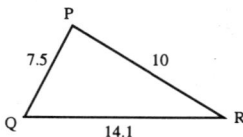

$$\cos P = \frac{7.5^2 + 10^2 - 14.1^2}{2 \times 7.5 \times 10}$$

$$= -0.2837$$

$$\therefore \boxed{P = 106.5°}$$

Find the size of each lettered side to 1 d.p.:

1.

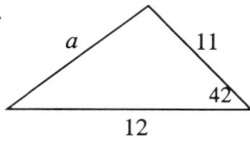

2.

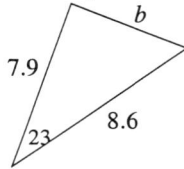

3.

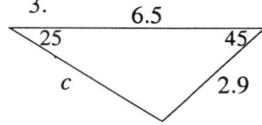

Find the size of each lettered angle to the nearest degree:

4.

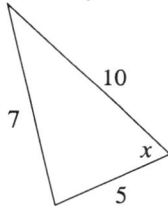

5.

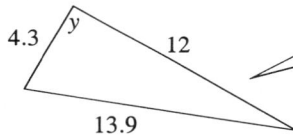

6.

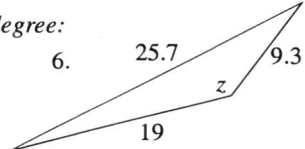

• *Check your answers.*

D6.2: The Sine Rule

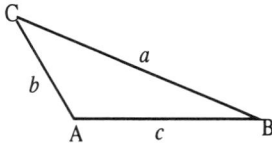

$$\frac{a}{\sin A} = \frac{b}{\sin B} = \frac{c}{\sin C}$$

or

$$\frac{\sin A}{a} = \frac{\sin B}{b} = \frac{\sin C}{c}$$

EXAMPLE   Find the longest side in this triangle to 1 d.p.

A: First we need to find the third angle.

$\angle L = 180° - (102° + 51°) = 27°$

Longest side is opposite the largest angle.

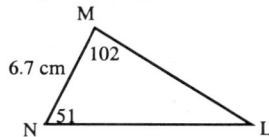

$$\frac{6.7}{\sin 27°} = \frac{m}{\sin 102°}$$

$\Rightarrow \qquad m \quad = \quad \dfrac{6.7 \times \sin 102°}{\sin 27°} = \boxed{14.4 \text{ cm}}$

Use the Sine Rule to find the size of each side and angle marked with a letter to 1 d.p.:

1.

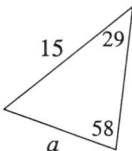

2.

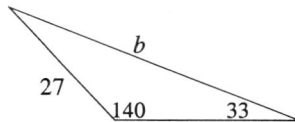

3.

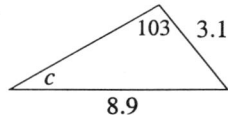

• *Check your answers.*

Section 7: Applications of ratio

In this section you will:
- divide in a given ratio
- do calculations involving similar triangles
- calculate areas and volumes of similar shapes.

DEVELOPMENT

The material in Section 7 is part of the **background knowledge** that all students are expected to be able to use in A-Level questions. Questions will not be set on this material. However, it may be assessed within questions focused on other material within the A-Level syllabus.

Students are advised to do as much as they need to develop/recall sufficient expertise with each technique.

D7.1: Dividing in ratio

EXAMPLE   The line MN is 42 cm long. P divides the line in the ratio 4 : 3 with P nearer to N. What is the length of MP ?

MP : PN = 4 : 3

$\boxed{\begin{array}{l}4 + 3 = 7 \\ \text{so divide 42cm} \\ \text{into 7 parts}\end{array}}$

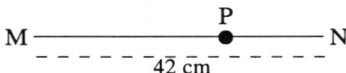

42 cm ÷ 7 = 6 cm

MP = 4 x 6 cm = $\boxed{24 \text{ cm}}$

M ———————————●————— N
P
$\overline{42 \text{ cm}}$

---

1. AP : PB = 4 : 1

   Work out the length of AP.

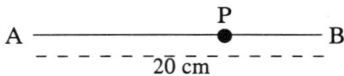

   A ——————————●———— B
   P
   $\overline{20 \text{ cm}}$

2. A 35 cm piece of string is cut in the ratio 2 : 5.
   What is the length of the shorter piece ?

3. A ladder leans against a wall. The base of the ladder, C,
   is 6 m from the wall and the top of the ladder, A, is 8 m
   above the ground. Pete stands at a point P on the ladder.
   AP : PC = 3 : 2. Calculate the distance PC.

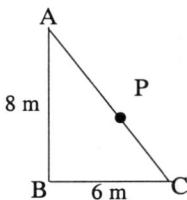

   (diagram: right triangle with vertical side 8 m = AB, horizontal side BC = 6 m, point P on hypotenuse AC)

4. XY is 40 cm long, Q divides the line XY in the ratio 3 : 5.
   Q is nearer to X than to Y. Work out the length of QY.

5. A is (2,3)   B is (6,11) as in the diagram.
   P divides the line AB so that AP : PB = 1 : 3
   If P divides AB in the ratio 1 : 3, then Q divides
   AC in the ratio 1 : 3 and R divides BC
   in the ratio 1 : 3. Work out the lengths AQ
   and CR. Hence work out the coordinates of P

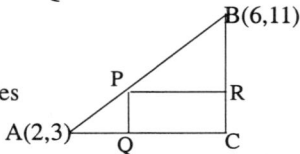

   (diagram: triangle with B(6,11), A(2,3), points P, R, Q, C)

6. A is (−1,1) B is (5,10) P divides AB in the ratio 1 : 2.
   Work out the coordinates of P

• Check your answers.

D7.2: Similar triangles

With some pairs of triangles it is often difficult to see which are the corresponding sides. This is a method that sorts out the corresponding sides.

EXAMPLE

Step 1 $\hat{A} = \hat{P}$ $\hat{B} = \hat{Q}$ $\hat{C} = \hat{R}$ (match up corresponding angles)

Step 2 $\dfrac{AB}{PQ} = \dfrac{BC}{QR} = \dfrac{AC}{PR}$ (line up corresponding angles under each other to make corresponding sides)

Step 3 $\dfrac{7}{y} = \dfrac{5}{10} = \dfrac{x}{12}$ (put sizes of sides into the equation)

Step 4 $\dfrac{7}{y} = \dfrac{5}{10} \Rightarrow \boxed{y = 14}$ (solve the equations)

$\dfrac{5}{10} = \dfrac{x}{12} \Rightarrow \boxed{x = 6}$

Similar triangles are the same shape but different sizes. The lengths of corresponding pairs of sides are in the same ratio.

Use this method to calculate the lengths of the sides in these triangles:

1. Find AC and QR

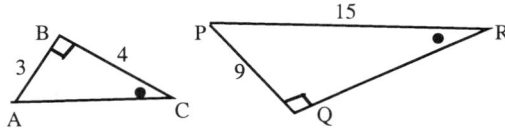

2. Find ZX and MN

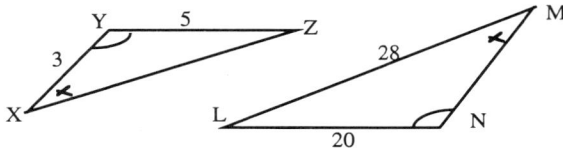

3.

4.

5.

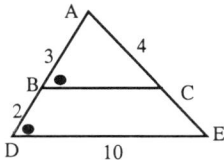

Consider triangles
ABC and ADE.
Work out BC and AE.

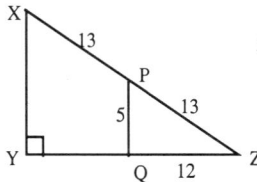

Which triangles are
similar here ?
Find XY and YQ.

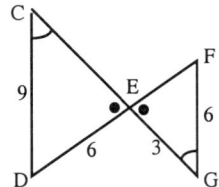

Work out CE and EF.

• *Check your answers*

D7.3: Areas of similar shapes

If two shapes are similar, lengths of corresponding sides are in the same ratio.
Let the corresponding sides have lengths in ratio $L_1 : L_2$
Any corresponding areas are also in ratio.
Let the corresponding areas be $A_1 : A_2$

$$\boxed{A_1 : A_2 = L_1{}^2 : L_2{}^2}$$

EXAMPLE Two similar triangles have base lengths 3 cm and 5 cm.
The area of the smaller triangle is 17 cm².
Calculate the area of the larger triangle.

A: $L_1 : L_2 = 3 : 5$

so $A_1 : A_2 = 3^2 : 5^2 = 9 : 25$

$\dfrac{A_2}{A_1} = \dfrac{25}{9}$ $\Rightarrow$ $\dfrac{A_2}{17} = \dfrac{25}{9}$

$A_2 = \dfrac{25}{9} \times 17 = \boxed{47.2 \text{ cm}^2 \text{ (to 3 s.f.)}}$

> Step 1: Work out ratio of areas
>
> Step 2: Write area ratio equation in fraction form
>
> Step 3: Solve equation

In each of these questions, the two shapes are similar.
Numbers inside shapes represent areas.
The capital letters represent unknown areas.
Work out each of the unknown areas.

1.
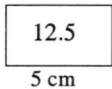 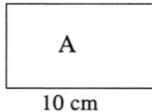

2.
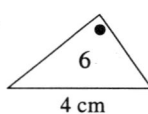 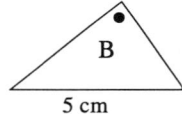

3.
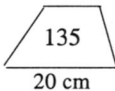 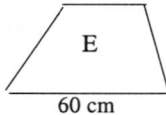

4.
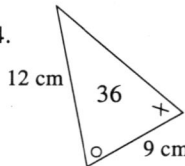 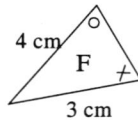

Work out the unknown lengths.

5.
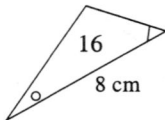 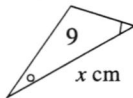

6.
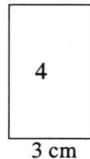 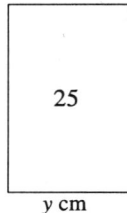

• *Check your answers.*

D7.4: Volumes of similar shapes

If two shapes are similar, lengths of corresponding sides are in the same ratio.
Let the corresponding sides have lengths in ratio $L_1 : L_2$
Any corresponding volumes are also in ratio.
Let the corresponding volumes be $V_1 : V_2$

$$\boxed{V_1 : V_2 = L_1{}^3 : L_2{}^3}$$

EXAMPLE 4   Q: Two similar bottles have diameters 4 cm and 6 cm.
The larger bottle holds 90 cl.
Work out the capacity of the smaller bottle to the nearest cl.

A: $L_s : L_l = 4 : 6 = 2 : 3$

so $V_s : V_l = 2^3 : 3^3 = 8 : 27$

$\dfrac{V_s}{V_l} = \dfrac{8}{27} \qquad \Rightarrow \qquad \dfrac{V_s}{90} = \dfrac{8}{27}$

$V_s = \dfrac{8}{27} \times 90 = \boxed{27\ cl}$ (to the nearest cl.)

In each of these questions, the two shapes are similar. Numbers inside shapes
represent volumes. The capital letters represent unknown volumes.
Calculate each of the unknown volumes to the nearest cm³.

1.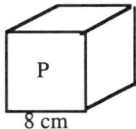
50
4 cm
P
8 cm

2.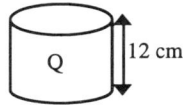
15   4 cm
Q
12 cm

3.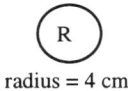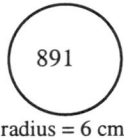
R
radius = 4 cm
891
radius = 6 cm

4.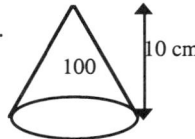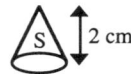
100
10 cm
S
2 cm

5. Two similar bowls have depths 9 cm and 12 cm. The smaller bowl holds 1500 cm³.
What is the capacity of the larger bowl ?

6. Two solid spheres are made of the same metal. Their diameters are 2.5 cm and 12.5
cm. The larger sphere weighs 25 kg. Work out the weight of the smaller sphere.

7. Two similar cylinders have volumes 16 cm³ and 250 cm³.
Find the ratio of   (a) their lengths (b) their surface areas

8. A wooden figure is 10 cm tall. A similar figure 20 cm tall is made of metal five
times as heavy as the wood. The wooden figure weighs 2 kg.
What is the weight of the metal figure ?

• *Check answers,*

Section 8: Proportion

In this section you will use direct and inverse proportion to solve problems

DEVELOPMENT

> The material in Section 8 is part of the **background knowledge** that all students are expected to be able to use in A-Level questions. Questions will not be set on this material. However, it may be assessed within questions focused on other material within the A-Level syllabus.
>
> Students are advised to do as much as they need to develop/recall sufficient expertise with each technique.

D8.1: Direct proportion

> If two variables, P and Q, are connected by an equation of the form
> $$P = kQ$$
> then we say that "P varies directly as Q"
> or "P is directly proportional to Q"
> k is called the constant of proportionality

EXAMPLE In a simple model, the distance, d km, of the horizon from an observer is related to the height, h m, of the observer above the earth's surface. d is proportional to the square root of h. When $d = 20$, $h = 36$. Calculate the height of the observer above the earth when $d = 10$.

A: $d = k\sqrt{h}$ Write the equation of variation

$\Rightarrow 20 = k\sqrt{36}$ Put the known values in

$\Rightarrow k = {}^{20}/_6 = {}^{10}/_3$ Work out k (leave as a fraction)

$\Rightarrow d = {}^{10}/_3 \sqrt{h}$ Put k in the equation of variation

When $d = 10$, $10 = {}^{10}/_3 \sqrt{h}$

$\Rightarrow \sqrt{h} = 3$

$\Rightarrow \boxed{h = 9}$

> **NOTE**
> Even though you are not asked explicitly to find the value of k, you are expected to find it. Marks will be given for finding k correctly.

All working must be clearly shown for each of these questions:

1. The number of roof tiles Dave lays is directly proportional to the time taken. He lays 130 tiles in 3 hours. How long would it take him to lay 380 tiles ?

2. A weight is hung on a string to make a pendulum. The period, T, (time in seconds for one swing) is proportional to the square root of the length of the string, l. With a string of length 0.95 m, the period is 1.95 s. Calculate the period of a pendulum of length 1.1 m, to 3 d.p.

3. The surface area of a hemisphere, S, is proportional to the square of its radius, r. When $r = 10$ cm, $S = 942$ cm^2. Calculate the surface area of a hemisphere of radius 8 cm, to 3 s.f. • *Check answers.*

D8.2: Direct and inverse proportion

> If P is **directly** proportional to Q, then $P = kQ$
>
> If P is **inversely** proportional to Q, then $P = \dfrac{k}{Q}$

EXAMPLE   On each lifeboat on a ship, there is an emergency pack of food. The number of days the food will last, N, is inversely proportional to the number of people in the lifeboat, p. The food will last 5 days if there are 20 people. How many days will the food last if there are 4 people in the lifeboat ?

A: $N = {}^{k}/_{p}$

     $\Rightarrow 5 = {}^{k}/_{20} \qquad \Rightarrow k = 100$

     $\Rightarrow N = {}^{100}/_{p}$

When $p = 4$, $N = {}^{100}/_{4} = \boxed{25}$

1. T is inversely proportional to v^2 When $v = 5$, $T = 48$.
   Work out (a) T when $v = 10$ (b) v when $T = 3$

2. The number of hours, H, taken to dig a ditch is inversely proportional to the number of labourers digging the ditch, n. It takes 5 labourers 3 hours to dig a particular ditch. How long would it have taken 2 labourers working at the same rate ?

EXAMPLE   S is directly proportional to $\sqrt{p}$ and t, and inversely proportional to v^2. When $t = 3$, $p = 25$ and $v = 4$, S = 1.5. Work out the value of S when $t = 10$, $p = 16$ and $v = 2$.

A: $S = \dfrac{k t \sqrt{p}}{v^2}$

     $\Rightarrow 1.5 = \dfrac{k 3 \sqrt{25}}{4^2} = k \dfrac{15}{16} \qquad \Rightarrow k = 1.6$

     $\Rightarrow S = \dfrac{1.6 t \sqrt{p}}{v^2}$

When $t = 10$, $p = 16$ and $v = 2$ $S = \dfrac{1.6 \times 10 \times \sqrt{16}}{2^2} = \boxed{16}$

3. V varies directly as x^2 and inversely as y. $V = 8$ when $x = 4$ and $y = 6$. Work out the value of the constant of proportionality, k. Hence work out the value of V when $x = 5$ and $y = 12$.

4. P varies directly as x and y, and inversely as t^2
   When $x = 5$, $y = 4$ and $t = 10$, $P = 8$.
   Work out P when $x = 6$, $y = 2$ and $t = 4$.

         • *Check answers.*

Section 9: Miscellaneous Techniques

In this section you will:
- work with HCFs and LCMs
- work with formulae for the volumes of cones & spheres and area of Δs

DEVELOPMENT

The material in Section 9 is part of the **background knowledge** that all students are expected to be able to use in A-Level questions. Questions will not be set on this material. However, it may be assessed within questions focused on other material within the A-Level syllabus.

Students are advised to do as much as they need to develop/recall sufficient expertise with each technique.

D9.1: Lowest common multiples (LCMs)

The multiples of 5 are 5, 10, 15, 20, …
The multiples of 4 are 4, 8, 12, 16, 20, …
The lowest common multiple (LCM) of 5 and 4 is $\boxed{20}$

Find the LCM of each set of numbers:

1. 3 and 4
2. 3 and 12
3. 8 and 20

EXAMPLE

$$\frac{3}{x} + \frac{5}{x+1} = \frac{3(x+1)}{x(x+1)} + \frac{5x}{x(x+1)}$$

$\boxed{\text{LCM of } x \text{ and } x+1 \text{ is } x(x+1)}$

$$= \frac{3(x+1) + 5x}{x(x+1)}$$

$$= \boxed{\frac{8x + 3}{x(x+1)}}$$

EXAMPLE

$$\frac{2}{x} + \frac{3}{x^2} = \frac{2x}{x^2} + \frac{3}{x^2}$$

$\boxed{\text{LCM of } x \text{ and } x^2 \text{ is } x^2}$

$$= \boxed{\frac{2x + 3}{x^2}}$$

Use LCMs to simplify these expressions:

4. $\dfrac{x}{2} + \dfrac{x+2}{3}$

5. $\dfrac{x-1}{3} + \dfrac{x+3}{2}$

6. $\dfrac{x}{5} - \dfrac{x-1}{2}$

7. $\dfrac{2}{x} + \dfrac{3}{x-1}$

8. $\dfrac{5}{x} - \dfrac{3}{2x-1}$

9. $\dfrac{3}{x-2} + \dfrac{4}{x+3}$

10. $\dfrac{3}{x(x+2)} + \dfrac{1}{x}$

11. $\dfrac{1}{x(x-1)} - \dfrac{1}{x-1}$

12. $\dfrac{5}{x(x+3)} + \dfrac{1}{x+3}$

• Check answers.

D9.2: Highest common factors (HCFs)

The factors of 6 are 1, 2, 3, 6   The factors of 21 are 1, 3, 7, 21

The **common factors** of 6 and 21 are 1 and 3

The **highest common factor (HCF)** of 6 and 21 is 3

Find the HCF of each set of numbers:

1. 12 and 18   2. 14 and 35   3. 27, 45 and 72

EXAMPLE   Factorise fully $ab^2c^3 - bc^4$

$$ab^2c^3 - bc^4 = bc^3(ab - c)$$

Note that

$bc^3(abc^2 - c^3)$

is NOT <u>fully factorised</u>

Factorise fully:

4. $x^3 - x^2y$ 5. $2ab - 4ac$ 6. $pqr + p^2qr$
7. $5n^2 - 2n^3 + n$ 8. $3mn^2 - 9m^2n$ 9. $ab^2c + a^2c + ac^2d$

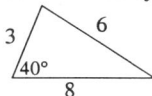

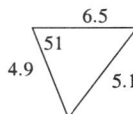

• *Check your answers.*

D9.3: Volumes of cones and spheres

For a cone: $V = \frac{1}{3}\pi r^2 h$

For a sphere: $V = \frac{4}{3}\pi r^3$

You need to KNOW these formulae.
They will <u>not</u> be given to you.

Yerwat

Give all answers to 3 s.f.

1. Calculate the volume of a sphere of radius 4.5 cm.
2. Calculate the volume of a cone of radius 6.2 cm and height 12.5 cm.
3. Work out the radius of a sphere with volume 500 cm^3
4. Work out the height of a cone, of radius 9.5 cm and volume 450 cm^3.
5. Calculate the volume of a hemisphere with base diameter 45 m.
6. A solid metal cone has radius 20 cm and height 22 cm. It is melted down and the metal reformed to make a sphere. Work out the radius of the sphere.

• *Check your answers.*

D9.4: Areas of triangles

The area of a triangle = $\frac{1}{2}ab \sin C$

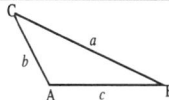

Work out the area of each triangle:

1.

3 / 6 / 40° / 8

2.

6.5 / 51 / 4.9 / 5.1

• *Check your answers.*

AIMING HIGH

Unit 2
Quadratic Expressions and Equations

CONTENTS

	OCR	AQA	Edexcel
Section 1	All	All	All
Section 2	All	All	All
Section 3	All	All	All
Section 4	All	All	All
Section 5	All	All	All
Section 6	All	All	All
Section 7	All	All	All
Section 8	All	—	—

D denotes topics which are covered in the DIAGNOSTIC TEST which follows.

D denotes topics which good students will have met earlier and with which they should have no problems.

Sections 3,6,7 should be done by all students.

It is recommended that D5.2 (section 5) be done by all students, even those who do not need to do D5.1

Diagnostic Test for Unit 2 (Quadratics)

Each question in the diagnostic test is related to part of Unit 2 (link is in brackets). For each question:
- if you have not met questions like this, or cannot do them, do the whole of the related part of the unit
- if you can do the question only after you have looked at the relevant part of the unit, you need to do some practice on this technique. Do as much practice as you feel you need.
- if you can do it easily, omit the related part of the unit.

You'll find this diagnostic test more useful if you cover up the answers while you are working on it.

1.	Factorise :	$x^2 + 4x - 21$	(D1.1 & 1.2)
2.	Factorise :	$6x^2 - 19x + 15$	(D1.3)
3.	Solve :	$(x - 3)(5x + 3) = 0$	(D2.1)
4.	Solve :	$12x^2 + 5x - 3 = 0$	(D2.2)
5.	Solve :	$x^2 + 7x = 0$	(D2.3)
6.	Solve :	$2(3x + 4) - 5 > 2x - 3$	(D4.1)

7. Use 'the formula to solve : $5x^2 - 7x - 13 = 0$ giving your answers to 2 d.p. (D5.1)

ANSWERS

1. $(x - 3)(x + 7)$ 2. $(2x - 3)(3x - 5)$ 3. $3, -\frac{3}{5}$

4. $\frac{1}{3}, -\frac{3}{4}$ 5. $0, -7$ 6. $x > -\frac{3}{2}$

7. $2.46, -1.06$

Unit 2: Quadratics
Section 1: Factorising quadratics

In this section you will factorise quadratic expressions.

DEVELOPMENT

D1.1: Systematic factorisation of type 1 quadratics

$(x+p)(x+q)$ $\xrightarrow{\text{multiplying out}}$ $x^2+(p+q)x+pq$

$x^2+(p+q)x+pq$ $\xrightarrow{\text{factorising}}$ $(x+p)(x+q)$

Type 1: $x^2 \pm bx + c$ + here tells you that the signs in both brackets are the same : ++ or − −

EXAMPLE $x^2 + 6x + 8$ = $(x + 4)(x + 2)$ Hints: $(x+p)(x+q)$
$p + q = 6$ & $pq = 8$

++ or − −   and, since it is + in front of the 6x, the signs will be ++

Check : $(x + 4)(x + 2) = x^2 + 6x + 8$ *Baggy*

EXAMPLE $x^2 − 6x + 8$ = $(x − 4)(x − 2)$ Hints: $(x+p)(x+q)$
$p + q = −6$ & $pq = 8$

++ or − −   and, since it is − in front of the 6x, the signs will be − −

Check : $(x − 4)(x − 2) = x^2 − 6x + 8$ *Baggy*

ALWAYS CHECK FACTORISATION IS CORRECT BY MULTIPLYING OUT THE FACTORS – *either on paper or in your head.*

Copy and complete:

1. $x^2 – 7x + 6 = (x\quad)(x\quad)$ | 6 = 1 × 6 |
    | = 2 × 3 |

2. $x^2 – 11x + 24 = (x\quad)(x\quad)$ | 24 = 1 × 24 |
    | = _ _ _ |
    | = _ _ _ |
    | = _ _ _ |

Factorise : [Write down both question & answer]

3. $x^2 + 6x + 5$ 4. $x^2 – 6x + 5$

• *Check your answers.*

D1.2: Systematic factorisation of type 2 quadratics

Type 2: $x^2 \pm bx - c$ — + here tells you that the signs in both brackets are different : $+ -$ or $- +$

EXAMPLE $\quad x^2 - 2x - 8 = (x - 4)(x + 2)$ — $+ -$ or $- +$

Hints: $(x+p)(x+q)$
$p + q = -2$ & $pq = -8$
and one of p, q is +ve and one is –ve

Baggy

Check : $(x - 4)(x + 2) = x^2 - 2x - 8$

Copy and complete:

1. $x^2 + 7x - 18 = (x \quad)(x \quad)$

$18 = 1 \times 18$
$\quad = 2 \times 9$
$\quad = 3 \times 6$

2. $x^2 - x - 20 = (\quad)(\quad)$

$20 =$

Factorise :   [*Write down both question & answer*]

3. $x^2 - x - 12$ 4. $x^2 - 2x - 15$ 5. $x^2 - 5x - 14$

6. $x^2 - 7x - 30$ 7. $x^2 - 7x + 6$ 8. $x^2 - 11x + 18$

9. $x^2 + 2x - 15$ 10. $x^2 - 7x - 18$ 11. $x^2 - 5x + 6$ 12. $x^2 + x - 20$

• *Check your answers.*

D1.3: More complex quadratics

EXAMPLE

signs are + +

$$2x^2 + 11x + 12 = (2x + 3)(x + 4)$$

product of coefficients of $x = 2$ $(= 1 \times 2)$

product of numbers $= 12$

$12 = 1 \times 12$
$\quad = 2 \times 6$
$\quad = 3 \times 4$

Try some numbers (in pencil) using what you know — until you find the right numbers.

Headbanger

Check : $(2x + 3)(x + 4) = 2x^2 + 11x + 12$

Factorise :

1. $2x^2 + 7x + 6$ 2. $2x^2 + 5x + 3$ 3. $3x^2 + 7x + 2$

4. $15x^2 + 11x + 2$ 5. $4x^2 - 23x + 15$ 6. $6x^2 + x - 35$

7. $24x^2 - 13x - 7$ 8. $2x^2 + 5x - 3$ 9. $30x^2 - 49x + 20$

10. $12x^2 + 7x - 5$ 11. $10x^2 + 9x - 1$ 12. $12x^2 - 4x - 21$

• *Check answers*

Section 2: Solving equations by factorisation

In this section you will solve quadratic and cubic equations by factorisation.

DEVELOPMENT

D2.1: Solving factorised equations

Consider the equation p x q = 0
The only possible solutions are p = 0 or q = 0

EXAMPLE $(x + 2)(x - 3) = 0$

Either $x + 2 = 0$ $\ or\ x - 3 = 0$

$\Rightarrow$ $\boxed{x = -2 \ or\ x = 3}$

Solve :

1. $(x - 1)(x - 9) = 0$
2. $(x + 5)(x - 6) = 0$
3. $x(x - 2) = 0$
4. $(x + 4)(x - 4) = 0$
5. $(x + 3)(2x + 1) = 0$
6. $x(x - 2)(3x + 2) = 0$

• *Check your answers.*

D2.2: Solving quadratic equations by factorisation

EXAMPLE Q: Factorise and solve $x^2 + x - 12 = 0$

A: $x^2 + x - 12 \quad = 0$

$\Rightarrow$ $(x - 3)(x + 4) = 0$

$\Rightarrow$ $x - 3 = 0 \ \ or\ x + 4 = 0$

$\Rightarrow$ $\boxed{x = 3 \quad or\ x = -4}$

Factorise and solve :

1. $x^2 - 2x + 1 \ = 0$
2. $x^2 + 3x + 2 \ \ = 0$
3. $x^2 - 8x + 15 \ = 0$
4. $x^2 + 3x - 4 \ \ = 0$
5. $x^2 + 10x - 24 = 0$
6. $2x^2 - 3x + 1 \ \ = 0$
7. $2x^2 + 5x + 2 \ = 0$
8. $2x^2 - 9x + 10 = 0$
9. $3x^2 + 11x - 4 = 0$

• *Check answers*

D2.3: Solving quadratics or cubics with x as a factor

EXAMPLE $x^2 - 3x \ = 0$

$\Rightarrow$ $x(x - 3) \ = 0$

$\Rightarrow$ $x = 0 \ or\ x - 3 = 0$

$\Rightarrow$ $\boxed{x = 0 \quad or\ x = 3}$

Factorise and solve :

1. $x^2 - 5x = 0$
2. $x^2 + 2x = 0$
3. $x^3 - 4x^2 = 0$

EXAMPLE $x^3 + 6x^2 + 8x = 0$

$\Rightarrow \quad x(x^2 + 6x + 8) = 0$

$\Rightarrow \quad x(x + 4)(x + 2) = 0$

$\Rightarrow \quad x = 0, x + 4 = 0, \; x + 2 = 0$

$\Rightarrow \quad \boxed{x = 0 \, , x = -4 \text{ or } x = -2}$

EXAMPLE $x^3 - 16x = 0$

$\Rightarrow \qquad x(x^2 - 16) = 0$

$\Rightarrow \quad x(x - 4)(x + 4) = 0$

$\Rightarrow \quad \boxed{x = 0 \, , x = -4 \text{ or } x = 4}$

$x^2 - 16$ is the difference of two squares
and $(a^2 - b^2) = (a - b)(a + b)$
– met in Unit 1

Gizmo

Factorise and solve :

4. $x^3 - 10x^2 + 16x = 0$ 5. $x^3 + 10x^2 + 21x = 0$ 6. $x^3 - 25x = 0$

7. $2x^3 - 18x = 0$ 8. $x^3 + 5x^2 + 4x = 0$ 9. $x^4 - 49x^2 = 0$

• *Check answers.*

PRACTICE
P2.4: Mixed factorisation practice

Factorise and solve:

1. $6x^2 + 29x - 5 = 0$ 2. $x^2 - 9x + 8 = 0$ 3. $x^2 - 5x = 0$

4. $x^2 - x - 20 = 0$ 5. $x^3 - 36x = 0$ 6. $x^2 + 14x + 45 = 0$

7. $12x^2 - 19x + 5 = 0$ 8. $x^3 - 8x^2 + 7x = 0$ 9. $4x^2 - 4x + 1 = 0$

10. $7x^2 + 27x - 4 = 0$ 11. $8x^2 + 13x - 6 = 0$ 12. $x^2 - 49x = 0$

• *Check answers.*

EXTENSION

EXTENSION PROBLEMS take you beyond the level of the basic techniques.
If you want to aim for the higher grades, you need to tackle as much of the extension
work as you can find time for. They will include A-Level examination-type questions.
This is where the top grades are earned.

E2.5: Factorisation challenge

Factorise and solve:

1. $2x^3 + 19x^2 - 10x = 0$ 2. $5x^2 + 7x + 2 = 0$ 3. $(x + 1)^2 - 16$

4. $x^4 - 81 = 0$ 5. $4x^2 - 9 = 0$ 6. $5(x + 1)^2 - 2x - 2 = 0$

• *Check answers.*

Section 3: Quadratic inequalities

In this section you will solve quadratic inequalities graphically.

DEVELOPMENT

D3.1: Solving quadratic inequalities

Sketching quadratic graphs

All quadratic graphs are shaped $\cup$ (if the coefficient of x^2 is positive)

or $\cap$ (if the coefficient of x^2 is negative)

The graph crosses the x-axis where $y = 0$

EXAMPLE (a) Sketch the graph of $y = (x + 2)(x - 4)$

(b) Use the graph to solve $(x + 2)(x - 4) < 0$

(a)

$y = (x + 2)(x - 4)$ crosses the x-axis where $y = 0$
$\Rightarrow (x + 2)(x - 4) = 0$
$\Rightarrow x = -2$ and $x = 4$

The solution of $(x - a)(x - b) < 0$
is the set of values of x for which $y < 0$

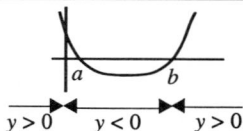

$y > 0 \quad y < 0 \quad y > 0$

(b) $\therefore (x + 2)(x - 4) < 0 \quad \Rightarrow \quad \boxed{-2 < x < 4}$

For each equation, sketch a graph and solve the inequality:

1. $(x - 1)(x - 3) < 0$ 2. $(x + 3)(x + 5) > 0$

3. $(x - 2)(5 - x) > 0$ [Note: the coefficient of x^2 is negative]

4.
$y = x^2 - 4$

(a) Work out the x-coordinates of A and B

(b) Solve $x^2 - 4 > 0$

5.

$y = 5 - x^2$

(a) Work out the exact x-coordinates of C and D

(b) Solve $5 - x^2 < 0$

For each equation, sketch a graph and solve the inequality:

6. $x^2 - 6x + 8 < 0$ 7. $x^2 - 5x - 6 \geq 0$

8. $2x^2 + 9x - 5 \leq 0$ 9. $x(x - 3) > 0$

> For questions like this, a sketch graph is required for full marks.

• *Check your answers.*

Section 4: Linear inequalities

In this section you will review solving linear inequalities.

DEVELOPMENT

D4.1: Review of linear inequalities

Linear inequalities are not quadratics, so strictly do not belong in this unit.
However, their use will be required in Section 6,
so it seems apposite to review them here.

Rules for solving algebraic inequalities

1. Any number may be added to, or taken away from, both sides of an inequality.

2. Both sides of an inequality may be multiplied or divided by the same POSITIVE number.

3. Both sides of an inequality may be multiplied or divided by the same NEGATIVE number, <u>provided the inequality sign is reversed</u>.

EXAMPLE

$$\frac{2x}{3} - 3 > 4$$
$$2x - 9 > 12$$
$$2x > 21$$
$$x > \frac{21}{2}$$

Multiply <u>every term</u> by 3 to remove the fraction.

Gizmo

Solve :

1. $3x + 1 > 5$

2. $4x - 2 > x + 5$

3. $2(3x + 1) < 2x + 1$

• *Check your answers.*

EXAMPLE   **Method 1**

$$3 - 7x \geq 12$$
$$-7x \geq 9$$
$$\Rightarrow \quad x \leq -\frac{9}{7}$$

$\geq$ changes to $\leq$ when ÷ by a −ve number

EXAMPLE   **Method 2**

$$3 - 7x \geq 12$$
$$3 \geq 12 + 7x$$
$$-9 \geq 7x$$
$$-\frac{9}{7} \geq x$$
$$\Rightarrow \quad x \leq -\frac{9}{7}$$

Remember:
You should show the same amount of working as in the example.

Solve :

4. $3(1 - 2x) \leq x$

5. $-3x < 6$

6. $\frac{2}{5}x \geq 3(1 - x)$

7. $\frac{3}{4}(x - 1) < \frac{1}{2}(1 - 2x) + 3$

• *Check answers*

Section 5: 'The formula'

In this section you will:
- meet 'the formula' for solving quadratic equations.

DEVELOPMENT

D5.1: Solving quadratic equations by formula

The solution of the quadratic equation $ax^2 + bx + c = 0$ is given by 'the formula'

$$x = \frac{-b \pm \sqrt{b^2 - 4ac}}{2a}$$

> You will learn how to derive 'the formula' when you meet 'completing the square'.

EXAMPLE Q: Use the formula to solve $3x^2 + 5x - 4 = 0$. (Answer to 2 dp)

A: $3x^2 + 5x - 4 = 0$ $\Rightarrow$ $a = 3, b = 5, c = -4$

$\Rightarrow x = \dfrac{-5 \pm \sqrt{25 - 4 \times 3 \times (-4)}}{6}$

$\Rightarrow x = \dfrac{-5 \pm \sqrt{25 + 48}}{6} = \dfrac{-5 \pm \sqrt{73}}{6}$

$\Rightarrow x = \dfrac{-5 \pm 8.544}{6}$

$\Rightarrow x = \dfrac{-5 + 8.544}{6} = \boxed{0.59}$ & $x = \dfrac{-5 - 8.544}{6} = \boxed{-2.26}$

Use the formula to solve each equation. Give each answer to 2 dp.

1. $x^2 + 7x - 2 = 0$ 2. $3x^2 - 4x + 1 = 0$ 3. $2x^2 - 10x + 7 = 0$

4. $6x^2 - 11x - 5 = 0$ 5. $2x^2 - 7x + 5 = 0$ 6. $x^2 + 5x + 2 = 0$

7. $6x^2 - 11x - 13 = 0$ 8. $4x^2 + 5x - 3 = 0$ 9. $10x^2 - 12x + 1 = 0$

- *Check your answers.*

D5.2: Choosing which method to use

Solve quadratic equations wherever possible by factorisation.
This method gives exact solutions. However, if the quadratic expression cannot be factorised, then solve the equation using the formula.

Solve, using the most relevant method:

1. $x^2 - 2x - 15 = 0$ 2. $x^2 + 7x = 0$ 3. $6x^2 + 11x + 3 = 0$

4. $x^2 + 6x - 7 = 0$ 5 $3x^2 - 6x = 0$ 6. $2x^2 + 9x + 4 = 0$

7. $x^2 - 4x + 2 = 0$ 8. $x^2 + x - 15 = 0$ 9. $3x^2 - 4x - 3 = 0$

10. $2x^2 - 3x - 5 = 0$ 11. $x^2 - 5x + 5 = 0$ 12. $2x^2 - 8x + 3 = 0$

13. $x^2 + x - 6 = 0$ 14. $x^2 + 3x - 70 = 0$ - *Check your answers.*

Section 6: The discriminant

In this section you will meet and use the discriminant.

DEVELOPMENT

D6.1 : Meet the discriminant

The solution of the quadratic equation $ax^2 + bx + c = 0$ is given by 'the formula'

$$x = \frac{-b \pm \sqrt{b^2 - 4ac}}{2a}$$

'$b^2 - 4ac$' is called "**the discriminant**" of the equation. It tells you the kind of roots (solutions) an equation has.

If $b^2 - 4ac = 0$ the equation has 2 real equal roots

If $b^2 - 4ac > 0$ the equation has 2 real distinct roots

If $b^2 - 4ac < 0$ the equation has no real roots

> The set of 'real numbers' is the set of all numbers that you have met so far.
>
> However, there is another set of numbers, 'complex numbers' which you have not yet met.
>
> A quadratic equation that has 'no real roots' has, in fact, two complex roots.

1. Use $x = \frac{-b \pm \sqrt{b^2 - 4ac}}{2a}$ to explain why the equation has no roots if $b^2 - 4ac < 0$.

2. Explain why the equation has just one root if $b^2 - 4ac = 0$.

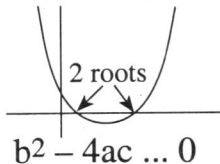

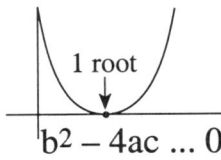

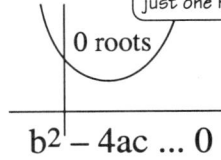

> If an equation has two real equal roots, it can also be described as having just one root.

3. *Copy and complete each diagram and statement:*

2 roots   1 root   0 roots

b2 – 4ac ... 0   b2 – 4ac ... 0   b2 – 4ac ... 0

• *Check your answers.*

D6.2 : Using the discriminant

EXAMPLE   Q: Determine how many roots $3x^2 - 2x - 1 = 0$ has.

A: For $3x^2 - 2x - 1 = 0$

$b^2 - 4ac = 2^2 - 4 \times 3 \times (-1)$

$= 4 + 12 > 0$

$\Rightarrow$ the equation has 2 roots

> Set each question out as in the example.

Determine how many roots each equation has. Do <u>not</u> solve the equations.

1. $2x^2 + 3x + 1 = 0$ 2. $3x^2 + 5x + 5 = 0$ 3. $3x^2 + 5x - 5 = 0$

4. $4x^2 + 4x + 1 = 0$ 5. $4x^2 - 3x + 2 = 0$ 6. $31x^2 - 57x - 101 = 0$

7. Explain what kind of roots an equation has if the discriminant is a perfect square.

• *Check your answers*

D6.3 : Further discriminant problems

Students sometimes have problems setting out answers to questions like these. Use the method demonstrated in the example and there should be no difficulty.

EXAMPLE   Q: For what values of p has $px^2 - 12x + p = 0$ two distinct roots?

A: For two distinct roots $b^2 - 4ac > 0$
$\Rightarrow \quad 12^2 - 4p^2 > 0$
$\Rightarrow \quad 144 > 4p^2$
$\Rightarrow \quad p^2 < 36$
$\Rightarrow \quad \boxed{-6 < p < 6}$

1. For what values of k has $x^2 + kx + 16 = 0$ no real roots ?

2. For what value of a has $2x^2 - 6x + a = 0$ two real equal roots (sometimes described as just one root) ?

> If $b^2 - 4ac > 0$, the quadratic equation has two distinct real roots.
> If $b^2 - 4ac = 0$, the quadratic equation has one distinct real root.
> Hence, if $b^2 - 4ac \geq 0$, the quadratic equation has real roots.

3. For what values of p has $3x^2 + 4x + p = 0$ real roots ?

• *Check your answers.*

EXTENSIONS

EXTENSION PROBLEMS take you beyond the level of the basic techniques. If you want to aim for the higher grades, you need to tackle as much of the extension work as you can find time for. They will include A-Level examination-type questions. This is where the top grades are earned.

E6.4 : Inequalities and the discriminant

EXAMPLE   For what values of p has the equation
$4x^2 + 8x - 8 = p(4x - 3)$ no real roots?

A : Writing the equation in standard quadratic form
$\Rightarrow \quad 4x^2 + x(8 - 4p) + (3p - 8) = 0$
For no real roots, $b^2 - 4ac < 0$
$\Rightarrow \quad (8 - 4p)^2 - 4 \times 4 \times (3p - 8) < 0$
$\Rightarrow \quad 64 - 64p + 16p^2 - 48p + 128 < 0$
$\Rightarrow \quad p^2 - 7p + 12 < 0$
$\Rightarrow \quad (p - 3)(p - 4) < 0 \quad \Rightarrow \quad$ $\quad \Rightarrow \quad \boxed{3 < p < 4}$

1. Find the condition that $x^2 + 2(a + 2)x + 9a = 0$ has no real roots

2. For what values of k has $x^2 + 2x + 7 = k(2x + 1)$ real roots?

3. Prove that $x^2 - 2px + p^2 - q^2 - r^2 = 0$ has real roots.

• *Check answers*

Section 7: Quadratic equations in disguise

In this section you will solve quadratic equations
that are not easily recognisable as quadratics.

DEVELOPMENT

D7.1: Rearrange and solve

Always rearrange a quadratic into the standard format
$ax^2+bx+c = 0$ before attempting to solve it.

Rearrange into standard form & solve. Where possible give <u>exact</u> answers.
Where exact answers are not possible, give answers to 2 dp.

1. $x^2 = 2x + 15$

2. $x^2 + 5x = 14$

3. $x^2 - 24 = 2x$

4. $4 - 3x - x^2 = 0$

5. $x(x + 2) = 7$

6. $12 - x^2 = x$

7. $(x - 3)^2 = 2(x + 1)$

8. $3x(x + 2) + 6 = x(x - 2)$ • *Check your answers.*

D7.2 : Quadratics in disguise

Students frequently fail to recognise quadratic equations which are not
in the standard format. This exercise sets out to remedy this problem.

EXAMPLE	EXAMPLE	Multiply
$x = 2 + \dfrac{15}{x}$	$\dfrac{2}{x} + \dfrac{2}{x + 1} = 3$	every term by the lowest common
$\Rightarrow \quad x^2 = 2x + 15$	$\Rightarrow 2(x + 1) + 2x = 3x(x + 1)$	multiple
$\Rightarrow x^2 - 2x - 15 = 0$	$\Rightarrow \quad 2x + 2 + 2x = 3x^2 + 3x$	(LCM) of the
$\Rightarrow (x + 3)(x - 5) = 0$	$\Rightarrow \quad 3x^2 - x - 2 = 0$	denominators.
$\Rightarrow \boxed{x = -3 \ \& \ 5}$	$\Rightarrow (3x + 2)(x - 1) = 0$	
	$\Rightarrow \boxed{x = {}^2/_3 \ \& \ 1}$	 *Didi*

Rearrange and solve each equation. Where possible give <u>exact</u> answers.
Where exact answers are not possible, give answers to 2 s.f.

1. $7 - \dfrac{2}{x} = x$

2. $\dfrac{2}{x} = x - 3$

3. $1 + \dfrac{3}{x} = 10x$

4. $\dfrac{2}{x} - \dfrac{2}{x + 1} = 3$

5. $4 = \dfrac{3}{x + 1} + \dfrac{3}{x - 1}$

6. $\dfrac{4}{x - 3} + \dfrac{4}{x} = 5$

7. $\dfrac{1}{2x - 1} - \dfrac{1}{x + 1} = \dfrac{3}{x + 5}$

8. $\dfrac{1}{x - 2} - \dfrac{4}{x + 3} = \dfrac{-5}{x + 6}$

• *Check your answers*

Section 8: Quadratic functions of *x*

In this section you will work with equations which are quadratic functions of *x*.

DEVELOPMENT

D8.1: Quadratics of functions of *x*

EXAMPLE

$$6x^4 - x^2 - 2 = 0$$
$$\Rightarrow \quad 6(x^2)^2 - x^2 - 2 = 0$$
$$\Rightarrow \quad (3x^2 - 2)(2x^2 + 1) = 0$$
$$\Rightarrow \quad x^2 = {}^2/_3 \qquad x^2 = -{}^1/_2$$
$$\Rightarrow \quad \boxed{x = \pm\sqrt{\frac{2}{3}}} \qquad no\ solution$$

$$\boxed{6x^4 - x^2 - 2 = 0}$$
This is called a quadratic in x^2

Alternative method

$$6x^4 - x^2 - 2 = 0$$
Let $y = x^2$
$$\Rightarrow \quad 6y^2 - y - 2 = 0$$
$$\Rightarrow \quad (3y - 2)(2y + 1) = 0$$
$$\Rightarrow \quad y = {}^2/_3 \qquad y = -{}^1/_2$$
$$\Rightarrow \quad x^2 = {}^2/_3 \qquad x^2 = -{}^1/_2$$
$$\Rightarrow \quad \boxed{x = \pm\sqrt{\frac{2}{3}}} \qquad no\ solution$$

Solve :

1. $x^4 - x^2 - 2 = 0$ 2. $x^6 + 7x^3 - 8 = 0$ 3. $18x^4 - 17x^2 + 4 = 0$

EXAMPLE

$$2^{2x} - 6 \times 2^x + 8 = 0$$
$$\Rightarrow \quad (2^x)^2 - 6\,(2^x) + 8 = 0$$
$$\Rightarrow \quad (2^x - 2)(2^x - 4) = 0$$
$$\Rightarrow \quad 2^x = 2\ \&\ 2^x = 4$$
$$\Rightarrow \quad \boxed{x = 1\ \&\ x = 2}$$

$$\boxed{2^{2x} - 6 \times 2^x + 8 = 0}$$
This is called a quadratic in 2^x

Solve :

4. $3^{2x} - 10 \times 3^x + 9 = 0$ 5. $20\dfrac{1}{x^2} - \dfrac{31}{x} + 12 = 0$

6. $2(\sin x)^2 - 3\sin x + 1 = 0$ [You may assume that *x* lies between 0° and 90°]

7. $x - 4\sqrt{x} + 3 = 0$ 8. $25x^4 - 25x^2 + 4 = 0$

9. Factorise $35x^2 - 16x - 3$.
   Hence, solve the equation $35y - 16\sqrt{y} - 3 = 0$

10. Solve $15x^2 + 2x - 8 = 0$
    Hence, find <u>exact values</u> for the four solutions of $15x^4 + 2x^2 - 8 = 0$

11. $^1/_2 = {}^3/_5 x^2 + {}^1/_4 x$ Rearrange this equation into standard quadratic form
    and solve it using the formula, giving answers to 3 d.p.

    Hence solve $0.5 = 0.6\ t^{2/3} + 0.25\ t^{1/3}$, giving answers to 3 d.p.

• *Check your answers.*

P1: Unit 2: Quadratic Expressions and Equations

Facts and formulae you need to learn

If $ax^2 + bx + c = 0$ then $x = \dfrac{-b \pm \sqrt{(b^2 - 4ac)}}{2a}$

If $b^2 - 4ac > 0$ the equation has two real distinct roots.

If $b^2 - 4ac = 0$ the equation has two real equal roots (*or* just one root).

If $b^2 - 4ac < 0$ the equation has no roots.

Competence Test P1.2

There are marks for the correct answer(s) and marks for the working out or explanation. (2M, 1A) means 2 marks for method and 1 mark for accuracy.
You may use your text book for reference.

Factorise:

1. $x^2 - 3x$ (1M,1A)

2. $x^2 + 2x - 15$ (1M, 1A)

3. $6x^2 - 5x - 4$ (1M,1A)

4. $2x^2 + 4x$ (1M, 1A)

Solve:

5. $x^2 + 13x + 36 = 0$ (1M,2A)

6. $x^2 + 8x - 9 = 0$ (1M, 2A)

7. $6x^2 - 5x = 0$ (1M,2A)

8. $4x^2 - 4x + 1 = 0$ (1M, 2A)

9. $15 - 2x < 3$ (1M,1A)

10. $\frac{4}{5}x \geq 4(x + 3)$ (1M, 2A)

11. $x^2 - 5x - 24 < 0$ (2M,2A)

12. $3x^2 - 2x - 1 > 0$ (2M, 2A)

13. $x = 4 + \dfrac{5}{x}$ (2M,2A)

14. $\dfrac{3}{x} - \dfrac{2}{x+1} = 5$ (2M,3A)

15. $4x^2 - 8x + 5 = 0$ How many roots does this equation have ?   (2M,2A)
Show how to use the discriminant to work it out.

16. Solve $x^3 - 4x^2 - 5x = 0$ (2M,3A)

Total (**AQA & Edexcel**) = 51

[OCR]

17. *Solve these quadratic equations:*

    (a) $3^{2x} - 12 \times 3^x + 27 = 0$ (b) $x + 3\sqrt{x} - 10 = 0$ (4M, 4A)

Total (**OCR**) = 59

AIMING HIGH

Unit 3
Coordinate Geometry and Graphs

CONTENTS
Section 1: Properties of lines and points
Section 2: $y = mx + c$
Section 3: Equations of straight lines
Section 4: Sketching graphs
Section 5: Related functions **[OCR and AQA only]**

	OCR	AQA	Edexcel
Section 1	All	All	All
Section 2	All	All	All
Section 3	All	All	All
Section 4	All	All	All
Section 5	All	All	—

Unit 3: Coordinate Geometry ...

Section 1: Properties of lines and points

In this section you will :
- calculate the distance between two points
- calculate the midpoint of a line joining two points
- calculate the gradient of a line joining two points

DEVELOPMENT

D1.1: Distance and midpoint formulae

The most common error, when working out midpoints, is to – instead of +.
Remember, the midpoint values are the mean values of the two endpoints, so you +

distance between A and B	coordinates of midpoint of AB
$d^2 = (x_2 - x_1)^2 + (y_2 - y_1)^2$	$(x_M, y_M) = (\frac{1}{2}[x_1 + x_2], \frac{1}{2}[y_1 + y_2])$

EXAMPLE   Calculate (a) the distance between P(1,2) and Q(3,–1)
and   (b) the coordinates of the midpoint of PQ.

A: (a) $d^2 = (1 - 3)^2 + (2 - (-1))^2$ $=$ $(-2)^2 + (3)^2 = 13$
$\Rightarrow$ $\boxed{\text{distance} = \sqrt{13}}$

(b)   midpoint $= (\frac{1}{2}[1 + 3], \frac{1}{2}[2 + (-1)]) = \boxed{(2, \frac{1}{2})}$

1. Calculate the distance between each of the following pairs of points:
   (a) (1,2),(3,7)   (b) (2,–5),(3,–1)   (c) (3,5),(–3,5)
   (d) (–4,–2),(–1,2)   (e) (–1,0)(–1,4)   (f) (0,a),(a,0)

2. Find the coordinates of the midpoints of the lines joining the pairs of points in question 1

3. For each △, calculate the lengths of the sides of △ ABC and determine whether the triangle is right angled. If it is right angled, say where the right angle is. Give each lengths as a surd (eg $\sqrt{21}$), since this is the exact value.
   (a)   A(0,0)   B(2,3)   C(1,4)
   (b)   A(3,–1)   B(1,7)   C(–7,5)

   'Equidistant' means "equal distances from"   *Chyps*

4. Prove that the point (4,4) is equidistant from the points (1,0) and (–1,4)

5. Prove that the triangle whose vertices are P(1,2), Q(3,4) and R(–1,6), is isosceles.

6. M is the midpoint of AB. A is (3,5), M is (0,2). Find the coordinates of B.

7. A,B,C are the points (7,3), (–4,1) and (–3,–2) respectively.
   (a) Show that △ ABC is isosceles
   (b) Find the midpoint of the base of △ABC and hence find the area of △ABC.

D1.2: Gradients of line segments

Gradient of line joining two points (x_1, y_1) and (x_2, y_2)

$$m = \frac{y_2 - y_1}{x_2 - x_1} = \frac{\text{difference in } ys}{\text{difference in } xs}$$

positive   negative   zero   infinite
gradient   gradient   gradient   gradient

1. Copy this sketch.
   (a) Work out the value of r and t and put them
       onto the sketch.
   (b) Write down the gradient of PQ
       as a fraction in its simplest form.

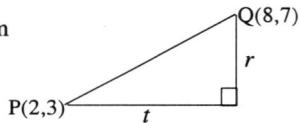

   P(2,3) t Q(8,7) r

2. Use the formula for the gradient given above to calculate the gradient of PQ.
   Show that it give the same value as in question 1.

3. Calculate the gradient of the line between each of the following pairs of points:
   (a) (1,2),(3,7)   (b) (2,–5),(3,–1)   (c) (–4,–2),(–1,2)

4. L is the point (1,2) and M is the point (1,4)
   (a) If you use the formula to calculate the gradient of LM, it does not work.
       Explain why it does not work.
   (b) Sketch the relative positions of the two points.
       What is the gradient of LM ? How could you have spotted this from the
       coordinates, without sketching the points ?

5. Sketch, (do not plot), each pair of lines on one diagram.
   Use a separate diagram for each pair of lines
   Write down the gradient of each line. Use integers or fractions – not decimals

   (a) Lines PQ and RS where P is (2,3), Q is (6,7), R is (6,3), S is (2,7)
   (b) Lines LM and MN where L is (2,1), M is (7,2), N is (6,7)
   (c) Line UV and WX where U is (4,11), V is (10,3), W is (3,4), X is (11,10)

Perpendicular lines
If m_1 is the gradient of one line and m_2 is the gradient of another line,
   and the two lines are perpendicular

   then $m_2 \times m_1 = -1$ or $m_2 = -1/m_1$

6. For each pair of lines in question 5, say whether they are perpendicular or not.
   • *Check your answers.*

D1.3 : Gradients and angles

EXAMPLE   Find the gradient of the line which is inclined at an angle of 120° to the positive direction of the x–axis.

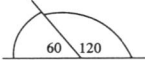

gradient = tan 120° = – tan 60° = –1.7321

Write down the gradients of the lines that are inclined at the following angles to the positive x–axis:

1. 45°   2. 135°   3. 90°

• *Check your answers.*

EXTENSIONS

EXTENSION PROBLEMS take you beyond the level of the basic techniques. If you want to aim for the higher grades, you need to tackle as much of the extension work as you can find time for. They will include A-Level examination-type questions. This is where the top grades are earned.

E1.4 : Altogether now

1. Find the gradients of the sides of the triangle whose vertices are the points A(5,4), B(2,–2), C(–6,2). Hence determine whether the triangle is right angled.

2. Find the gradient of the line joining the points on the curve $y = x^3$, whose x-coordinates are 1 and 3.

3. A set of points are <u>collinear</u> if they lie in a straight line. Determine, by comparing gradients, whether the three points given are collinear.:

   (a) (0,–1), (1,1), (2,3)
   (b) (1,–3), (0,–1), (–1,2)
   (c) (–6,–5), (1,–3), (8,–1)

4. The distance between the points $(\alpha,0)$ and $(0,\alpha)$ is equal to the distance between the points (1,2) and (–1,3). Find α (2 possible values).

5. The distance of the point (a,b) from the origin is equal to its distance from the point (–2,3). Find an equation connecting a and b.

6. Find the gradient of the straight line joining the points of intersection of the curve $y = x^2$ and the line $y = x + 2$.

7. The straight line $x/_3 + y/_4 = 1$ meets the x- and y- axes at the point A and B respectively. Find the length and gradient of AB.

• *Check your answers.*

Section 2: $y = mx + c$

In this section you will:
- recognise whether an equation represents a straight line, or not
- work out the gradient of a line from its equation
- determine whether lines are parallel, perpendicular, or neither.

DEVELOPMENT

D2.1: The standard equation of a straight line

$y = mx + c$
is the standard equation of a straight line

m = gradient of line

c = y–intercept

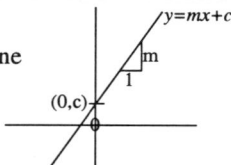

EXAMPLE   Q. Sketch the lines given by $y = 2x + 3$ and $2y - 4x + 3 = 0$

A: $y = 2x + 3$ has gradient 2
and y–intercept 3

The second equation needs rearranging into $y = mx + c$ format, first.

$2y - 4x + 3 = 0$
$\Rightarrow \quad 2y = 4x - 3$
$\Rightarrow \quad y = 2x - \frac{3}{2}$ which has gradient 2
and y–intercept $-\frac{3}{2}$

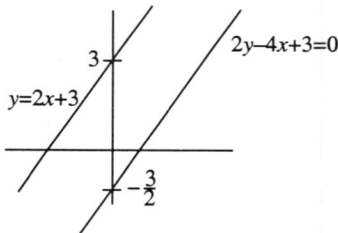

1. On one diagram sketch (do not plot!) each of the following lines :
    (label each one clearly)

    $y = x$ $\qquad$ $y = 3x$ $\qquad$ $y = 0$ $\qquad$ $y = \frac{1}{3}x$

    $y + x = 0$ $\qquad$ $y + 2x = 0$ $\qquad$ $x = 0$

2. On one diagram, sketch and label each of the following lines :

    $y = x$ $\qquad$ $y - x = 2$ $\qquad$ $2y + 5 = 2x$ $\qquad$ $2y + 7 - 2x = 0$

3. Find the gradients of each line by rearranging the equation into standard format:

    (a) $5x - 2y = 3$ $\qquad$ (b) $x = 3y - 4$ $\qquad$ (c) $y + 3x = 6$

    (d) $\frac{y}{3} + x = 2$ $\qquad$ (e) $7y - 4x = 3$ $\qquad$ (f) $7x - 4y = 8$

    (g) $\frac{x}{2} - \frac{y}{3} = 1$ $\qquad$ (h) $ax - by = c$

• *Check your answers.*

D2.2 : Is it a straight line, or not ?

> An equation represents a straight line if it could be rearranged into the form
> $$y = mx + c$$

1. Which of these equations represents a straight line ?

   A: $y = 3 - 2x$ B: $y = \dfrac{5}{x} + 3$ C: $3y = 2x + 5$ D: $xy = 2x + 3$

   E: $4x + 2y = 7$ F: $y = 3x^2 + 2x + 1$ G: $\dfrac{y}{x+1} = 5$ H: $2y + 3x + 5 = 0$

2. *Rearrange each of these equations into the form y = mx + c:*

   (a) $y = 5 - 7x$ (b) $3y = 5x + 1$ (c) $3x + 2y = 5$ (d) $\dfrac{y}{x+4} = 2$

   • *Check your answers.*

D2.3: Parallel and perpendicular lines

Parallel lines	Perpendicular lines
$m_2 = m_1$	$m_1 \times m_2 = -1$ or $m_2 = -1/m_1$

EXAMPLE Determine whether y $-7x = 3$ and $7y + x = 5$ are parallel, perpendicular, or neither.

$y - 7x = 3$ can be written as $y = 7x + 3$.   Its gradient is 7

$7y + x = 5$ can be written as $y = -\frac{1}{7}x + \frac{5}{7}$. Its gradient is $-\frac{1}{7}$

$m_1 \times m_2 = 7 \times (-\frac{1}{7}) = -1$

$\Rightarrow$ the lines are perpendicular.

Determine whether each pair of lines is parallel, perpendicular, or neither:

1. $4y = 6x + 1$ $2y - 3x + 5 = 0$ 2. $21y = 33x + 4$ $7y - 11x + 31 = 0$

3. $y + 5x = 0$ $5y = x - 3$ 4. $y + ax = 0$ $a^2x - ay = 1/a$

5. $3y - 4x = 2$ $4x - 3y = 4$ 6. $py - p^2x = 0$ $p^2y + px = 0$

7. Prove that the lines OA and OB are perpendicular where A is (4,3) and B is (3,–4). O is the origin.

   • *Check your answers.*

Section 3: Equations of straight lines

In this section you will meet and use the formula for a straight line, when you have been given:
- the gradient of a line and a point on the line
- two points on the line

DEVELOPMENT

D3.1 : Straight line equations

1. (3,4) is a given point on this line.
   The gradient of the line is 2.
   (x,y) is a general point on the line.

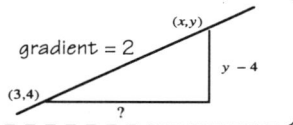

   gradient = 2

   (x,y)

   (3,4)

   $y - 4$

   ?

   (a) Explain why the marked side of the triangle is $y - 4$
   (b) Find a similar expression for the bottom line of the triangle (? in diagram)
   (c) Express the gradient in terms of x and y.
   (d) Explain why $\dfrac{y-4}{x-3} = 2$
   (e) Show how to rearrange the equation in (d) to give $y = 2x - 2$

2.

   gradient = 3

   (x,y)

   (1,2)

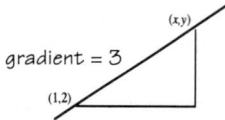

   Use the method of question 1 to show that the equation of this line is $y = 3x - 1$

3. A straight line passes through (3,7) and has gradient –1.
   Work out the equation of the line. Show all working.

4. A straight line passes through (x_1, y_1) and has gradient m.
   Show that the equation of the line is given by $\dfrac{y - y_1}{x - x_1} = m$

   • *Check your answers.*

D3.2 : A formula for equations of straight lines

Equation of a straight line with gradient m passing through the point (x_1, y_1)

$\dfrac{y - y_1}{x - x_1} = m$

From now on, you should use this formula to derive the equation of a straight line.
Driller

1. Work out the equation of the line passing through (2,7) with gradient 2.
   Give the equation in the form $y = mx + c$.

2. Work out the equation of the line passing through (2,5) with gradient $^3/_2$.
   Give the equation in the form $ax + by + c = 0$.

EXAMPLE   Work out the equation of the straight line that passes through (5,–1) and (–2,3).

Method 1

gradient $= \dfrac{(3-(-1))}{-2-5} = \dfrac{4}{-7} = -\dfrac{4}{7}$

$\dfrac{y-(-1)}{x-3} = -\dfrac{4}{7}$

$\Rightarrow \quad y+1 = \dfrac{-4}{7}(x-3)$

$\Rightarrow \quad y+1 = \dfrac{-4x}{7} + \dfrac{12}{7}$

$\Rightarrow \quad 7y+7 = -4x + 12$

$\Rightarrow \quad 7y = -4x + 5$

Method 2

gradient $= \dfrac{(3-(-1))}{-2-5} = \dfrac{4}{-7} = -\dfrac{4}{7}$

$\dfrac{y-(-1)}{x-3} = -\dfrac{4}{7}$

$\Rightarrow \quad 7(y+1) = -4(x-3)$

$\Rightarrow \quad 7y+7 = -4x + 12$

$\Rightarrow \quad 7y = -4x + 5$

Method 2 is much simpler because it gets rid of the fractions as early as possible.

Letmewin

3. *Work out the equations of each line:*

   (a) gradient – 5, passing through (0,0)

   (b) gradient $\frac{1}{3}$, passing through (1, – 2)

4. *Work out the equations of the straight lines joining the following pairs of points:*

   (a) (1,4) (2, 9)   (b) (–1, 1) (1, –2)   (c) (3, 4) (–4, 3)

5. Show that the equation of the line that passes through (–7,1) and (3,13) is $5y = 6x + 47$

6. Find the equation of the line that passes through (–4,–1) and (17,23). Give the equation in the form $ax + by + c = 0$

7. Work out the equation of the line parallel to $3x – y = 7$ which passes through the point (–1, 3)

8. Find the equation of the line perpendicular to the line $y + 2x = 8$ which passes throught the point (3,1)

9. Find the equation of the straight line which passes through the point of intersection of the lines $y = -x$ and $y = 2x + 3$ and the point (1, –5)

10.

(8,8)

perpendicular bisector

(0,0)

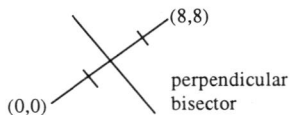

What is the equation of the perpendicular bisector of the line joining the points (0,0) and (8,8).

You will be expected to KNOW what is meant by 'perpendicular bisector'.

Big Edd

• *Check your answers.*

D3.3 : Setting out problems

To achieve high marks at AS/A-Level, it is not sufficient just to get the right answers.
You need to be able to explain clearly how you get the answers.
The following example shows you how to set out more complex questions.

EXAMPLE The coordinates of P, Q, R are $(1,5), (7,9), (9,6)$ respectively.
PQRS is a rectangle. Find the coordinates of S.

Step 1: Put all the information you are given onto a sketch.
Step 2: Plan what you need to do to solve the problem.

Driller

S is at the intersection of PS and RS
You need to find the equations of PS and RS

You know the point P and need to find the $\Rightarrow$ equation of PS
gradient of PS. Grad of PS = grad of RQ

You know the point R and need to find the $\Rightarrow$ equation of RS
gradient of RS. Grad of RS = grad of PQ

Solve the equations for PS and RS simultaneously to find
the coordinates of S.

Grad PS = grad RQ $= \dfrac{9-6}{7-9} = \dfrac{3}{-2} = \dfrac{-3}{2}$

Equation of PS:
$\dfrac{y-5}{x-1} = \dfrac{-3}{2}$ $\Rightarrow 2y - 10 = -3x + 3$

$\Rightarrow 2y = -3x + 13$ —— (1)

Grad RS = grad PQ $= \dfrac{9-5}{7-1} = \dfrac{4}{6} = \dfrac{2}{3}$

Equation of RS:
$\dfrac{y-6}{x-9} = \dfrac{2}{3}$ $\Rightarrow 3y - 18 = 2x - 18$

$\Rightarrow 3y = 2x$ —— (2)

OR, you could use the fact that RS is perpendicular to PS, to get the gradient of RS

Idea

(2) $\Rightarrow y = {}^2/_3 x$ and putting this into (2) $\Rightarrow {}^4/_3 x = -3x + 13$

$\Rightarrow 4x = -9x + 39$ $\Rightarrow 13x = 39$ $\Rightarrow x = 3$

(2) $\Rightarrow y = 2$

$\therefore$ S is (3,2)

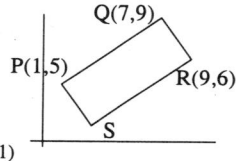

1. Find the equation of the chord joining the points on the curve $y = x^3$ whose y–coordinates are 0 and -1

2. P(0,1), Q(3,2), R(–1,7), S(–3,1) are the vertices of a quadrilateral PQRS. Find the equations of the diagonals PR and QS. Find the point of intersection of the diagonals.

---

3. A is the point (0,2). A perpendicular is drawn from this point to the line $2x - 3y = 5$. Find the equation of this perpendicular. Hence find the coordinates of the foot of the perpendicular (the point where it meets the line).

4. W(0,0), X(2,3), Y(3,5) are three vertices of a parallelogram WXYZ.
   Sketch and label the parallelogram.
   Find :   (a) the gradients of WX and XY
             (b) the equation of the line through W parallel to XY
             (c) the equation of the line through Y parallel to WX
             (d) the coordinates of Z

5. EFGH is rectangle where E(−3,−1), G(−8,4) and H(−2,1)
   Sketch and label the rectangle.
   Find: (a) the equation of the line through G perpendicular to GH
             (b) the equation of the line through E perpendicular to EH
             (c) the coordinates of F

6. KLMN is a parallelogram. K is (3,5), L is (−4,2), N is (1,0)
   (a) Work out the coordinates of M
   (b) Find the equation of KM

• *Check your answers*

E3.4: Line challenges

1. ABCD is a parallelogram. A(8,6) and C(1,2) are opposite corners.
   BC and CD lie along the lines $x + 7y = 15$ and $y = x + 1$ respectively.
   Work out the coordinates of B and D.

2. The line $2x + y = 8$ cuts the x–axis at A and the y–axis at B.
   Find the equation of the perpendicular bisector of AB.
   The perpendicular bisector cuts the y –axis at C.
   Find the gradient of the line AC.

3. P has y–coordinate 4 and lies on the curve $y^2 = 16x$.
   A line through P goes through the point F(4,0) and
   meets the curve again at Q.
   Find the equation of PQ and the coordinates of Q

4. Work out the perpendicular distance of the
   point (3,−5) from the line $3x - 4y + 1 = 0$

5. Find the equation of the perpendicular bisectors of the lines joining the pairs of points (2,1), (6,3) and (6,3), (8,1). Show that the point of intersection of these bisectors is on the x-axis.

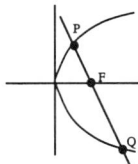

• *Check your answers*

Section 4: Sketching graphs

In this section you will work with sketch graphs of $y = kx^n$, $y = \sqrt{x}$, $y = ax^2 + bx + c$ and $y = f(x)$ where $f(x)$ is the product of at most 3 linear factors, not necessarily all distinct.

DEVELOPMENT

D4.1: Graphs of $y = kx^n$

Sketch graphs you need to know

$y = x$ $y = x^2$ $y = x^3$ $y = x^4$ $y = x^5$

$y = x^{-1}$ $y = x^{-2}$ $y = x^{-3}$ $y = x^{-4}$

$y = \pm\sqrt{x}$

$y = \sqrt{x}$

$y = -f(x)$ is the reflection of $y = f(x)$ in the x-axis. For example:

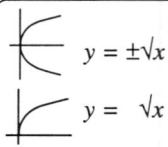

$y = -x^2$

$y = x^2$

$y = f(x)$ means 'y is a function of x' or 'y equals an expression involving only x'

For each function below, sketch $y = f(x)$ and $y = -f(x)$. Label each graph.
1. $y = x^3$ 2. $y = x^4$ 3. $y = \sqrt{x}$ 4. $y = \frac{1}{x}$ 5. $y = \frac{1}{x^2}$

$y = kf(x)$ is the graph of $y = f(x)$ stretched by a factor k in the y-direction (a y-scaling of factor k)

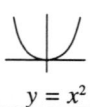

$y = x^2$ $y = 2x^2$

Sketch each pair of functions, side-by-side :

6. $y = x^3$ 7. $y = \sqrt{x}$ 8. $y = x^2$ 9. $y = \frac{1}{x}$

    $y = 3x^3$ $y = 2\sqrt{x}$ $y = \frac{x^2}{4}$ $y = -\frac{2}{x}$

10.(a) Sketch the graph of $y = k\sqrt{x}$.
   (b) $y = k\sqrt{x}$ passes through $(9, 6)$. What is the value of k ?

11. This is the graph of $y = k\,x^n$, where k is an integer less than 100.
   (a) Give two values that n could be.
   (b) The point $(2, 16)$ is on the graph. Determine the values of k and n.

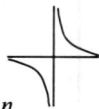

• *Check your answers.*

D4.2: Intersecting lines and curves

1. Use the graph to solve these simultaneous equations:

   (a) $y = 2x + 3$
   $y = {}^2/_x$

   (b) $2y = x - 3$
   $y = {}^2/_x$

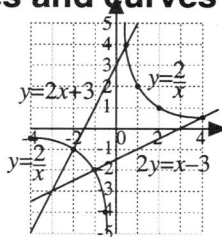

2. Use simultaneous equations to show that $y = x^2 - 2x + 3$ and $y = 2x$ intersect at two points, and find the coordinates of these points.

To find the points of intersection of the curve $y = f(x)$ and a line $y = mx + c$, you solve the equation $f(x) = mx + c$.

If this equation has two distinct roots, then the line cuts the curve twice.

If this equation has one root, then the line is tangent to the curve.

EXAMPLE   Use simultaneous equations to show that $y = x - 4$ is a tangent to $y = x^2 - x$ and find the point of intersection.

$y = x - 4$ intersects $y = x^2 - x$ when $x^2 - x = x - 4$

$\Rightarrow$ $x^2 - 2x + 4 = 0$

$\Rightarrow$ $(x - 2)^2 = 0$

There is just one root to this equation, so $\boxed{\text{the line is a tangent to the curve.}}$

When $x = 2$, $y = -2$ $\therefore$ point of intersection is $\boxed{(2, -2)}$

---

3. Show that $y = 2 - x$ is a tangent to the curve $y = {}^1/_x$.

4. Is the line $y = 2x - 6$ a tangent to the curve $y = x^2 - x - 6$? Find the point(s) of intersection.

5. Is the line $y = 5 - 2x$ a tangent to the curve $y = 4 - x^2$? Find the point(s) of intersection.

6. **[OCR only]**

   Sketch the curve $y = \sqrt{x}$.

   Show that the line $y = {}^1/_4 x + 1$ is a tangent to the curve $y = \sqrt{x}$ and find the coordinates of the point of intersection.

• *Check your answers.*

D4.3: Factorisable quadratics

Sketching quadratic graphs

All quadratic graphs are shaped ⌣ (if the coefficient of x^2 is positive)

or ⌢ (if the coefficient of x^2 is negative)

The graph crosses the x-axis where $y = 0$

EXAMPLE   Sketch the graph of $y = (x + 2)(x - 4)$

$y = (x + 2)(x - 4)$ crosses the x-axis where $y = 0$

$\Rightarrow \quad (x + 2)(x - 4) = 0$

$\Rightarrow \quad x = -2$ and $x = 4$

Always label any points where the curve crosses the x-axis.

Sketch the graph of each of these:

1. $y = (x - 1)(x + 2)$ 2. $y = x(x - 2)$ 3. $y = 5x - x^2$

To find the points of intersection of the curve $y = ax^2 + bx + c$ and the line $y = 0$, you solve the equation $ax^2 + bx + c = 0$.

[This gives the points where the curve crosses the x-axis.]

If this equation has two distinct roots, then the curve cuts the x-axis twice.

If this equation has one root, then the x-axis is tangent to the curve.

EXAMPLE   Sketch the graph of $y = (x - 2)^2$

$y = (x - 2)^2$ crosses the x-axis where $y = 0$

$\Rightarrow \quad (x - 2)(x - 2) = 0$

$\Rightarrow \quad x = 2$ is the only point where it crosses the x-axis.

Sketch the graph of each of these:

4. $y = (x - 3)^2$ 5. $y = -(x - 1)^2$ 6. $y = (x + 3)^2$

7. (a) Sketch the graph of $y = (x + 1)(x - 3)$

   (b) All quadratic graphs are symmetrical. The vertex is the turning point of the graph. Work out the coordinates of the vertex.

   (c) What is the minimum value of $(x + 1)(x - 3)$?

8. (a) Sketch the graph of $y = (x + 1)(5 - x)$

   (b) Work out the coordinates of the vertex.

   (c) What is the maximum value of $(x + 1)(5 - x)$?

   (d) Solve $(x + 1)(5 - x) > 0$

• *Check your answers.*

D4.4: Factorisable cubics

Cubics

$y=(x-a)(x-b)(x-c)$ is of

the form

This is similar to $y=x^3$

$y=(x-a)(x-b)(c-x)$

is like this

and $y=-x^3$ is

Remember : If the coefficient of x^3 is +ve the the graph is ╱ (like $y = x^3$)
and if the coefficient of x^3 is −ve then
the graph is ╲ (like $y = -x^3$)

1. $y = x(x-3)(x+4)$
    (a) For what value of x does the graph cross the x-axis?
    (b) Sketch the graph of $y = x(x-3)(x+4)$
    (c) Use the graph to solve $x(x-3)(x+4) > 0$

2. (a) Sketch the graph of $y = x(x-2)^2$
    (b) For what value of x is the x-axis a tangent to the curve ?
    (c) Solve $x(x-2)^2 < 0$ • *Check your answers.*

EXTENSIONS
E4.5: Intersecting graphs

1. (a) Work out the coordinates of A,B,C and D.
    (b) For what values of x is $x + 5 < 4x + 5 - x^2$?
    (c) Solve $x + 5 > 4x + 5 - x^2$

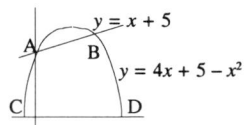

2. (a) Sketch the graph of $y = x^2 - 2x$
    (b) On the same graph sketch $y = x$
    (c) Work out the solution of $x^2 - 2x = x$
    (d) Use the graph and the answers to (c) to solve $x^2 - 2x < x$

3. (a) Sketch the graph of $y = (x-1)(x+4)(3-x)$
    (b) Solve $(x-1)(x+4)(3-x) \geq 0$
    (c) On the same graph, sketch $y = x + 4$
    (d) Solve $(x-1)(x+4)(3-x) \leq x + 4$

• *Check your answers.*

Section 5: Related functions

In this section you will :
  • work with graphs of related functions;
  • use the rules for drawing graphs of related functions.

DEVELOPMENT

D5.1: Graphs of some related functions

1. *Sketch the graphs of:*
   (a) $y = x^3 + 3$
   (b) $y = x^3 - 1$

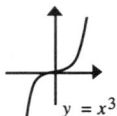

Adding k to the function moves the graph up k units.

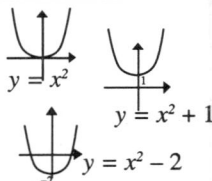

$y = x^2$

$y = x^2 + 1$

$y = x^2 - 2$

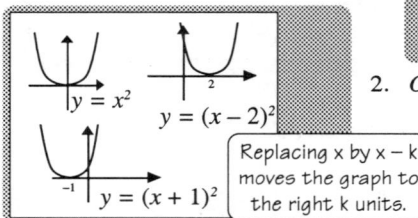

$y = x^2$

$y = (x - 2)^2$

$y = (x + 1)^2$

Replacing x by x – k moves the graph to the right k units.

2. *On separate diagrams sketch the graphs of:*
   (a) $y = (x - 2)^3$
   (b) $y = (x + 1)^3$
   (c) $y = (x + 3)^3 + 1$

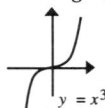

$y = x^3$

3.

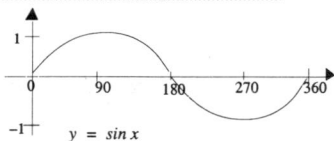

$y = \sin x$

Multiplying a function by k stretches the graph by a factor of k in the y-direction

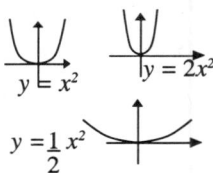

$y = x^2$

$y = 2x^2$

$y = \frac{1}{2}x^2$

On separate diagrams sketch the graphs of:
   (a) $y = 2\sin x$ (b) $y = 2\sin x + 1$ (c) $y = \frac{1}{2}\sin x$ (d) $y = 3x^3$

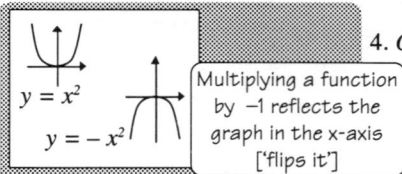

$y = x^2$

$y = -x^2$

Multiplying a function by –1 reflects the graph in the x-axis ['flips it']

4. *On separate diagrams sketch the graphs of:*
   (a) $y = -x^3$ (b) $y = -2x^2$
   (c) $y = -\sin x$ (d) $y = 1 - x^2$

5. *On separate diagrams sketch the graphs of:*
   (a) $y = 1 + 2\cos x$ $[0° \le x \le 360°]$
   (b) $y = 2(x - 3)^2$ (c) $y = -\frac{1}{x}$
   (d) $y = \dfrac{1}{x + 2}$ (e) $y = 3(x + 1)^2 - 2$
   (f) $y = 2 - \cos x$ $[-180° \le x \le 180°]$

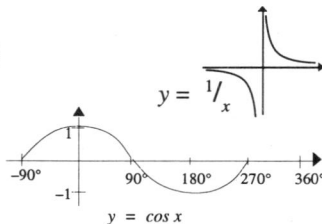

$y = \frac{1}{x}$

$y = \cos x$

   • *Check answers.*

D5.2: A systematic look at graph transformations

Type 1
When y is replaced by $y - k$
the graph moves a distance k
in the positive y–direction.

$y = f(x)$ becomes $y - k = f(x)$

Same as $y = f(x) + k$

Type 2
When x is replaced by $x - a$
the graph moves a distance a
in the positive x–direction.

$y = f(x)$ becomes $y = f(x - a)$

Type 3
When y is replaced by y / p
the graph is stretched by a factor p
in the y–direction.

$y = f(x)$ becomes $y/p = f(x)$

Same as $y = p\,f(x)$

Type 4
When x is replaced by x / q
the graph is stretched by a factor q
in the x–direction.

$y = f(x)$ becomes $y = f(x/q)$

Type 5
When y is replaced by $-y$
the graph is reflected in the x–axis

$y = f(x)$ becomes $-y = f(x)$

Same as $y = -f(x)$

Type 6
When x is replaced by $-x$
the graph is reflected in the y–axis

$y = f(x)$ becomes $y = f(-x)$

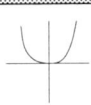

$y = x^2$

$y = x^3$

$y = 1/x$

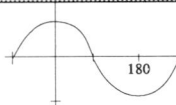

$y = \cos x$

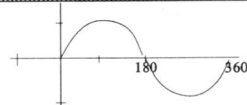

$y = \sin x$

On separate diagrams sketch the graphs of:

1. $y = (x - 3)^2 - 1$

2. $y = 4(x + 1)^3$

3. $y = \sin x/2$

4. $y = \sin 2x$

5. $y = 2 + \sin x$

6. $y = 2 \sin x$

7. $y = -x^2$

8. $y = 2 - x^2$

9. $y = -1/x$

10. $y = 1/(x + 3)$

11. $y + 4 = 1/x$

12. $y = 2 + 1/(x + 2)$

13. $y = \sin (x - 90°)$

14. $y = \cos (x + 180°)$

15. $y = 2(x - 3)^2 + 1$

16. $y = \sin (-x)$

17. $y = 2 \sin 3x$

18. $y = 2 \sin (90° - x)$

• *Check your answers.*

P1: Unit 3: Coordinate Geometry and Graphs

> **Facts and formulae you need to know:**
> Distance between two points $\qquad d^2 = (x_2 - x_1)^2 + (y_2 - y_1)^2$
> Midpoint $\qquad (x_m, y_m) = (\frac{1}{2}(x_1 + x_2), \frac{1}{2}(y_1 + y_2))$
> Condition for perpendicular lines $\qquad m_1 \times m_2 = -1$
>
> Gradient $\qquad m = \dfrac{y_2 - y_1}{x_2 - x_1}$
>
> Equation of a straight line $\qquad \dfrac{y - y_1}{x - x_1} = m$

Competence Test P1.3

1. Find the equation of each of these lines : $\hfill$ (4M, 4A)
   (a) passes through (−1,4) with gradient −2 (b) passes through (7,1) & (−1,3)

2. Sketch each of the following graphs : $\hfill$ (6A)
   (a) $y = x(x - 1)(x + 3)$ (b) $\quad 3x + 2y = 7$ (c) $\quad y = x^3$
   (d) $y = \sqrt{x}$ (e) $\quad y = \frac{2}{x}$ (f) $\quad y = -\frac{1}{x}$

3. (a) Sketch the graph of $y = (x - 3)(x + 1)$ $\hfill$ (2M, 3A)
   (b) Work out the coordinates of the vertex of the graph.
   (c) What is the minimum value of the function ?

4. Find the equation of the straight line passing through the point of intersection of
   the lines $3y - x + 2 = 0$ and $y - 5x = 4$ and perpendicular to the line $y - 2x = 3$
   $\hfill$ (4M,4A)

5. Determine whether PQ is parallel or perpendicular to RS, or neither where:
   (a) P is (1,0), Q is (5,2), R is (6,−2), S is (10,0)
   (b) P is (1,0), Q is (6,1), R is (5,−1), S is (4,3) $\hfill$ (2M,2A)

6. The points A(2,2), B(7,4), C(0,7) form a triangle ABC.
   Prove that the triangle is right angled and find its area. $\hfill$ (3M,4A)

7. Prove that the quadrilateral with vertices (2,1), (2,3), (5,6), (5,4) is a
   parallelogram and find the point of intersection of the diagonals. (4M,4A)

8. The coordinates of A,B,C are (0,2), (−2,0), (1,−3) respectively. ABCD is a
   rectangle. Find the coordinates of D. $\hfill$ (4M,4A)

> Total = 54

AIMING HIGH

Unit 4
Surds, Powers, Simultaneous Equations, Radians

CONTENTS

	OCR	AQA	Edexcel
Section 1	All	All	All
Section 2	All	All	All
Section 3	All	All	All
Section 4	All	All	All
Section 5	All	All	All
Section 6	All	All	All
Section 7	—	—	All

Unit 4: Surds, Powers and …
Section 1: Working with surds

In this section you will learn techniques for working with surds.

DEVELOPMENT

D1.1: Basic simplification

A **surd** is an irrational number of the form $\sqrt{n}$
where n is a positive integer, which is not a perfect square.

Addition and Subtraction	**Multiplication**	**Division**
$2\sqrt{7} + \sqrt{7} = 3\sqrt{7}$	$\sqrt{2} \times \sqrt{3} = \sqrt{6}$	$\sqrt{6} \div \sqrt{3} = \sqrt{2}$
$3\sqrt{5} - \sqrt{5} = 2\sqrt{5}$	$(\sqrt{2})^2 = 2$	
but $\sqrt{5} + \sqrt{2}$ cannot be simplified	$2\sqrt{5} \times 3\sqrt{2} = 6\sqrt{10}$	

EXAMPLE

$5\sqrt{3} + 2\sqrt{2} - \sqrt{3}$
$= \boxed{4\sqrt{3} + 2\sqrt{2}}$

EXAMPLE

$\sqrt{3}(3 + 2\sqrt{3})$
$= \boxed{3\sqrt{3} + 6}$

$\sqrt{3} \times 2 \times \sqrt{3}$
$= 2 \times \sqrt{3} \times \sqrt{3} =$
$2 \times 3 = 6$

EXAMPLE
$12\sqrt{6} \div 3\sqrt{2} = \dfrac{\cancel{12}^{\,4}\cancel{\sqrt{6}}^{\,\sqrt{3}}}{\cancel{3}_{1}\cancel{\sqrt{2}}_{1}} = \boxed{4\sqrt{3}}$

Always start by writing down the expression you have been given. **Why?**

1. If the expression you have been given is written next to your working out, you are less likely to make mistakes.

2. If you make a mistake, and it is in the first line of working out, you will never find it if the original expression is not there on the page.

3. If you do not start with the expression that you have been given, the solution is incomplete.

Driller

Simplify wherever possible:

1. $2\sqrt{3} + 6\sqrt{3}$
2. $2\sqrt{5} + 3\sqrt{5}$
3. $4\sqrt{3} - \sqrt{3}$
4. $\sqrt{3} \times \sqrt{3}$
5. $\sqrt{2}(\sqrt{2} + 1)$
6. $\sqrt{2} \times \sqrt{3}$
7. $\sqrt{15} \div \sqrt{3}$
8. $\sqrt{5} \times \sqrt{5}$
9. $8\sqrt{10} \div 2\sqrt{2}$
10. $3\sqrt{2} \times 5\sqrt{3}$
11. $3\sqrt{13} - \sqrt{13}$
12. $\sqrt{2}(\sqrt{2} + 2\sqrt{3})$
13. $3(\sqrt{2} + \sqrt{3})$
14. $\sqrt{5} + 2\sqrt{3}$
15. $\sqrt{2}(2 + 3\sqrt{2})$
16. $2\sqrt{3}(\sqrt{3} + \sqrt{2})$
17. $10\sqrt{6} \div 5\sqrt{3}$
18. $\sqrt{5}(2\sqrt{5} + 5)$
19. $12\sqrt{15} \div 18\sqrt{3}$
20. $2(\sqrt{3})^2$

• *Check answers.*

D1.2: Brackets and surds

EXAMPLE

$(\sqrt{2} + 3)(\sqrt{2} + 1)$
$= \sqrt{2}(\sqrt{2} + 1) + 3(\sqrt{2} + 1)$
$= 2 + \sqrt{2} + 3\sqrt{2} + 3$
$= \boxed{5 + 4\sqrt{2}}$

Multiply out and simplify:

1. $(\sqrt{2} - 1)(\sqrt{2} + 1)$
2. $(\sqrt{3} - 2)(\sqrt{3} - 1)$
3. $(\sqrt{5} + 2)(2\sqrt{5} - 1)$
4. $(3 - \sqrt{2})(2 + \sqrt{3})$
5. $(\sqrt{2} - 1)^2$
6. $(\sqrt{3} + 1)^2$
7. $(\sqrt{x} - 1)(\sqrt{x} + 1)$
8. $(\sqrt{x} + \sqrt{y})(\sqrt{x} - \sqrt{y})$

D1.3: Simplest form

EXAMPLE	Q: *Write $\sqrt{8}$ in simplest form*
A:	$\sqrt{8} = \sqrt{(4 \times 2)} = \sqrt{4} \times \sqrt{2} = \boxed{2\sqrt{2}}$

This must be the largest possible square number.

Write in simplest form:

1. $\sqrt{32}$ 2. $\sqrt{50}$ 3. $\sqrt{12}$ 4. $\sqrt{18}$ 5. $\sqrt{48}$ 6. $\sqrt{125}$ 7. $\sqrt{300}$

CHECK ANSWERS BEFORE CONTINUING.

EXAMPLE	Q: *Simplify $\sqrt{27} - \sqrt{12}$*
A:	$\sqrt{27} = \sqrt{(9 \times 3)} = 3\sqrt{3}$
	$\sqrt{12} = \sqrt{(4 \times 3)} = 2\sqrt{3}$
$\Rightarrow$	$\sqrt{27} - \sqrt{12} = 3\sqrt{3} - 2\sqrt{3} = \boxed{\sqrt{3}}$

Simplify:

8. $\sqrt{3} + 2\sqrt{12}$ 9. $\sqrt{27} + 2\sqrt{3}$ 10. $\sqrt{7} \times \sqrt{7}$ 11. $\sqrt{3} \times \sqrt{24}$

12. $\sqrt{10} \times \sqrt{2}$ 13. $3\sqrt{3} - \sqrt{12}$ 14. $3\sqrt{20} \div 4\sqrt{5}$ 15. $\sqrt{200} \div 5\sqrt{2}$

16. $5\sqrt{3} + \sqrt{48}$ 17. $\sqrt{32} + 3\sqrt{8}$ 18. $\sqrt{3}(\sqrt{27} - 1)$ 19. $\sqrt{5}(\sqrt{5} + \sqrt{20})$

20. $\sqrt{2}(\sqrt{8} - 3)$ 21. $\sqrt{3}(3\sqrt{3} - \sqrt{12})$ 22. $\sqrt{72} + \sqrt{8} - \sqrt{98} + \sqrt{50}$

• *Check your answers.*

D1.4: Rationalising the denominator

Surds are irrational numbers.
To **'rationalise the denominator'** means to replace a fraction that has a surd in the denominator, with an equivalent fraction that has a rational denominator.

EXAMPLE	*Rationalise the denominator, and simplify where possible:*

(a) $\dfrac{2}{\sqrt{3}} = \dfrac{2}{\sqrt{3}} \times \dfrac{\sqrt{3}}{\sqrt{3}} = \boxed{\dfrac{2\sqrt{3}}{3}}$

(b) $\dfrac{2}{\sqrt{12}} = \dfrac{2}{\sqrt{12}} \times \dfrac{\sqrt{12}}{\sqrt{12}} = \dfrac{\overset{1}{\cancel{2}}\sqrt{12}}{\cancel{12}_{6}} = \dfrac{\overset{1}{\cancel{2}}\sqrt{3}}{\cancel{6}_{3}} = \boxed{\dfrac{\sqrt{3}}{3}}$

Multiplying numerator and denominator of a fraction by the same number gives an equivalent fraction.

Rationalise the denominator and simplify where possible:

1. $\dfrac{1}{\sqrt{2}}$ 2. $\dfrac{1}{\sqrt{5}}$ 3. $\dfrac{3}{\sqrt{7}}$ 4. $\dfrac{5}{\sqrt{3}}$ 5. $\dfrac{3}{\sqrt{6}}$

6. $\dfrac{2}{\sqrt{8}}$ 7. $\dfrac{3}{\sqrt{18}}$ 8. $\dfrac{2}{\sqrt{32}}$ 9. $\dfrac{3}{\sqrt{125}}$ 10. $\dfrac{2\sqrt{2}}{\sqrt{50}}$

• *Check your answers.*

D1.5: More complex rationalising

EXAMPLE   Rationalise the denominator of $\dfrac{3}{\sqrt{2}+1}$

$$\dfrac{3}{\sqrt{2}+1} = \dfrac{3}{(\sqrt{2}+1)} \times \dfrac{(\sqrt{2}-1)}{(\sqrt{2}-1)}$$

The aim is to remove any surds from the denominator of the fraction.

$$= \dfrac{3(\sqrt{2}-1)}{2-1}$$

$$= \boxed{3\sqrt{2}-3}$$

$$(a-b)(a+b) = a^2 - b^2$$
$$\Rightarrow (\sqrt{a} - \sqrt{b})(\sqrt{a} + \sqrt{b}) = a - b$$

Rationalise the denominator and simplify:

1. $\dfrac{1}{\sqrt{5}+1}$

2. $\dfrac{1}{\sqrt{3}-1}$

3. $\dfrac{1}{2+\sqrt{3}}$

4. $\dfrac{\sqrt{5}}{2+\sqrt{5}}$

5. $\dfrac{2}{2\sqrt{3}-3}$

6. $\dfrac{3}{2-\sqrt{3}}$

7. $\dfrac{1}{2\sqrt{3}+\sqrt{2}}$

8. $\dfrac{\sqrt{7}}{2-\sqrt{7}}$

9. $\dfrac{2+\sqrt{3}}{2-\sqrt{3}}$

10. $\dfrac{\sqrt{2}-1}{2\sqrt{2}+1}$

11. $\dfrac{\sqrt{6}-\sqrt{2}}{\sqrt{6}+\sqrt{2}}$

12. $\dfrac{\sqrt{5}-1}{3+\sqrt{5}}$

• *Check your answers.*

EXTENSIONS

EXTENSION PROBLEMS take you beyond the level of the basic techniques.
If you want to aim for the higher grades, you need to tackle as much of the extension work as you can find time for.
They will include A-Level examination-type questions.
This is where the top grades are earned.

E1.6: Surd challenges

Simplify, leaving the denominator in rational form:

1. $\dfrac{1}{\sqrt{2}+1} + \dfrac{1}{\sqrt{2}-1}$

2. $\dfrac{1}{\sqrt{x}+2} + \dfrac{1}{\sqrt{x}-2}$

3. $\dfrac{\sqrt{x}}{\sqrt{x}+1}$

4. $\dfrac{x-y}{\sqrt{x}+\sqrt{y}}$

5. $\dfrac{\sqrt{x}+2}{\sqrt{x}}$

6. $\left(\sqrt{x}+\dfrac{1}{\sqrt{x}}\right)\left(\sqrt{x}-\dfrac{1}{\sqrt{x}}\right)$

7. $\dfrac{1}{1+\sqrt{x}} + \dfrac{1}{1-\sqrt{x}} + \dfrac{1}{1-x}$

• *Check your answers.*

Section 2: Positive powers

In this section you will review the rules of indices for positive powers.

DEVELOPMENT

D2.1: Basic Rules

RULES	EXAMPLES
$a^m \times a^n = a^{m+n}$	$3^4 \times 3^6 = 3^{10}$
$a^m \div a^n = a^{m-n}$	$2^7 \div 2^3 = 2^4$
$(a^m)^n = a^{mn}$	$(5^2)^3 = 5^6$
$a^1 = a$	$3^1 = 3$

Note: $\dfrac{a}{b}$ means $a \div b$

Yusual

Copy and complete :

1. $5^3 \times 5^5 = 5^?$
2. $3^7 \times 3^{10} = 3^?$
3. $4^5 \div 4^3 = 4^?$
4. $10^3 \times 10^2 \times 10^4 = 10^?$

5. $3^2 \times 3 = 3^?$
6. $4^7 \div 4 = 4^?$
7. $3^9 \times 3^2 \div 3^4 = 3^?$
8. $5^7 \times 5^3 \div 5 = 5^?$

EXAMPLE	Q: Work out the value of $(4^3 \times 4^2)^2 \div 4$ in index form.

A: $(4^3 \times 4^2)^2 \div 4 = \dfrac{(4^3 \times 4^2)^2}{4} = \dfrac{(4^5)^2}{4^1} = \dfrac{4^{10}}{4^1} = \boxed{4^9}$

Remember:
You should show the same amount of working as in the example.

Gizmo

Work out the values of each of these, in index form :

9. $(2^3)^3$
10. $(3^7)^2$
11. $(5^4)^3$
12. $(7^2)^4$

13. $(5^3)^2$
14. $(10^4)^5$
15. $(3^4)^3 \times 3^2$
16. $(5^5)^2 \times 5$

17. $(4^3)^7 \div 4^5$
18. $(3^7)^2 \div 3^7$
19. $(4^6 \times 4)^2$
20. $(5^3 \div 5)^3$

21. $\dfrac{3^4}{3^2}$
22. $\dfrac{5^4 \times 5}{5^3}$
23. $\dfrac{6^9}{6 \times 6^3}$
24. $\dfrac{4^8}{4^3 \times 4}$
25. $\dfrac{(3^7 \times 3)^3}{(3 \times 3^4)^2}$

• *Check answers.*

PRACTICE

P2.2: Basic practice

Do as many of these as you need. Check your answers regularly.

Batch A : *Work out the values of each of these, in index form :*

1. $5^2 \times 5^3$
2. $(3^7)^3$
3. $4^3 \div 4$
4. $3^5 \times 3^2$
5. $(4^6)^3$

6. $(4^3 \times 4)^2$
7. $2^9 \times 2 \div 2^7$
8. $6^4 \div 6^2$
9. 3×3^4
10. $(3^2 \times 3^5)^2$

11. $6^4 \div 6$
12. $\dfrac{2^5}{2^3}$
13. $\dfrac{3^6 \times 3}{3^4}$
14. $\dfrac{5^2 \times 5^3}{5}$
15. $\dfrac{(6^3)^2 \times 6}{6^4}$

DEVELOPMENT

D2.3: Powers and algebra

EXAMPLE   *Simplify each of these expressions:*

(a) $a^5 \times a^2 \;=\; a^7$

(b) $(n^3)^4 \;=\; n^{12}$

(c) $\dfrac{c^4}{c} = \dfrac{c^4}{c^1} = c^3$

(d) $(2a)^3 \;=\; 8a^3$

$\boxed{(2a)^3 = (2a) \times (2a) \times (2a)}$

> **Remember:**
> Don't just write down the answer.
> Write down the original expression. any
> necessary working — and then the answer.

Gizmo

Simplify :

1. $n^3 \times n^2$ 2. $x^9 \div x^5$ 3. $m^4 \times m^3 \div m^2$ 4. $(v^3)^2$ 5. $t^5 \times t$

6. $c^3 \div (c \times c^4)$ 7. $(3n)^2$ 8. $(5p^2)^3$ 9. $(x^2)^3$ 10. $(2x^2)^3$

EXAMPLE Q : *Simplify* $5a^2bc^3 \times 3ab^2$

A : $5a^2bc^3 \times 3ab^2 \;=\; \boxed{15a^3b^3c^3}$

$5 \times 3 \;\; a^2 \times a \;\; b \times b^2$ $\boxed{\text{This line is not needed in your answers.}}$

Simplify :

11. $2p^2q \times 3pq$ 12. $5mn^2 \times 4m^2$ 13. $3p^3q^2r \times 5pqr$

14. $(6\dot{u}v^3)^2$ 15. $3(2mn^2)^3$ 16. $(3x^2y^3z)^2$

           • *Check answers.*

PRACTICE

P2.4: Powers and algebra practice

Simplify :

1. $e^4 \times e^2$ 2. $k^3 \div k$ 3. $(a^2)^4$ 4. $h^8 \div h^3$

5. $u^2 \div u$ 6. $(3x)^2$ 7. $5xy \times 3xy^2$ 8. $6ab^2 \times 2a^2b^3$

9. $5(3p^2q)^2$ 10. $m^6 \times m$ 11. $3xy^2z \times 2xy$ 12. $4a^2b^2d^3 \times 2ad$

           • *Check answers*

D2.5: Simplifying by cancelling

EXAMPLE   Q: *Simplify* $(5^2 \times 4^4) \div (5^3 \times 4^2)$

A: $(5^2 \times 4^4) \div (5^3 \times 4^2) = \dfrac{{}^1 \cancel{5^2} \times \cancel{4^4}^{\,4^2}}{\cancel{5^3}_{\,5} \times \cancel{4^2}_{\,1}} = \boxed{\dfrac{4^2}{5}}$

$\div$ top and bottom by 5^2 ⟵ ⟶ $\div$ top and bottom by 4^2

Simplify by cancelling. Show all working. Leave answers in index form.

1. $(2^5 \times 3^3) \div (2^2 \times 3^2)$ 2. $(6^3 \times 3^4) \div (6 \times 3^2)$

3. $\dfrac{(8^5 \times 5^2 \times 3)}{(8^3 \times 3^2)}$ 4. $\dfrac{(8^4 \times 3^2)}{(3^5 \times 8^3)}$

5. $(7^4 \times 5^3) \div (7^2 \times 5)$ 6. $(4^3 \times 7^2) \div (4 \times 7^4)$

7. $\dfrac{(10^4 \times 8^4)}{(10^2 \times 8)}$ 8. $\dfrac{(2^5 \times 5^3 \times 3)}{(2^2 \times 5 \times 3^3)}$

• *Check your answers*

EXAMPLE :   Q: *Simplify* $(n^3 \times p^2) \div (n \times p^5)$

A: $(n^3 \times p^2) \div (n \times p^5) = \dfrac{{}^{n^2} \cancel{n^3} \times \cancel{p^2}^{\,1}}{\cancel{n}_{\,1} \times \cancel{p^5}_{\,p^3}} = \boxed{\dfrac{n^2}{p^3}}$

$\div$ top and bottom by n^2 ⟵ ⟶ $\div$ top and bottom by p^3

Simplify by cancelling. Show all working.

9. $6xy^3z^2 \div 2xz$ 10. $10d^4be \div d^3e$

11. $\dfrac{8a^2b^4c}{4abc^2}$ 12. $\dfrac{16p^6q^4r^2}{4p^3q^4r}$

13. $\dfrac{15m^3n^2r^2}{5mn^3r}$ 14. $\dfrac{2pr^3x}{6p^2rx}$

15. $\dfrac{8p^2q^3r}{2pq^4r^2}$ 16. $\dfrac{3p^2x^3y}{12px^2y}$

Note: it is usual, but not essential, to write algebraic expressions in alphabetical order, with the number at the front of the letters.

Bonkaz

• *Check your answers*

Section 3: Negative powers and roots

In this section you will :
- work with negative and zero powers
- use powers to represent roots

DEVELOPMENT

D3.1: Negative and zero powers

$$a^{-n} = \frac{1}{a^n} \qquad \text{eg} \quad 2^{-3} = \frac{1}{2^3} = \frac{1}{8}$$

$$a^0 = 1 \qquad \text{eg} \quad 17^0 = 1$$

The value of 2^{-3} is $\frac{1}{8}$

Write down the value of each of these as fractions or whole numbers.

1. 3^{-2} 2. 10^{-1} 3. 5^{-1} 4. 4^{-3} 5. 5^0

6. 132^0 7. 57^{-1} 8. 6^{-2} 9. 5^{-3} 10. 10^{-4}

EXAMPLE   *Find the value of* $(4^{-3} \times 4^2)^{-2}$. *Give the answer in index form.*

$$(4^{-3} \times 4^2)^{-2} = (4^{-1})^{-2} = \boxed{4^2}$$

Find the value of each of these.
Give the answers in index form.

11. $2^4 \times 2^{-2}$ 12. $(3^4 \times 3^{-1})^2$

13. $5^{-1} \times 5^2$ 14. $(3^3 \times 3^{-2})^{-1}$

15. $(4^3)^{-2}$ 16. $(2^{-1})^2$

17. $(3^{-2})^{-2}$ 18. $\dfrac{2^5 \times 2^{-2}}{2^{-3}}$

> **Remember:**
> Don't just write down the answer.
> Write down the original expression. any
> necessary working – and then the answer.
>
> *Gizmo*

Find the value of each of these. Give the answers NOT in index form.

19. $(4^2 \times 4^{-1})^2$ 20. $\dfrac{3^4 \times 3^{-2}}{3^3}$ 21. $6^{-2} \times 6^2$ 22. $(5^3 \times 5^{-4})^{-1}$

23. $(2^{-2} \times 2^{-1})^{-2}$ 24. $(17^3)^0$ 25. $(4^{-2} \times 4^5)^{-1}$ 26. $(2^6 \times 2^{-1})^2 \div 2^4$

• *Check answers.*

P3.2: Power practice

Do as many of these as you need. Check your answers regularly.

Batch A : *Simplify:*

1. $5^3 \times 5^{-1}$ 2. $3^5 \div 3^{-3}$ 3. $x^5 \times x^{-4}$ 4. $m^3 \times m^{-3}$ 5. $n^2 \times n^{-3}$

6. $3^6 \times 3 \times 3^{-3}$ 7. $t^4 \times t^{-3} \times t$ 8. $(3n)^2$ 9. $(2p^2)^{-1}$ 10. $(3p^{-1})^4$

11. $3b^2c^{-2} \times 2b^3c^4$ 12. $(m^3 \times m^{-2})^2$ 13. $5x^{-2}y \times 2x^2y^3$

14. $(3m^{-2}n^3)^2$ 15. $2pq \times p^{-1}q^{-2}$

Batch B : *Simplify:*

1. $m^4 \times m^{-2}$ 2. $(3^4 \times 3^{-1})^2$ 3. $6^{-1} \times 6^2$ 4. $8^4 \times 8^{-2}$ 5. $(2^{-3})^2$

6. $(7^{-1} \times 7^4)^{-1}$ 7. $(3^{-2} \times 3^{-3})^{-2}$ 8. $6^5 \times 6^{-2} \div 6^{-2}$ 9. $(3m^{-1})^{-2}$ 10. $5pq^{-1} \times 2p^{-2}q$

11. $\dfrac{2^4 \times 2^{-2}}{2^3}$ 12. $a^3 \times a^{-2} \times a$ 13. $a^2 \times ab^{-2}$ 14. $(p^2q^4)^{1/2}$ 15. $9m^2n^3 \div 3mn^{-1}$

Batch C: *Simplify:*

1. $c^5 \times c^{-5}$ 2. $s^5 \times (2s)^3$ 3. $m^4 \div m^4$ 4. $(c^4)^2 \times c^{-3}$

5. $4v^2w^3 \times v^{-1}w^{-1}$ 6. $(2n^2 \times n^{-3})^2$ 7. $(6n^{-3})^{-1}$ 8. $(5p^2q^{-3})^2$

9. $(5v)^2$ 10. $(4m)^{-2}$ 11. $5(5p^2q^{-3})^{-2}$ 12. $(p^3q^{-3}r^2)^{-1}$

D3.3 : Powers and roots

$$\sqrt{n} = n^{1/2} \qquad \text{eg} \qquad 9^{1/2} = \sqrt{9} = 3$$
$$\sqrt[3]{n} = n^{1/3} \qquad \text{eg} \qquad 8^{1/3} = \sqrt[3]{8} = 2$$

Write down the value of :

1. $16^{1/3}$ 2. $125^{1/3}$ 3. $64^{1/2}$ 4. $64^{1/3}$ 5. $(64^{1/3})^2$

6. $25^{1/2}$ 7. $1000^{1/3}$ 8. $27^{1/3}$ 9. $49^{1/2}$ 10. $1^{1/2}$

Evaluate :

11. $144^{1/2}$ 12. $81^{1/4}$ 13. 53^0 14. $(3^2)^{1/2}$ 15. $(4^{1/2})^2$

16. $32^{1/5}$ 17. $(8^{1/3})^2$ 18. $(4^{1/2})^3$ 19. $(100^{1/2})^3$ 20. $169^{1/2}$

• *Check answers*

Section 4: A very important technique

In this section you will write complex expressions as sums of powers of x.

DEVELOPMENT

D4.1: Writing expressions as sums of powers of x

The most important set of mathematical techniques that you will meet at A-Level is Calculus. Whenever a University course, such as Engineering, demands A-Level Mathematics as a pre-requisite, it is because that course requires the student to be competent in Calculus.

It is essential that the algebraic technique met in this section is mastered before you tackle Calculus, where it will be required.

EXAMPLE   Q: *Write* $\frac{x}{\sqrt{x}}$ *in the form* x^n

A: $\quad \dfrac{x}{\sqrt{x}} \quad = \quad \dfrac{x^1}{x^{1/2}} \quad = \quad \boxed{x^{1/2}}$

Remember:
You should show the same amount of working as in the example.

Write in the form x^n

1. $\dfrac{1}{x}$ 2. $\dfrac{x}{x^3}$ 3. $\dfrac{\sqrt{x}}{x}$ 4. $x\sqrt{x}$ 5. $\dfrac{1}{\sqrt{x}}$ 6. $\dfrac{\sqrt{x}}{x^2}$

7. $\dfrac{x\sqrt{x}}{x^2}$ 8. $\dfrac{1}{\sqrt[3]{x}}$ 9. $\dfrac{\sqrt[3]{x}}{x}$ 10. $\dfrac{x^2}{\sqrt{x}}$ 11. $x^2\sqrt{x}$ 12. $\dfrac{x^2\sqrt{x}}{x}$

EXAMPLE :   *Write as sums of powers of x*

(a) $(x + 1)(2x - 3) \ = \ \boxed{2x^2 - x - 3}$

(b) $\quad x(3\sqrt{x} + x) \ = \ 3x\sqrt{x} + x^2 = \boxed{3x^{3/2} + x^2}$

x^2 & x *are powers of* x — *but so is* 1 *since* $1 = x^0$

Write each as a sum of powers of x :

13. $(x + 1)(x + 2)$ 14. $x(x^2 - 3)$ 15. $\sqrt{x}(x + 1)$

16. $\sqrt{x}(\sqrt{x} + 3)$ 17. $\sqrt{x}(2x - 1)$ 18. $x\sqrt{x}(3x - \sqrt{x})$

Big Edd

EXAMPLE :   *Write as a sum of powers of x*

$\dfrac{x^2+1}{\sqrt{x}} \ = \ \dfrac{x^2 + 1}{x^{1/2}} \ = \ \dfrac{x^2}{x^{1/2}} + \dfrac{1}{x^{1/2}} \ = \ \boxed{x^{3/2} + x^{-1/2}}$

Note:
It is usual to write $x^{3/2}$ rather than $x^{1\frac{1}{2}}$

Write each as a sum of powers of x:

19. $\dfrac{x^2 + 5x}{x}$ 20. $\dfrac{x^2 - 5x}{x^3}$ 21. $\dfrac{x^2 - 3x}{\sqrt{x}}$

22. $\dfrac{\sqrt{x} + 2x + 1}{x}$ 23. $\dfrac{3\sqrt{x} - x\sqrt{x} - 4}{x}$ 24. $\dfrac{5\sqrt{x} + 2x\sqrt{x} - 2x}{\sqrt{x}}$

25. $\dfrac{\sqrt{x}(3\sqrt{x} - 1)}{x}$ 26. $\dfrac{\sqrt[3]{x} - 3x^2\sqrt{x} + 2}{x}$ 27. $\dfrac{(\sqrt{x} - 2)(x + 1)}{x\sqrt{x}}$

• *Check answers*

Section 5: More complex techniques with powers

In this section you will:
- evaluate complex powers including $a^{m/n}$
- solve equations involving powers

DEVELOPMENT

D5.1: Evaluating complex powers by simplifying

EXAMPLE   *Simplify:*

(a) $\left[\frac{1}{2}\right]^{-2} = [2]^2 = 4$

(b) $4^{1/3} \times 2^{1/3} = 8^{1/3} = 2$

(c) $\left[\frac{25}{36}\right]^{1/2} = \frac{25^{1/2}}{36^{1/2}} = \frac{5}{6}$

(d) $\left(1\frac{1}{3}\right)^2 = \left(\frac{4}{3}\right)^2 = \frac{16}{9}$

Note: $\dfrac{1}{{}^a/_b} = \dfrac{b}{a}$

eg: $\dfrac{1}{{}^3/_2} = \dfrac{2}{3}$

Fission

Simplify :

1. $\left[\frac{1}{3}\right]^{-2}$

2. $\left[\frac{100}{9}\right]^{1/2}$

3. $\left[\frac{10}{7}\right]^{-2}$

4. $\left[1\frac{1}{4}\right]^{-2}$

5. $27^{1/3}$

6. $27^{-1/3}$

7. $(-1)^{1/3}$

8. $\left[\frac{125}{49}\right]^{0}$

9. $\left[\frac{36}{25}\right]^{1/2}$

10. $18^{1/2} \times 2^{1/2}$

11. $64^{-1/3}$

12. $\left[\frac{125}{27}\right]^{1/3}$

• *Check answers.*

D5.2: Evaluating $a^{m/n}$

$$a^{m/n} = (a^{1/n})^m = (\sqrt[n]{a})^m$$

EXAMPLE   *Simplify:*

$27^{2/3} = (27^{1/3})^2 = 3^2 = \boxed{9}$

Simplify :

1. $8^{2/3}$ 2. $9^{3/2}$ 3. $16^{3/4}$ 4. $25^{3/2}$ 5. $125^{4/3}$ 6. $100^{5/2}$

EXAMPLE   *Simplify:*

$\left[\frac{125}{8}\right]^{-2/3} = \left[\frac{8}{125}\right]^{2/3} = \left[\frac{8^{1/3}}{125^{1/3}}\right]^2 = \left[\frac{2}{5}\right]^2 = \boxed{\frac{4}{25}}$

Simplify :

7. $\left(\frac{1}{3}\right)^{-2}$ 8. $\left(\frac{1}{9}\right)^{5/2}$ 9. $\left(\frac{1}{4}\right)^{-3/2}$ 10. $\left(\frac{100}{81}\right)^{-3/2}$ 11. $\left(\frac{8}{27}\right)^{2/3}$ 12. $\left(\frac{4}{9}\right)^{-3/2}$ 13. $\left[\frac{125}{27}\right]^{-2/3}$

• *Check answers*

D5.3: Solving equations

EXAMPLE   *Solve* $\left(\frac{3}{5}\right)^x = \left(\frac{25}{9}\right)$

$\left(\frac{3}{5}\right)^2 = \left(\frac{9}{25}\right) \quad \Rightarrow \quad \left(\frac{3}{5}\right)^{-2} = \left(\frac{25}{9}\right) \Rightarrow \boxed{x = -2}$

Solve :

1. $3^x = 81$ 2. $3^x = \frac{1}{9}$ 3. $3^x = 1$ 4. $3^x = \sqrt{3}$

5. $(2^x)^2 = 2$ 6. $\left(\frac{2}{3}\right)^x = \frac{3}{2}$ 7. $\left(\frac{2}{3}\right)^x = \frac{8}{27}$ 8. $\left(\frac{2}{3}\right)^x = 1$

$$a^{m/n} = (a^{1/n})^m = (\sqrt[n]{a})^m$$

Solve :

9. $(\sqrt[3]{x})^2 = 9$ 10. $25^{3/2} = 5^x$ 11. $27 = (9^{1/2})^x$ 12. $125 = 25^{x/2}$

13. $a^{x/2} \div a = a^{1/2}$ 14. $8^{4/3} = 2^x$ 15. $81^{x/4} = 243$ 16. $(\sqrt[3]{2^6} \times x)^2 = 144$

EXAMPLE   *Solve* $4^x = 2^6$

$\qquad\qquad\qquad 4^x = 2^6$

$\Rightarrow \qquad\quad (2^2)^x = 2^6$

$\Rightarrow \qquad\qquad 2^{2x} = 2^6$ — *equating*

$\Rightarrow \qquad\qquad 2x = 6$ — *indices*

$\Rightarrow \qquad\qquad \boxed{x = 3}$

Remember:
You should show the same amount of working as in the example.

Headbanger

Solve :

17. $5^4 = 25^x$ 18. $8^x = 4^x \times 2^3$ 19. $8^x = 4^{x+1}$ 20. $27^x = 9^{x-1}$

• *Check answers.*

Section 6 : Simultaneous Equations

In this section you will :
- review elimination, substitution and graphical methods for solving simultaneous linear equations
- solve linear simultaneous equations in three unknowns
- solve linear and quadratic simultaneous equations

DEVELOPMENT

D6.1: Basic methods for solving simultaneous equations

Method 1 – Elimination

$$5m - 3n = 9 \quad \text{............ ①}$$
$$3m + 2n = 13 \quad \text{.......... ②}$$

$2×①$ $10m - 6n = 18 \quad \text{.......... ③}$
$3×②$ $9m + 6n = 39 \quad \text{.......... ④}$

$③+④$ $19m = 57$
             $m = 3 \quad \text{............. ⑤}$

$⑤ \text{ into } ②$ $9 + 2n = 13$
              $2n = 4$
              $n = 2$

$\boxed{\text{Solution} : m = 3, n = 2}$

Method 2 – Substitution

$$2m + n = 13 \quad \text{...... ①}$$
$$5m - 4n = 13 \quad \text{...... ②}$$

$① \Rightarrow$ $n = 13 - 2m$ ③
$③ \text{ into } ② \Rightarrow 5m - 4(13 - 2m) = 13$
         $5m - 52 + 8m = 13$
         $13m = 65$
         $m = 5 \quad \text{...... ④}$

$④ \text{ into } ③$ $n = 13 - 10 = 3$

$\boxed{\text{Solution} : m = 5, n = 3}$

Method 3 – Graphical method

Solve $y = x^2$ & $y + x = 3$ graphically

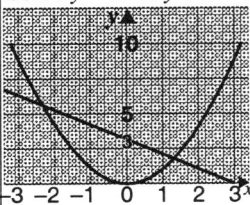

The solutions of the simultaneous equations are given by the values of x and y at the points of intersection

$\Rightarrow$ Solutions are $\left. \begin{array}{l} x = 1.3 \\ y = 1.7 \end{array} \right\}$

and $\left. \begin{array}{l} x = -2.3 \\ y = 5.3 \end{array} \right\}$

Important note :
The solution of two simultaneous equations is given by the coordinates of the points where the graphs cross.
CONVERSELY
the coordinates of the points where two lines cross is the simultaneous solution of their equation

Zuk

Solve using the method of elimination :

1. $4x + y = 14$ 2. $5m + 6p = 23$
    $x + 5y = 13$ $m + 3p = 10$

Solve using the method of substitution

3. $2x + 3y = 4$ 4. $2m + n = 5$
    $x + 2y = 1$ $m + 3n = 5$

Solve using either the elimination or the substitution method:

5. $7p + 3q = 13$ 6. $5y = 11 + 3x$ 7. $2c + d = 0$
    $5p + q = 7$ $2x + 7y = 3$ $c + 2d = 3$

8. *Use this graph to solve the following pairs of simultaneous equations :*

(a) $y = x^2 - 4x + 3$
$x + y = 3$

(b) $x + y = 3$
$y = x$

(c) $y = x^2 - 4x + 3$
$y = 0$

• *Check answers.*

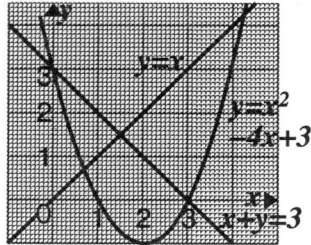

D6.2 : When one equation is not linear

| EXAMPLE | Solve $x^2 + y^2 = 25$ .... ① | **Remember:** You should show the same amount of working as in the example. |
| | & $y = x - 1$ .... ② | |

Subst. from ② into ① $x^2 + (x-1)^2 = 25$

$x^2 + x^2 - 2x + 1 = 25$

$2x^2 - 2x - 24 = 0$

$x^2 - x - 12 = 0$

$(x + 3)(x - 4) = 0$

$\Rightarrow$ $\left. \begin{array}{l} x = -3 \\ \& \, y = -4 \end{array} \right] \& \left. \begin{array}{l} x = 4 \\ y = 3 \end{array} \right]$

Solutions must link corresponding pairs of x and y

Icee

Solve these equations. Any quadratic equations can be factorised.

1. $y = x^2$
   $y = x + 6$

2. $y = x^2$
   $y = 3 - 2x$

3. $y^2 + x^2 = 20$
   $2y = x$

| EXAMPLE | Solve $x^2 - y^2 = 8$ .... ① |
| | & $2x + y = 7$ .... ② |

Rearrange ② $y = 7 - 2x$ ... ③

Subst. from ③ into ① $x^2 - (7 - 2x)^2 = 8$

$x^2 - (49 - 28x + 4x^2) = 8$

$-3x^2 + 28x - 49 = 8$

$3x^2 - 28x + 57 = 1$

$(x - 3)(3x - 19) = 0$

$\Rightarrow$ $\left. \begin{array}{l} x = 3 \\ \& \, y = 1 \end{array} \right] \& \left. \begin{array}{l} x = {}^{19}/_3 \\ y = {}^{-17}/_3 \end{array} \right]$

There are two possible substitutions

$y = 7 - 2x$ & $x = \frac{1}{2}(7 - y)$

Think which is easier to square to put into the other equation - then choose !

Solve these equations. Any quadratic equations can be factorised.

4. $xy = 4$
   $y = 2x + 2$

5. $y^2 = 4x$
   $2x + y = 4$

6. $4y^2 - 3x^2 = 1$
   $x - 2y = 1$

7. $x^2 + xy + y^2 = 7$
   $2x + y = 1$

8. $5x^2 - 6xy + 4y^2 = 3$
   $3x - 2y = 2$

• *Check your answers.*

D6.3 : Simultaneous quadratic equations AQA only

EXAMPLE   Find the coordinates where the graphs of
$$y = 3x^2 + 2x - 3 \text{ and } y = 2x^2 - 4x + 4 \text{ cross.}$$

A: $y = 3x^2 + 2x - 3$ and $y = 2x^2 - 4x + 4$ cross
where $3x^2 + 2x - 3 = 2x^2 - 4x + 4$

$\Rightarrow \quad x^2 + 6x - 7 = 0$

$\Rightarrow \quad (x - 1)(x + 7) = 0$

$\Rightarrow \quad \boxed{x = 1} \text{ and } \boxed{x = -7}$
$\boxed{y = 2} \qquad \boxed{y = 130}$

1. Show that there is only one solution to the simultaneous equations
$$y = x^2 + 4x - 1 \qquad \text{and} \qquad y = x^2 + 2x + 3 \qquad \text{and find it.}$$

2. Find the coordinates where the graphs of
$$y = x^2 + 6x - 1 \qquad \text{and } y = 7 - x^2 \qquad \text{cross.}$$

3. Find the solutions to the pair of simultaneous equations
$$y = 4x^2 - 3x - 7 \qquad \text{and} \qquad y = x^2 + 5x + 1$$
giving your answers to 2 d.p.

• *Check your answers.*

EXTENSIONS

EXTENSION PROBLEMS take you beyond the level of the basic techniques.
If you want to aim for the higher grades, you need to tackle as much of the extension work as you can find time for. They will include A-Level examination-type questions.
This is where the top grades are earned.

E6.4: Simultaneous equation challenges

1. *Solve:* $2x + 5y = 1$
$x^2 + 5xy - 4y^2 = -10$

2. $x^2 + y^2 + 4x + 6y - 40 = 0$ is a circle. Find the coordinates of the two points where the line $x - y = 10$ crosses the circle.

3. *Solve:* $3x + 2y - z = -1$ 4. *Solve:* $x + y + z = 4$
$2x + 5y = 16$ $2x + 3y - z = 7$
$z = 3$ $x - y = -1$

5. Show that the exact x value of one of the solutions of the pair of simultaneous equations $y = 5x^2 + 3x - 1$ and $y = 2x^2 + 5x + 3$
is $x = {}^2/_3(1 + \sqrt{13})$ and find the exact x value of the other solution.
Find the corresponding y values to 2 d.p.

• *Check your answers.*

Section 7: Circular Measure

In this section you will:
- meet and use radians to measure angles
- calculate arc lengths and sector areas

DEVELOPMENT
D7.1 Radians and degrees

1 radian = angle in sector of radius and arc length r

Until now, you have always measured angles in degrees. Now you will learn to use a new measurement for angles, **the radian**.

$$\pi \text{ radians} = \pi^c = 180°$$

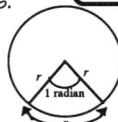

$$180° = \pi^c \qquad\qquad 1° = \frac{\pi}{180}^c$$
$$360° = 2\pi^c$$
$$90° = \frac{\pi^c}{2} \quad \text{(read as "}\pi\text{ by 2 radians")}$$

c = radians (originally from 'circular measure')

1. *Write these angles in degrees:*
   (a) $\frac{\pi^c}{3}$ (b) $\frac{\pi^c}{4}$ (c) $\frac{\pi^c}{10}$ (d) $2\pi^c$ (e) $\frac{\pi^c}{8}$ (f) $\frac{3\pi^c}{8}$ (g) $\frac{2\pi^c}{9}$

EXAMPLE Change 45° to radians

$$45° = \frac{180°}{4} = \boxed{\frac{\pi^c}{4}}$$

---

2. *Write these angles in radians (as fractions or multiples of π):*
   (a) 18° (b) 90° (c) 60° (d) 30° (e) 270° (f) 720°

EXAMPLE Change 17° to radians

$$180° = \pi \text{ radians} \quad\longleftarrow\quad \text{Start with this}$$
$$\Rightarrow 1° = {}^\pi/_{180} \text{ radians}$$
$$\Rightarrow 17° = {}^\pi/_{180} \times 17 = \boxed{{}^{17\pi}/_{180}{}^c}$$

---

3. *Write these angles in radians (as fractions or multiples of π):*
   (a) 72° (b) 54° (c) 162° (d) 240° (e) 15° (f) 35°

EXAMPLE Change 1.4^c to degrees

$$\pi \text{ radians} = 180° \quad\Rightarrow\quad 1 \text{ radian} = {}^{180°}/_\pi{}^\circ$$
$$\Rightarrow 1.4^c = {}^{180°}/_\pi{}^\circ \times 1.4 = \boxed{{}^{252}/_\pi{}^\circ \text{ or } 80.2°}$$

---

4. *Write these angles in degrees (to the nearest degree):*
   (a) 2^c (b) 1.2^c (c) 0.8^c

Note: if an angle is given in terms of π you should assume that it is in radians.

5. *Put your calculator into radian mode. Evaluate each of these:*
   (a) $\sin {}^\pi/_6$ (b) $\sin {}^{3\pi}/_8$ (c) $\cos {}^\pi/_7$ (d) $\tan {}^{5\pi}/_4$
   (e) $\sin {}^{5\pi}/_6$ (f) $\cos {}^{2\pi}/_9$ (g) $\sin 0.35^c$

- *Check your answers.*

D7.2: Arcs and sectors of circles

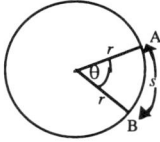

$$\frac{\text{length of arc AB}}{\text{circumference}} = \frac{\theta}{2\pi}$$

θ = theta

$$\Rightarrow \frac{s}{2\pi r} = \frac{\theta}{2\pi}$$

$$\Rightarrow \boxed{s = r\theta} \quad \text{where } \theta \text{ is in radians}$$

$$\frac{\text{area of sector AOB}}{\text{area of circle}} \quad \frac{\theta}{2\pi}$$

$$\Rightarrow \frac{\text{area of sector}}{\pi r^2} = \frac{\theta}{2\pi}$$

$$\Rightarrow \boxed{\text{area of sector} = \tfrac{1}{2} r^2 \theta} \quad \text{where } \theta \text{ is in radians}$$

EXAMPLE   Find the arc length and area of this sector.

First, we need the angle in radians.

$$180° = \pi^c$$
$$1° = \frac{\pi^c}{180}$$
$$72° = \frac{72\,\pi^c}{180} = \frac{2\pi^c}{5}$$

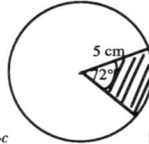

5 cm, 72°

It is usual to leave answers in terms of π

| Arc length | $= r\theta$ | $= 5 \times {}^2/_5\,\pi$ | $= \boxed{2\pi \text{ cm}}$ |

| Area of sector | $= \tfrac{1}{2} r^2 \theta$ | $= \tfrac{1}{2} \times 25 \times {}^2/_5\,\pi =$ | $\boxed{5\pi \text{ cm}^2}$ |

Mishrak

1. *Work out the arc lengths of the following sectors:*
    (a) radius 6 cm, angle at centre = 36°
    (b) radius 4 cm, angle at centre = 90°
    (c) radius 10 cm, angle at centre = 0.2^c
    (d) radius 15 cm, angle at centre = 0.5^c
    (e) radius 20 cm, angle at centre = 144°

2. Work out the area of each sector in question 1.

3. Work out the angle, in radians, subtended by an arc of length 10 cm, at the centre of a circle of radius 8 cm.

4. The area of a sector is 7.079 cm², and its angle is 30°.
    Work out the radius of the circle.

• *Check your answers.*

D7.3: Segments of circles

EXAMPLE 3: Find the area of the minor segment of a circle of radius 10 cm, given that the arc of the segment subtends an angle $\pi/_6$ at the centre of the circle.

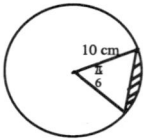

segment $\big)$ = sector $\triangleleft\!\big)$ − triangle $\triangleleft$

Area of sector	$= \frac{1}{2}r^2\theta = \frac{1}{2} \times 10^2 \times \pi/_6$	$= 26.18 \text{ cm}^2$

Area of Δ = $\frac{1}{2}\,ab\sin C$

Area of Δ $= \frac{1}{2} \times 10^2 \times \sin \pi/_6$ $= 25$

Area of segment $= 26.18 - 25$ $= \boxed{1.18 \text{ cm}^2}$

1. Work out the area of the minor segment, to 2 decimal places, given that
   (a) $\theta = \pi/_2$ (b) $\theta = 2\pi/_3$

2. Work out the area of a sector of a circle with radius 5 cm which is bounded by an arc of length 8 cm.

3. A circle of radius 8 cm is divided into two segments by a chord 8 cm long. Work out the area of each of these segments, to 2 d.p.

• *Check your answers.*

EXTENSIONS

EXTENSION PROBLEMS take you beyond the level of the basic techniques. If you want to aim for the higher grades, you need to tackle as much of the extension work as you can find time for.
They will include A-Level examination-type questions.
This is where the top grades are earned.

E7.4: Circular challenges

1. The radius of a cycle wheel is 35 cm. How many radians does the wheel turn through when travelling 1 m ?

2. Work out the area enclosed by two concentric circles of radii 12 cm and 9 cm and two radii inclined at an angle of 50° to each other. Give your answer as a multiple of π.

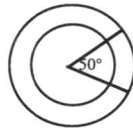

3. The radius of a circle is 15 cm. Work out the length of an arc of this circle if the length of the chord of the arc is 15 cm.

4. A cylindrical log of radius 30 cm and length 10 m, is floating with its axis horizontal and its highest point 5 cm above the level of the water.
   Work out the volume of the log below the water.

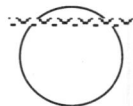

• *Check your answers.*

P1: Unit 4: Surds, Powers, Simultaneous Equations, Radians

Facts and formulae you need to know:

$a^m \times a^n = a^{m+n}$ $\quad a^m \div a^n = a^{m-n}$ $\quad (a^m)^n = a^{mn}$ $\quad a^1 = a$ $\quad a^0 = 1$ $\quad a^{-n} = \dfrac{1}{a^n}$

$\sqrt[n]{} = n$

Edexcel only area of triangle = $\frac{1}{2} ab \sin C$ $\quad$ [θ must be in radians]

π rads = 180° $\quad$ arc length = $s = r\theta$ $\quad$ area of sector = $\frac{1}{2} r^2 \theta$

Competence Test P1.4

1. *Simplify wherever possible:*
   (a) $2\sqrt{3} + 4\sqrt{3} + 3\sqrt{2}$ $\quad$ (b) $\sqrt{3} \times \sqrt{5}$ $\quad$ (c) $\sqrt{3} + \sqrt{5}$ $\quad$ (d) $\sqrt{2}(2 + \sqrt{2})$ $\qquad$ (4A)

2. *Write in simplest form:* (a) $\sqrt{12}$ $\qquad$ (b) $\sqrt{800}$ $\qquad\qquad$ (2A)

3. *Simplify:* (a) $5\sqrt{3} - \sqrt{12}$ (b) $\sqrt{10} \times \sqrt{8}$ (c) $\sqrt{32} - \sqrt{8}$ (d) $(\sqrt{3} + 1)^2$ $\qquad$ (4M,4A)

4. *Write down the values of these in index form:*
   (a) $(3^4)^2 \times 3^{-2}$ $\quad$ (b) $6m^2n^3 \div 2(mn^2)^3$ $\quad$ (c) $27^0 \times 27^{1/3} \times 3^{-2}$ $\qquad$ (3M,3A)

5. *Find the values of each of these NOT in index form:*
   (a) $(3^2 \times 3^{-1})^{-2} \div 3$ $\quad$ (b) $25^{1/2} \times 4^{-1/2}$ $\quad$ (c) $\left[\dfrac{125}{27}\right]^{-2/3}$ $\qquad$ (3M,3A)

6. *Write in the form x^n:*
   (a) $\dfrac{\sqrt{x}}{x}$ $\quad$ (b) $x^2 \sqrt{x}$ $\quad$ (c) $\sqrt{x}(x + x\sqrt{x})$ $\quad$ (d) $\dfrac{(\sqrt{x} - 1)(\sqrt{x} + 2)}{x}$ $\qquad$ (4M,4A)

7. *Solve:* $\quad x + 2y = 5 \quad 2x^2 - y^2 = 2$ $\qquad$ (3M,3A)

8. *Solve:* (a) $3^x = 81$ $\quad$ (b) $(3^x)^{1/2} = 3\sqrt{3}$ $\quad$ (c) $\left[\dfrac{5}{4}\right]^x = \dfrac{4}{5}$ $\quad$ (d) $8^x = 4^{x+1}$ $\qquad$ (1,2,1,2)

$$\boxed{\text{Total (AQA \& OCR)} = 44}$$

[Edexcel only]

9. Write in radians (in terms of π) (a) 30° (b) 45° $\quad$ (c) 18° $\quad$ (d) 5° $\qquad$ (1M,4A)

10. Write in degrees $\qquad\qquad$ (a) $\pi/2$ (b) 2π $\quad$ (c) 0.3 $\qquad$ (1M,3A)

11. An arc of a sector of a circle of radius 6 cm subtends an angle of 60° at the
    centre of the circle. $\qquad\qquad\qquad\qquad\qquad\qquad\qquad$ (4M,4A)
    Calculate: (a) the length of the arc $\qquad$ (b) the area of the sector

$$\boxed{\text{Total (\textbf{Edexcel})} = 61}$$

AIMING HIGH

Unit 5
Differential Calculus

CONTENTS

	OCR	AQA	Edexcel
Section 1	All	All	All
Section 2	All	All	All
Section 3	All	All	All
Section 4	—	All	—
Section 5	All	All	All
Section 6	All	All	All
Section 7	All	—	All

It is essential that Unit 4, section 4 has been done before a student works on Unit 5, Section 3, D3.3.

Unit 5: Differential Calculus
Section 1: Gradients of lines and curves

In this section you will:
- review gradients of straight lines;
- find lines of numerical sequences;
- work out gradients of some curved lines using limits.

DEVELOPMENT

D1.1: Gradients of straight lines

The gradient is a measure of the slope of a line.

Gradient of straight line = $\dfrac{\text{rise}}{\text{tread}}$

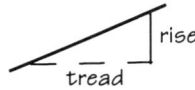

Work out the gradient of each of these lines:

1. $(9,4)$ $(3,1)$
2. $(11,15)$ $(5,2)$
3. $(-3,5)$ $(2,3)$

Work out the gradient of each of these lines:

4. $(x+h, y+k)$ (x,y)
5. $(x^2,(x+1)^2)$ $(x,x+1)$
6. $(x^2,(x+h)^2)$ $(x,x+h)$

• *Check your answers.*

D1.2: Limits of numerical sequences

EXAMPLE   State the limit of this sequence 1.9, 1.99, 1.999. 1.9999, …

A: The limit =   2

The terms approach closer and closer to 2, even though they will never reach 2.

We say that this sequence converges to 2 or the limit of this sequence is 2

State the limit of each sequence:

1. 0.3, 0.33, 0.333, 0.3333, …
2. $\frac{1}{2}$, $\frac{1}{4}$, $\frac{1}{8}$, $\frac{1}{16}$, …
3. 2.4, 2.04, 2.004, 2.0004, 2.00004, …
4. 5.26, 5.18, 5.22, 5.195, 5.203, 5.1995, 5.2012, …
5. 0.1, 0.01, 0.001, 0.0001, …

Blurbl

• *Check your answers*

D1.3: Gradients of curves

The gradient of a curve at a point P is defined as the gradient of the tangent at that point.

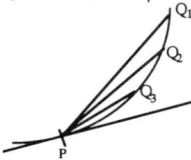

The gradient of the tangent at P is the limit of the gradients of the chords PQ_1, PQ_2, PQ_3, ...

We write this as:

grad at P = lim [gradPQ]
          Q–>P

Read this as

" gradient at P = the limit of the gradient of PQ, as Q approaches P".

Task 1: You are going to work out the gradient of the curve $y = x^2$ at the point (2,4)

Copy and complete the information in the box with broken lines:

PR	0.1	0.01	0.001	0.0001	0.00001
OT	2.1	2.01			
TQ	4.41				
QR	0.41				
QR/PR	4.1				

grad at P = lim [grad PQ] = ...
           Q–>P

$y = x^2$

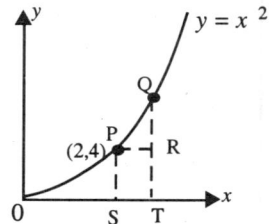

Task 2: *Copy and complete this information to work out the gradient at P(3,9):*

PR	0.1	0.01	0.001	0.0001	0.00001
OT					
TQ					
QR					
QR/PR					

grad at P = lim [grad PQ] = ...
           Q–>P

$y = x^2$

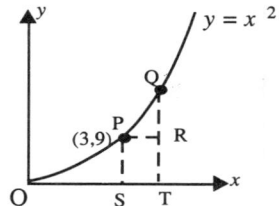

You cannot just write down the gradient. In order to justify the value of the gradient, the whole of this statement must be written.

Icee

Task 3:

$y = 3x^2$

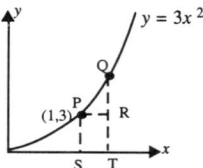

P is the point (1,3) on the curve $y = 3x^2$ and Q is a nearby point on the curve. Complete a table like that in Tasks 1 and 2 and deduce the gradient of $y = 3x^2$ at the point (1,3).

• *Check your answers.*

D1.4: Gradient functions

> **The gradient function** is the algebraic expression which gives the gradient at any point in terms of x
>
> For example :
> for $y = x^2$
>
> | x | 1 | 2 | 3 | 4 |
> |---|---|---|---|---|
> | gradient | 2 | 4 | 6 | 8 |
>
> For $y = x^2$, the gradient function = 2x

1. For $y = 3x^2$, the gradient values are given here:

x	1	2	3	4
gradient	6	12	18	24

   What is the gradient function for $y = 3x^2$?

2. For $y = x^3$, the gradient values are given here:

x	1	2	3	4	5
gradient	3	12	27	48	75

   What is the gradient function for $y = x^3$?

3. For $y = x^4$, the gradient values are given here:

x	1	2	3	4	5
gradient	4	32	108	192	500

   What is the gradient function for $y = x^4$?

• *Check answers.*

Section 2: Deriving gradient formulae

In this section you will:
- work out some gradient functions from first principles;
- establish a rule for gradient functions of powers of x;
- work out gradient functions of expressions involving powers of x.

DEVELOPMENT

D2.1: Gradient at a point from first principles

New notation:	δx stands for 'a small increase in the x direction' read δx as 'delta x'
	δy stands for 'a small increase in the y direction' read δy as 'delta y'

PLEASE NOTE: Here you are going to use the fact that
$$\text{gradient at P} = \lim_{Q \to P} [\text{grad PQ}] = \lim_{\delta x \to 0} \frac{\delta y}{\delta x}$$

EXAMPLE   Find the gradient of $y = x^2$ at any point, from first principles.

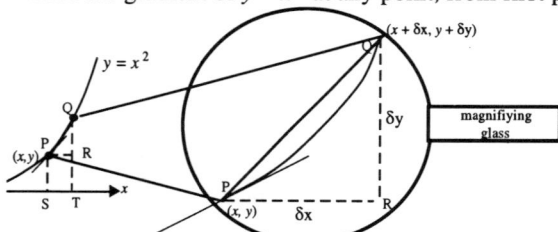

If $y = x^2$

then $y + \delta y = (x + \delta x)^2$

$\Rightarrow$ $\delta y = (x + \delta x)^2 - x^2$

  $= x^2 + 2x\delta x + (\delta x)^2 - x^2$

  $= 2x\delta x + (\delta x)^2$

Hence $\dfrac{\delta y}{\delta x} = 2x + \delta x$

Gradient $= \lim\limits_{\delta x \to 0} \dfrac{\delta y}{\delta x} = \lim\limits_{\delta x \to 0} (2x + \delta x)$

$\Rightarrow$ Gradient $= 2x$

Step 1 : work out the distance δy
Note that, when simplified, all remaining terms should have δx or $(\delta x)^2$ in them

Step 2 : Work out $\dfrac{\delta y}{\delta x}$

Step 3 : Use limits to evaluate the gradient function

Step 1: in $y = x^2$ you replace y by $y + \delta y$ and replace x by $x + \delta x$

Your task: Find the gradient of $y = 3x^2$ at any point, from first principles.

YOU WILL NOT BE ASKED TO USE THIS METHOD IN A TEST OR EXAM.

This is purely so you can see where the $\frac{dy}{dx}$ notation comes from.

• *Check your answers.*

D2.2: Gradient of x^n

1. Information:

Equation of line	$y = x^2$	$y = x^3$	$y = x^4$	$y = x^5$	$y = x^6$
Gradient function	$2x$	$3x^2$	$4x^3$	$5x^4$	$6x^5$

What will the gradient function be for:

(a) $y = x^7$ (b) $y = x^{12}$ (c) $y = x^{35}$ (d) $y = x^p$?

2. Information:

Equation of line	$y = x^2$	$y = 4x^2$	$y = x^3$	$y = 2x^3$	$y = 5x^6$
Gradient function	$2x$	$8x$	$3x^2$	$6x^2$	$30x^5$

What will the gradient function be for:

(a) $y = 5x^4$ (b) $y = 3x^7$ (c) $y = 2x^{10}$ (d) $y = kx^t$?

3. Information:

Equation of line	$y = 3x$	$y = 4x$	$y = x$	$y = x^2 + x$	$y = 3x^2 + 3x$
Gradient function	3	4	1	$2x + 1$	$6x + 3$

What will the gradient function be for:

(a) $y = 5x$ (b) $y = 7x$ (c) $y = x^2 + 2x$ (d) $y = 5x^2 + 10x$?

4. Information:

Equation of line	$y = x^2 + x^3$	$y = 4x^2 + 3x$	$y = x^3 + 2x^5$
Gradient function	$2x + 3x^2$	$8x + 3$	$3x^2 + 10x^4$

What will the gradient function be for:

(a) $y = 2x^4 + 5x$ (b) $y = 7x^3 - 4x$ (c) $y = 2x^3 + 3x^{10}$ (d) $y = 15x + 6x^5$?

> By now, you should have worked out some of the rules.
> Let us try to formalise these rules.

5. What will the gradient function be for:

(a) $y = x^n$ (b) $y = kx^n$ (c) $y = ax^n + bx^m$?

> You have seen that the rule for the gradient function for $y = x^n$
> works when n is a positive whole number.
> It also works when n is negative or not a whole number.

6. Information:

Equation of line	$y = x^{-2}$	$y = 2x^{-3}$	$y = x^{-2.4}$	$y = x^{1/2}$	$y = x^{2/3}$
Gradient function	$-2x^{-3}$	$-6x^{-4}$	$-2.4x^{-3.4}$	$\frac{1}{2}x^{-1/2}$	$\frac{2}{3}x^{-1/3}$

What will the gradient function be for:

(a) $y = x^{-7}$ (b) $y = 2x^{3.5}$ (c) $y = x^{-4}$ (d) $y = x^{1/3}$ (e) $y = 5x^{7/5}$?

7. What will the gradient function be for:

(a) $y = 3x^5 - 2x^8 + 6x$ (b) $y = 3x^{1.2} + 5x^{-3} + 10x^2$ (c) $y = \frac{1}{x}$

$$\boxed{\frac{1}{x} = x^{-1}}$$

• Check answers.

Section 3: Terminology and rules

In this section you will:
- meet and use words and phrases used in differentiation;
- meet and use the basic rules for differentating polynomials.

DEVELOPMENT

D3.1: Terminology

What do we know so far...
... the gradient function of x^2 is $2x$
... the gradient function of x^3 is $3x^2$
... the gradient function of x^n is nx^{n-1}
... the gradient $= \lim\limits_{\delta x -> 0} \dfrac{\delta y}{\delta x}$

Now we need to learn that ...
... the gradient function is also called the derived function.
... the gradient function is also called the derivative.
... $\dfrac{dy}{dx} = \lim\limits_{\delta x -> 0} \dfrac{\delta y}{\delta x}$
... $\dfrac{dy}{dx} =$ the derivative of y with respect to x
... $\dfrac{dy}{dx} =$ the rate of change of y with respect to x
... the process of obtaining the derivative is called **differentation.**

> $\dfrac{dy}{dx}$ is read as
>
> dee-y by dee-x   *Chyps*

If you are asked to differentiate a function, you may be asked in one of several ways:

Case 1: Find $\dfrac{dy}{dx}$ if $y = x^2$ A: $\begin{aligned} y &= x^2 \\ \dfrac{dy}{dx} &= 2x \end{aligned}$	Get into the habit of writing $y = \ldots\ldots$ first and then $\dfrac{dy}{dx} = \ldots\ldots\ldots$ underneath it.

Find $\dfrac{dy}{dx}$ if :
1. $y = 3x^2 + 4x$
2. $y = x^5 - 3x^7$
3. $y = 3x^3 + 2x^2$

> $\dfrac{d(x^2)}{dx}$ is read as
>
> "dee by dee-x of x^2"

Case 2: Find $\dfrac{d(x^2)}{dx}$	A: $\dfrac{d(x^2)}{dx} = 2x$
Literally: find the derivative of x^2	Literally: the derivative of x^2 is $2x$

Find :
4. $\dfrac{d(x^4)}{dx}$
5. $\dfrac{d(2x^4 + 3x^6)}{dx}$
6. $\dfrac{d(5x + 7x^4)}{dx}$

Case 3: If $f(x) = x^2$, find $f'(x)$	A: $f'(x) = 2x$	$f'(x)$ is read as "ef dashed x"
Literally: find the derived function	Literally: the derived function is $2x$	

Find $f'(x)$ if :   7. $f(x) = 2x^2 + 5x^3$ 8. $f(x) = x^6 - 3x^7$ 9. $f(x) = 5x + 9x^2$

• *Check your answers.*

D3.2: Rules for differentiating polynomials

A polynomial is an expression which is the sum of powers of x
e.g. $a + bx + cx^2 + dx^3 + ...$ where $a, b, c, d, ...$ are constants

Rules	Examples	
1. $\dfrac{d}{dx}(c) = 0$	$\dfrac{d}{dx}(3) = 0$	rate of change of a constant is zero
2. $\dfrac{d}{dx}(ax) = a$	$\dfrac{d}{dx}(3x) = 3$	gradient of $y = ax$ is a
3. $\boxed{\dfrac{d}{dx}(x^n) = nx^{n-1}}$	$\dfrac{d}{dx}(x^4) = 4x^3$	
4. $\dfrac{d}{dx}(ax^n) = anx^{n-1}$	$\dfrac{d}{dx}(5x^4) = 20x^3$	
5. $\dfrac{d}{dx}(f(x) + g(x)) = \dfrac{d}{dx}(f(x)) + \dfrac{d}{dx}(g(x))$	$\dfrac{d}{dx}(3x^5 + 2x^7 + 3) = 15x^4 + 14x^6$	

Find the derivative with respect to x $\left[\dfrac{dy}{dx}\right]$

1. $y = 4x^2 + 3x$ 2. $y = 3x^{-1} + 5x^{1.5}$ 3. $y = 2x^{-2} + 7x^{3.8}$

4. $y = x^{1/2} + 7$ 5. $y = 3x^{-1/3} + 2x^{1/3}$ 6. $y = 3x^{-1.2} + 4x^{1/2}$

Work out :   7. $\dfrac{d}{dx}(5x + 2x^{-1})$ 8. $\dfrac{d}{dx}(3x^{1/4} + 5x^{-3})$ 9. $\dfrac{d}{dx}(5 + 2x - 3x^{-2})$

Find the derivative with respect to t $\left[\dfrac{ds}{dt}\right]$

10. $s = 3t^2 + 1$ 11. $s = 2t^{-2} + 3t^{1/4}$ 12. $s = 4t^{-3} - 4t^{3/2}$

• *Check your answers.*

D3.3: Differentiating powers of x

In order to differentiate some expressions,
you must first write them as sums of powers of x

$$\frac{d(x^n)}{dx} = x^{n-1}$$

EXAMPLE Differentiate $y = \sqrt[3]{x}$

$$y = \sqrt[3]{x} = x^{1/3}$$

$$\frac{dy}{dx} = \boxed{\frac{1}{3} x^{-2/3}}$$

EXAMPLE Differentiate $y = \frac{1}{x^4}$

$$y = \frac{1}{x^4} = x^{-4}$$

$$\frac{dy}{dx} = \boxed{-4x^{-5}}$$

Differentiate:

1. $y = 2 + \dfrac{1}{x}$ 2. $y = 3x^4 - \dfrac{1}{x^2}$ 3. $y = \sqrt{x}$ 4. $y = \sqrt{(x^3)}$

EXAMPLE Differentiate $y = (2x + 1)(x + 1)$

$$y = (2x + 1)(x + 1) = 2x^2 + 3x + 1$$

$$\Rightarrow \qquad \frac{dy}{dx} = \boxed{4x + 3}$$

---

5. $y = x(x + 1)$ 6. $(x + 1)(x - 4)$ 7. $y = \sqrt{x}(x - 2)$ 8. $y = (1 - 3x)^2$

EXAMPLE Differentiate $y = \dfrac{x^2 + 1 + 3x}{x}$

$$y = \frac{x^2 + 1 + 3x}{x} = x + x^{-1} + 3$$

$$\Rightarrow \qquad \frac{dy}{dx} = \boxed{1 - x^{-2}}$$

Differentiate:

9. $y = \dfrac{x^3 + 4}{x}$ 10. $y = \dfrac{x^2 - 7x + 1}{x^3}$ 11. $y = \dfrac{2x + \sqrt{x}}{x}$ 12. $y = \dfrac{x - 3}{\sqrt{x}}$

13. $y = 3x - \dfrac{3}{x}$ 14. $y = \dfrac{(x + 1)(2x - 3)}{x^2}$ 15. $y = \dfrac{1}{\sqrt{x}}$ 16. $y = \dfrac{x(x + 1)}{\sqrt{x}}$

Work out $f'(x)$:

17. $f(x) = x^2(5 - \sqrt{x})$ 18. $f(x) = \sqrt{x}(3x - \sqrt{x})$ 19. $f(x) = (x + 1)(5 - \sqrt{x})$

20. $f(x) = \dfrac{x^2 - 3x}{\sqrt{x}}$ 21. $f(x) = \dfrac{\sqrt{x} - 2x\sqrt{x} - 7}{x}$ 22. $f(x) = \dfrac{(2x + 1)(3 - x)}{x\sqrt{x}}$

$$f(x) = 2x^{-1}$$
So $f'(x) = -2x^{-2}$

Stripee

$$\boxed{f(x) = \frac{1}{2x}}$$

$f'(x) = -\frac{1}{2}x^{-2}$

Spottee

This is the most common
standard mistake!

23. Spottee was correct.
    Explain what Stripee did wrong.   • *Check your answers.*

Section 4: From first principles

AQA
only

> In this section you will differentiate functions from first principles using function notation.

DEVELOPMENT

D4.1: Differentation from first principles

EXAMPLE   Differentiate $f(x) = x^2$ from first principles.

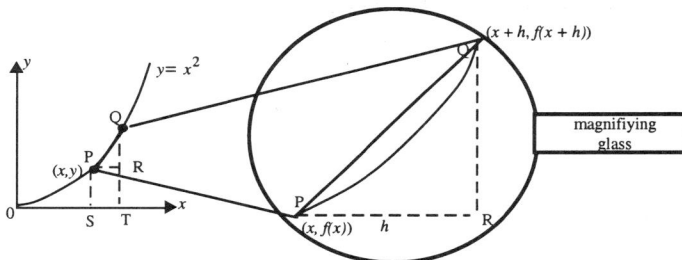

Gradient of PQ $= \dfrac{QR}{PR} = \dfrac{f(x + h) - f(x)}{h}$

$= \dfrac{(x + h)^2 - x^2}{h}$

$= \dfrac{x^2 + 2xh + h^2 - x^2}{h}$

$= \dfrac{2xh + h^2}{h} = 2x + h$

Gradient of curve $= \lim_{h \to 0}$ (gradient of PQ) $= \lim_{h \to 0} (2x + h) = 2x$

$f'(x) = \boxed{2x}$

Differentiate from first principles:

1. $y = 2x^2$

2. $y = x^2 + 1$

3. $y = 4x - 1$

4. $y = \dfrac{1}{x}$

5. $y = 6x - x^2$

6. If $v = 3r^2 + 2r$ find $\dfrac{dv}{dr}$ from first principles.

• *Check your answers.*

Section 5: Gradients, tangents & normals

In this section you will:
- calculate gradients of curves;
- find equations of tangents and normals;
- do problems using tangents and normals to curves.

DEVELOPMENT

D5.1: Calculating gradients

> **EXAMPLE** Find the gradient of the curve $y = (x + 1)(x + 2)$ at the point where $x = 3$
>
> A: $y = (x + 1)(x + 2) = x^2 + 3x + 2$
>
> $\dfrac{dy}{dx} = 2x + 3$ and, when $x = 3$, $\dfrac{dy}{dx} = 9$
>
> $\Rightarrow$ gradient = 9

Find the gradient of the curve at the given point:

1. $y = x^5 - 3$ where $x = 1$
2. $y = 4x^3 - 1$ where $x = 2$
3. $y = \sqrt{x}$ where $x = 3$
4. $y = \frac{1}{x}$ where $x = 4$
5. $y = (x - 2)(x + 1)$ where $x = -2$
6. $y = \frac{(2x - 1)}{x}$ where $x = \frac{1}{2}$

> **EXAMPLE** Find the coordinates of the point at which $y = \frac{2}{x^2}$ has gradient $\frac{1}{2}$
>
> A: $y = \dfrac{2}{x^2} = 2x^{-2} \Rightarrow \dfrac{dy}{dx} = -4x^{-3}$
>
> $\dfrac{dy}{dx} = \dfrac{1}{2} \Rightarrow -4x^{-3} = \dfrac{1}{2} \Rightarrow x^3 = -8 \Rightarrow x = -2$
>
> When $x = -2$, $y = \frac{1}{2} \Rightarrow$ point = $(-2, \frac{1}{2})$

Find the coordinates of the point(s) on the curve at which the gradient has the given value:

7. $y = 2x^2 - 3x + 4$: gradient = 5
8. $y = 5 - 3x^3$: gradient = -9
9. $y = (x - 2)(x + 2)$: gradient = 6
10. $y = x^3 + x^2$: gradient = 1
11. $y = \frac{1}{\sqrt{x}}$: gradient = $-\frac{1}{2}$
12. $y = 3 + \frac{1}{x}$: gradient = $-\frac{1}{4}$

13. Find the gradients of the curve $y = 3x^2 + 1$ at the points where the line $y = 3x + 1$ cuts the curve.

14. Find the coordinates of the points on the curve $y = \frac{1}{3}x^3 - \frac{1}{2}x^2 - 11x + 7$ where the tangent makes an angle of $45°$ with the positive direction of the x–axis.

• *Check your answers.*

D5.2: Tangents and normals

Not AQA

You already know how to find the equation of a line given a point and the gradient. We will now use calculus to work out the value of the gradient.

Equation of line passing through point (x_1, y_1) with gradient m is
$$\frac{y - y_1}{x - x_1} = m$$

EXAMPLE   Find the equations of the tangents to the curve $y = 2x^2 - x - 2$ at (a) the point $(-1,1)$ (b) the point where it cuts the positive x-axis.

(a) The gradient of the tangent at $(-1,1)$ is the value of $\frac{dy}{dx}$ when $x = -1$

$$y = 2x^2 - x - 2$$
$$\Rightarrow \frac{dy}{dx} = 4x - 1$$
When $x = -1$, the gradient $= -5$

Equation of tangent :
$$\frac{y - 1}{x + 1} = -5$$
$$\Rightarrow \quad y - 1 = -5x - 5$$
$$\boxed{y = -5x + 4}$$

(b) First, we must find where it cuts the x-axis.
$$y = 2x^2 - x - 2 \text{ cuts the } x\text{-axis where } y = 0$$
$$\Rightarrow 2x^2 - x - 2 = 0$$
$$\Rightarrow (2x + 1)(x - 2) = 0$$
$$\Rightarrow x = -\tfrac{1}{2} \text{ \& } x = 2 \quad \Rightarrow \quad \text{it cuts the positive } x\text{-axis where } x = 2, y = 0$$
When $x = 2$, the gradient $= 7$
Equation of tangent :
$$\frac{y - 0}{x - 2} = 7 \quad \Rightarrow \quad \boxed{y = 5x - 14}$$

Find the equation of the tangent to each curve at the given point:

1. $y = 3x^2$ at $x = 2$ 2. $y = 5x - 3x^2 + 1$ at $x = 0$ 3. $y = \frac{1}{x}$ at $x = -1$

4. $y = (x - 1)(3x^2 + 1)$ at $x = 1$ 5. $y = (2x - 1)^2$ at $x = 3$

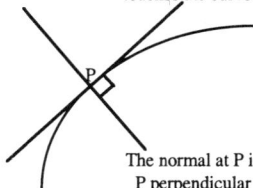

the tangent at P touches the curve at P

The normal at P is a line through P perpendicular to the tangent

To find the equation of a normal, use the same method as that for finding the equation of a tangent BUT first find the gradient of the normal.

If two lines are perpendicular their gradients are related.
$$m_1 \times m_2 = -1 \quad \text{or} \quad m_2 = \frac{-1}{m_1}$$

6. Show that the equation of the normal to the curve $y = 2x^2 - x - 2$ at the point $(-1,1)$ is $5y = x + 6$

7. Find the equation of the normal to the curve $y = 5x - 3x^2 + 1$ at the point $(0,1)$

• *Check your answers.*

P1 Unit 5: Differential Calculus: Section 5   *p 91*

D5.3: Setting out more complex problems

> To achieve high marks at AS/A-Level, it is not sufficient just to get the right answers.
> You need to be able to explain clearly how you get the answers.
>
> Step 1: Put all the information you are given onto a sketch.
> Step 2: Plan what you need to do to solve the problem.

1. Find the equation of the tangent to the curve $y = 4x^2 + 3x - 2$ at the point where the curve cuts the y – axis.

2. Find the coordinates of the point on $y = x^2$ at which the gradient is 6. Hence, find the equation of the tangent to $y = x^2$ with gradient 6.

3. Find the equation of the normal to $y = x^2 - 3x + 4$ which has gradient 0.5.

4. Find the equation of the tangent to the curve $y = 10x - 5x^2$ at the point where $x = 2$ and find where this tangent meets the line $y = 5x$

5. Find the coordinates of the point of intersection of the normal to the curve $y = x^3 - 3x^2 + 3x + 2$ at the point where $x = 2$, and the line $y = 2x - 7$

$y = x^3 - 3x^2 + 3x + 2$

- *Check your answers.*

EXTENSION

E5.4: Differentiation challenges

$xy = 2$

1. (a) Copy this sketch of the curve $xy = 2$.
      Mark in and label the point where $x = 1$.
      Draw the tangent and the normal at this point.

   (b) Work out the coordinates of the point where the normal intersects the curve again.

2. The tangents to the curve $y = 5 - 3x - 2x^2$ at the points whose x–coordinates are 1 & -1 meet at T. Work out the coordinates of T.

3. Find the equations of the normals to the curve $y = (x-2)(x+1)$ at the points where the curve cuts the x–axis. Find the coordinates of the points of intersection of these normals.

4. Find the point of intersection of the normals to the curve $x^2 = 25y$ at the ends of the chord with equation $x = 2y + 2$.

5. Find the two values of k for which $y = 3x + k$ is normal to $y = 1 - x^3$

6. The tangent and the normal at the point P(4,0) on the curve $y = x(4 - x)$ meet the y–axis at the points T and N respectively. Calculate the lengths of PT and PN.

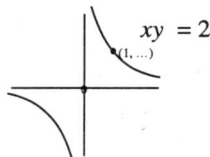

- *Check your answers.*

Section 6: Stationary values & turning points

In this section you will:
- associate increasing and decreasing functions with properties of gradients;
- calculate stationary values and locate turning points on graphs;
- meet three different kinds of turning points;
- find and classify turning points of curves and use them to sketch the curves.

DEVELOPMENT

What is calculus for ?

What is so important about gradients ?

Is calculus only used with graphs ?

Calculus is one of the most important and useful branches of mathematics. It is a very powerful tool and is used in research, in business, in engineering, science, design and technology ... At University, it is a standard pre-requisite for many higher level courses in engineering, science and technology as well as in mathematics.

What is calculus ?

Imagine you have set up a series of equations linking several variables that are important to your business : the costs of various raw materials, the cost of diesel, distribution costs, production costs, prices, wages, time etc – and, of course, profits. You want to be able to maximise profits, minimise production costs etc. If you alter one variable, how does it affect others ? Is any increase/decrease rapid, slow or somewhere in between. How can you measure the rate of change (increase or decrease) ? The derivative is a measure of the rate of change. Maximum values come when the function stops increasing – when the rate of change is zero.

In real-life problems, there are usually more than two variables but, at A–Level, we develop the basic calculus techniques using just two variables. Once the basics of calculus are established, it is not difficult to extend the techniques to deal with more than two variables, but this is usually done at University level.

Why is so much calculus to do with graphs ?

Calculus is to do with the rate of change of functions – but it is much easier to visualise what is happening, if you show the relationship between two variables as a graph.

An ex-student came into school and into a Y12 lesson. "I never believed her when she said that calculus was used in fields like engineering. But I build bridges in the Far East and I use it regularly. I promised myself that I would come in and tell her – and the A–Level students !"

D6.1: Stationary values

1. For what part(s) of this curve ...

   (a) ... is $f(x)$ increasing ?

   (b) ... is $f(x)$ decreasing ?

   (c) ... is $f(x)$ stationary
   (neither increasing nor decreasing) ?

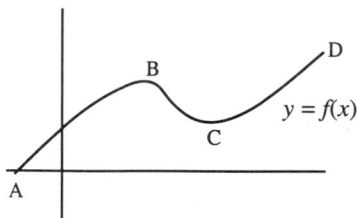

$f'(x)$ is the derived function (or gradient function) of $f(x)$

$f(x)$ is increasing	$\Leftrightarrow$	$f'(x) > 0$
$f(x)$ is decreasing	$\Leftrightarrow$	$f'(x) < 0$
$f(x)$ is stationary	$\Leftrightarrow$	$f'(x) = 0$

EXAMPLE   Find the values of x at which the function $x^4 - 4x^3$ has stationary values and find the stationary values.

Let $\quad f(x) \quad = \quad x^4 - 4x^3$

$\Rightarrow \quad\quad f'(x) \quad = \quad 4x^3 - 12x^2$

For stationary values $f'(x) = 0$ $\quad\quad \Rightarrow \quad\quad 4x^2(x - 3) = 0$

$\quad\quad\quad\quad\quad\quad\quad\quad\quad\quad\quad\quad\quad \Rightarrow \quad\quad\quad x = 0$ and $x = 3$

Stationary values occur when $x = 0$ and $x = 3$
Stationary values are $f(0)$ and $f(3)$, that is 0 and 27

Find the values of x at which the following functions have stationary values:

  2. $x^2 - 3$ $\quad\quad\quad\quad\quad$ 3. $x^2 - 6x + 5$ $\quad\quad\quad\quad$ 4. $x^3 - 12x - 4$

Find the stationary values of each of the following functions:

  5. $x^2 - 10x$ $\quad\quad\quad\quad$ 6. $x + {}^1/_x$ $\quad\quad\quad\quad\quad\quad$ 7. $3x^3 - 4x + 3$

$\quad\quad\quad\quad\quad\quad\quad\quad\quad\quad\quad\quad\quad\quad\quad\quad\quad\quad\quad\quad\quad\quad\quad$ • *Check your answers.*

D6.2: Stationary values and turning points

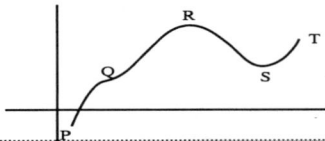

At Q, R and S the function $f(x)$ has
stationary values.

At Q, R and S the graph of $y = f(x)$ has
turning points.

At R ...	**At S ...**
... the stationary value is a maximum.	... the stationary value is a minimum.
... the turning point is a maximum	... the turning point is a minimum
turning point.	turning point.

At Q ...

... the function $f(x)$ has a stationary value.

... the graph of $y = f(x)$ has a turning point.

... the stationary value is neither a maximum nor a minimum.

... the turning point is not a maximum or min imum turning point.

... the turning point is **a point of inflexion.**

A point of inflexion is a kink in the curve
i.e. a point where the graph changes direction.

<table>
<tr><td colspan="3" align="center">**Classifying turning points**</td></tr>
<tr>
<td>At a maximum turning point, the gradient changes from +ve to −ve</td>
<td>At a minimum turning point, the gradient changes from −ve to +ve</td>
<td rowspan="2">At a point of inflexion, the gradient has the same sign before and after the point of inflexion.</td>
</tr>
</table>

At a maximum turning point, the gradient changes from +ve to −ve

At a minimum turning point, the gradient changes from −ve to +ve

At a point of inflexion, the gradient has the same sign before and after the point of inflexion.

EXAMPLE   Find and classify the turning points or the curve $y = x^3 - 3x$. Sketch the curve.

$y = x^3 - 3x \qquad \Rightarrow \quad \dfrac{dy}{dx} = 3x^2 - 3$

Turning points occur when $\dfrac{dy}{dx} = 0 \quad \Rightarrow \quad 3x^2 - 3 = 0$

$\Rightarrow \; 3(x^2 - 1) = 0 \qquad \Rightarrow \qquad x = \pm 1$

When $x = 1$, $y = -2$

When $x = 0.9$, $\dfrac{dy}{dx} = 3 \times 0.81 - 3 < 0$

When $x = 1.1$, $\dfrac{dy}{dx} = 3 \times 1.21 - 3 > 0$ $\Rightarrow$ $\Rightarrow$ a minimum t.p. at $(1, -2)$

When $x = -1$, $y = 2$

When $x = -1.1$, $\dfrac{dy}{dx} = 3 \times 1.21 - 3 > 0$

When $x = -0.9$, $\dfrac{dy}{dx} = 3 \times 0.81 - 3 < 0$ $\Rightarrow$ $\Rightarrow$ a maximum t.p. at $(-1, 2)$

Also, when $x = 0$, $y = 0$
When $y = 0$ $x(x^2 - 3) = 0$
$\quad x = 0$ & $x = \pm \sqrt{3}$

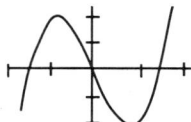

Find and classify the turning points on each of these curves. Sketch each graph.

1. $y = 3x - x^2$ 2. $y = x^2 - 4x + 3$ 3. $y = 2x^3$

4. $y = 3x^6$ 5. $y = 5 - x^3$ 6. $y = (2x - 1)(x + 1)$

• Check your answers.

Curve sketching by finding turning points is more accurate than plotting graphs.
When you calculate and plot points on a graph, you only know what is happening at those points, not at the points between them. In between two plotted points, you could have a smooth curve or a zig-zag line or several turning points. You don't know.

When you calculate the positions of all the turning points, you must have smooth lines between these points because there can be no other turning points than the ones you have calculated.

D6.3: Maximum and minimum values of functions

EXAMPLE   Find the minimum value of the function $9 - 2x + x^2$

Let $f(x) = 9 - 2x + x^2$

$\Rightarrow f'(x) = -2 + 2x$

For a maximum or a minimum $f'(x) = 0$ $\Rightarrow -2 + 2x = 0$

                                            $\Rightarrow x = 1$

$f'(0.9) = -2 + 1.8 < 0$ $\Rightarrow$ $\searrow\nearrow$ $\Rightarrow$ a minimum when $x = 1$
$f'(1.1) = -2 + 2.2 > 0$

Hence, the minimum value is $f(1) = \boxed{8}$

Points to note:

- the maximum/minimum value is the value of $f(x)$ <u>not</u> the value of x.
- it is not sufficient just to find the stationary value.
  For full marks you must show whether it is a maximum or a minimum
  (or a point of inflection)

1. Find the maximum value of $3x(4 - x)$.

2. Find the greatest value of $(1 - 2x)(1 + x)$

3. What is the minimum value of $(2 - 3x)^2$?

4. Find the value of p which makes $\dfrac{p^2 + 1}{p}$ a minimum

• Check your answers.

EXTENSIONS
E6.4: Max-min challenges

1. A fluid flows along a straight shallow channel with parallel sides. At a point x cm
   from one side of the channel, the speed, v cm^{-1}, of the fluid is given by
   $$v = 3.4 + 0.051x - 0.0003x^2$$
   (i) Find by differentiation the maximum speed of the fluid as x varies, giving your
   answer correct to 2 significant figures.
   (ii) Assuming that the speed of the fluid is greatest at a point half-way across the
   channel, find the width of the channel.   *(OCR)*

2. Figure 1 shows the part of the curve with equation
   $y = 5 - \frac{1}{2}x^2$ for which $y \geq 0$.
   The point $P(x,y)$ lies on the curve and O is the origin.

   (a) Show that $OP^2 = \frac{1}{4}x^4 - 4x^2 + 25$

   Taking $f(x) \equiv \frac{1}{4}x^4 - 4x^2 + 25$,

   (b) find the values of x for which $f'(x) = 0$
   (c) Hence, or otherwise, find the minimum distance from O to the curve,
         showing that your answer is a minimum.   *(Edexcel)*

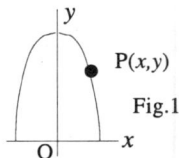

P(x,y)

Fig.1

Section 7: The second derivative

In this section you will:
- meet and use the second derivative
- use the second derivative test to classify turning points
- use calculus with practical problems.

DEVELOPMENT

D7.1: Meet the second derivative

> w.r.t. means 'with respect to'

If y is a function of x, $\dfrac{dy}{dx}$ is the rate of change of y w.r.t. x

The rate of change of $\dfrac{dy}{dx}$ w.r.t. x is $\dfrac{d}{dx}\left(\dfrac{dy}{dx}\right)$ which is written as $\dfrac{d^2y}{dx^2}$

EXAMPLE   If $y = 5x - x^3$ work out the value of $\dfrac{d^2y}{dx^2}$ when $x = 2$

$$y \quad = \quad 5x - x^3$$
$$\Rightarrow \quad \frac{dy}{dx} \quad = \quad 5 - 3x^2$$
$$\Rightarrow \quad \frac{d^2y}{dx^2} \quad = \quad -6x$$
$$\Rightarrow \quad \text{when } x = 2 \quad \boxed{\frac{d^2y}{dx^2} \quad = \quad -12}$$

1. If $y = 3x^4 + 2x^2$, work out the value of $\dfrac{d^2y}{dx^2}$ when $x = 3$

2. If $p = t^3 - 3t^2$, work out the value of $\dfrac{d^2p}{dt^2}$ when $t = 2$

Using function notation

If $y = f(x)$, $f'(x)$ is the rate of change of y w.r.t. x

The rate of change of $f'(x)$ is $f''(x)$, which is read as "ef double dash x"

EXAMPLE If $f(x) = 3x + 2x^3 + 5$ work out the value of $f''(x)$ when $x = 5$

$$f(x) \quad = \quad 3x + 2x^3 + 5$$
$$\Rightarrow \quad f'(x) \quad = \quad 3 + 6x^2$$
$$\Rightarrow \quad f''(x) \quad = \quad 12x$$
$$\Rightarrow \quad \text{when } x = 5 \quad \boxed{f''(x) \quad = \quad 60}$$

3. If $f(x) = 2x^3 - x^4 - 7$ work out the value of $f''(x)$ when $x = 2$

4. If $f(p) = p^5 + 3p^3 + 2p$ work out the value of $f''(p)$ when $p = 3$

5. The area of a water patch in mm² at time t seconds after it is spilt is given by $A = 3t^3 + 2t$. Find the time when $\dfrac{d^2A}{dt^2}$ has the value 27mm²/s².

D7.2: The second derivative test

Here are two related graphs. On the lower graph, the gradient $\frac{dy}{dx}$ of the upper graph is plotted against x.

A and B are turning points. Here the gradients are zero.

Between A and B, the gradient is negative, and this is shown as below the axis on the lower graph.

The parts of the curve where the gradient is positive give positive values on the lower graph.

The gradient of the lower graph is the rate of change of $\frac{dy}{dx}$

A is a maximum turning point. $\frac{dy}{dx} = 0$ & $\frac{d^2y}{dx^2} < 0$

B is a minimum turning point. $\frac{dy}{dx} = 0$ & $\frac{d^2y}{dx^2} > 0$

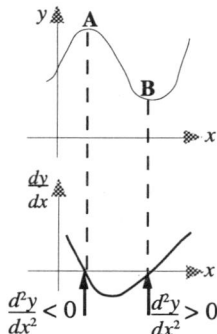

$\frac{d^2y}{dx^2} < 0$ $\qquad$ $\frac{d^2y}{dx^2} > 0$

The second derivative test

If $\frac{dy}{dx} = 0$ & $\frac{d^2y}{dx^2} < 0$ then there is **a maximum turning point.**

If $\frac{dy}{dx} = 0$ & $\frac{d^2y}{dx^2} > 0$ then there is **a minimum turning point.**

However, if $\frac{dy}{dx} = 0$ & $\frac{d^2y}{dx^2} = 0$, then the turning point may be a maximum, a minimum or a point of inflection. In this case, the gradients on either side of the point must be considered.

EXAMPLE Find and classify any turning points of the curve $y = x^3 - 12x$

$$y = x^3 - 12x$$
$$\Rightarrow \quad \frac{dy}{dx} = 3x^2 - 12$$
$$\Rightarrow \quad \frac{d^2y}{dx^2} = 6x$$

For turning points, $\frac{dy}{dx} = 0$ $\Rightarrow$ $3x^2 - 12 = 0$
$\Rightarrow$ $3(x^2 - 4) = 0$ $\Rightarrow x^2 - 4 = 0$
$\Rightarrow$ $x = \pm 2$

When $x = 2$, $y = -16$ and $\frac{d^2y}{dx^2} = 12 > 0$ $\Rightarrow$ $\boxed{\text{min t.p. at } (2,-16)}$

When $x = -2$, $y = 16$ and $\frac{d^2y}{dx^2} = -12 < 0$ $\Rightarrow$ $\boxed{\text{max t.p. at } (-2,16)}$

Find and classify any turning points of the following curves:

1. $y = 2x^3 - 9x^2 + 12x - 4$
2. $y = x^3 - 6x^2 + 12x - 11$

3. $y = x + \dfrac{1}{x} + 1$

• *Check your answers.*

D7.3: Problem solving with calculus

If s is distance travelled in t seconds,
then velocity $= v = \dfrac{ds}{dt}$ and acceleration $= \dfrac{d^2s}{dt^2}$

EXAMPLE If $s = 3t^3 - 4t^2$ where $s =$ the distance (in m) moved in t seconds, find the velocity and acceleration after 3 seconds.

$s = 3t^3 - 4t^2$

$v = \dfrac{ds}{dt} = 9t^2 - 8t$ | when $t = 3$, velocity $= 9 \times 9 - 8 \times 3 = \boxed{57 \text{ m/s}}$

$a = \dfrac{d^2s}{dt^2} = 18t - 8$ | acceleration $= 18 \times 3 - 8 = \boxed{46 \text{ m/s}^2}$

EXAMPLE The area A cm^2 of a blot of ink is growing so that, after t seconds, $A = 2t^2 - t$. Find the rate at which the area is increasing after 2 s.

$A = 2t^2 - t \quad \Rightarrow \quad \dfrac{dA}{dt} = 4t - 1$

When $t = 2$, the rate of increase $= \boxed{7 \text{ cm}^2/\text{s}}$

1. A body travels s m in t s, where $s = 4t^2 - 6t + 2$. Find the velocity and accleration of the body after 3 seconds. At what time is the body at rest ?

2. The velocity v m/s of a particle is $(1 - 2t)^2$, where t is the time in seconds after the start of the motion. Find the acceleration after t seconds.
   When is the body at rest ? What is the acceleration at this moment ?

3. A stone thrown into the air rises s m in t s, where $s = 12t - 4.9t^2$. Find the velocity of the stone when $t = 1$ s and $t = 2$ s. What is the meaning of the negative velocity?

4. The acceleration of a body is equal to $3t(t - 5)$ m/s^2, where t is the time in seconds. Find when the acceleration is a minimum and find its minimum value.

• *Check your answers.*

EXTENSIONS

E7.4: Challenging problems

1. The diagram shows an open rectangular tank, of height h metres, with a horizontal square base of side x metres. The tank can hold a volume of 13.5 m^2 of water and the internal surface area of the tank is S m^2.

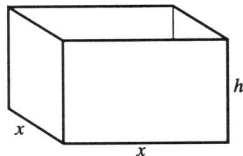

   (i) Show that $S = x^2 + \dfrac{54}{x}$

   (ii) Differentiate S with respect to x and hence find the dimensions of the tank when S is a minimum. Show clearly that, in this case, S is a minimum and not a maximum. *(OCR)*

P1 Unit 5: Differential Calculus: *Section 7* p 99

2. Find the exact coordinates of the stationary point on the curve $y = x^{3/2} - 5x$
   Show that this stationary point is a minimum point. *(OCR)*

3. A glass window consists of a rectangle with sides of
   length $2r$ cm and h cm and a semicircle of radius r cm.
   The total area of one surface of the glass is 500 cm².

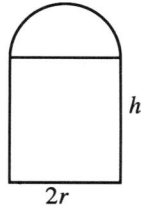

   (a) (i) Write down a formula connecting h and r.
       (ii) The perimeter of the window is p cm.
       By eliminating h, show that

   $$p = (2 + \tfrac{\pi}{2})r + \frac{500}{r}$$

   (b) (i) Determine the positive value of r for which p has a stationary value, giving
       your answer correct to 3 significant figures.

       (ii) Calculate $\frac{d^2p}{dr^2}$ and hence determine whether this stationary value is a
       maximum or a minimum value. *(AQA)*

4. Figure 4 shows an open tank for storing water, ABCDEF. The sides ABFE and
   CDEF are rectangles. The triangular ends, ADE and BCF are isosceles and
   $\angle AED = \angle BFC = 90°$. The ends ADE and BCF are vertical and EF is horizontal.
   Given that AD = x metres,

   (a) show that the area of $\triangle ADE$ is $\frac{1}{4}x^2$ m².

   Given also that the capacity of the container is
   4000 m³ and that the total area of the two triangular
   and two rectangular sides of the container is S m²,

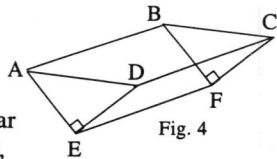

   (b) show that $S = \dfrac{x^2}{2} + \dfrac{16\,000\sqrt{2}}{x}$

   Given that x can vary,
   (c) use calculus to find the minimum value of S,
   (d) justify that the value of S you have found is a mimimum. *(Edexcel)*

5. The volume of a circular, cylindrical block is 800 cm³. Show that the total surface
   area is given by $S = 2\pi r^2 + 1600/r$, where r is the radius. Work out the exact value
   of r that makes the surface area a minimum.

6. A closed rectangular box is made of thin card. The length of the box is twice
   its width. The box has a volume of 243 cm³. If its width is x cm, show that its
   surface area is $4x^2 + 729/x$ cm².
   Find the dimensions of the box which has the least surface area.

   • *Check your answers.*

P1: Unit 5: Differential calculus

Facts and formulae you need to know:

Condition for perpendicular lines $\quad m_1 \times m_2 = -1$

Equation of a straight line given a point and its gradient $\quad \dfrac{y - y_1}{x - x_1} = m$

The gradient function is also called the derived function or the derivative

$\dfrac{dy}{dx}$ = the derivative of y with respect to x = the rate of change of y with respect to x

The process of obtaining the derivative is called **differentation.**

Rules for differentiating polynomials

1. $\dfrac{d}{dx}(c) = 0$ $\quad$ 2. $\dfrac{d}{dx}(ax) = a$ $\quad$ 3. $\boxed{\dfrac{d}{dx}(x^n) = nx^{n-1}}$ $\quad$ 4. $\dfrac{d}{dx}(ax^n) = nx^{n-1}$

5. $\dfrac{d}{dx}(f(x) + g(x)) = \dfrac{d}{dx}(f(x)) + \dfrac{d}{dx}(g(x))$

Competence Test P1.5

1. Find $\dfrac{dy}{dx}$ if $y = 3x^2 - 3$ $\quad$ (2A) $\qquad$ 2. $f(x) = 2x^{-1/2}$ Write down $f'(x)$ $\quad$ (2A)

2. *Differentiate the following w.r.t. x:* $\qquad\qquad$ (1M,2A for each = 27marks)

(a) $\sqrt{x}$ $\qquad$ (b) $(2x - 1)(x + 3)$ $\qquad$ (c) $\dfrac{x^2 - 3x + 4}{x}$ $\qquad$ (d) $\dfrac{1}{x^2}$ $\qquad$ (e) $\dfrac{1}{3x}$

(f) $(x^2 - 1/x^2)^2$ $\quad$ (g) $(3x^2 - 5)\sqrt{x}$ $\qquad$ (h) $\sqrt{x}(x + 3x^2)$ $\qquad$ (i) $\dfrac{1 - 5x^2}{4x^3}$

3. Find the gradient of the curve $y = (x + 1/x)^2$ at the point where $x = 2$. $\quad$ (2M,2A)

4. Find the gradients of the curve $y = x(x - 1)(x - 4)$ at the points where the the the curve cuts the x–axis. Also, find the coordinates of the curve at the points where the tangent to the curve is parallel to the x–axis. Sketch the curve. $\qquad$ (4M,11A)

5. $x^3 y = 5$. Find the value of $\dfrac{dy}{dx}$ and $\dfrac{d^2y}{dx^2}$ when $x = 2$. $\qquad\qquad$ (3M, 4A)

6. Find and classify the turning points of the curve $y = 5 + 12x - 3x^2 - 2x^3$. Sketch the curve. $\qquad\qquad$ (4M,8A)

$\boxed{\text{Total (AQA)} = 69}$

[OCR and Edexcel]

7. Find the equations of the tangent and the normal to the curve $y = x(3 - x)$ at the point where $x = 4$. (6M,7A)

$\boxed{\text{Total (OCR \& Edexcel)} = 82}$

AIMING HIGH

Unit 6
Completing the Square

CONTENTS
Section 1: The basic technique
Section 2: Maximum and minimum values (including sketching curves of quadratics in completed square form)
Section 3: Solving quadratic equations (including deriving 'the formula')
Section 4: More quadratic inequalities

	OCR	AQA	Edexcel
Section 1	All	All	All
Section 2	All	All	All
Section 3	All	All	All
Section 4	All	All	All

Unit 6: Completing the Square
Section 1: Completed square form

In this section you will put quadratic expressions into completed square form.

▨▨DEVELOPMENT▨▨

D1.1: The basic technique

1. Explain why $(x + 3)^2 = x^2 + 6x + 9$ rather than $x^2 + 9$.

$$(x + a)^2 = x^2 + 2\underline{ax} + a^2$$

$\boxed{\text{twice the product}}$

Write down the expansions of:

2. $(x + 4)^2$ 3. $(x - 1)^2$ 4. $(x + 5)^2$ 5. $(x - 3)^2$

Copy and complete each of these:

6. $x^2 + 6x + 9 \quad = \quad (x + ...)^2$ 7. $x^2 + 20x + 100 \quad = \quad (.........)^2$

8. $x^2 - 12x + 36 = \quad (x - ...)^2$ 9. $x^2 - 18x + 81 \quad = \quad (.........)^2$

10. $x^2 + 14x + ... = \quad (.........)^2$ 11. $x^2 - 40x + ... \quad = \quad (.........)^2$

12. $x^2 - 22x + ... = \quad (.........)^2$ 13. $x^2 + 24x + ... \quad = \quad (.........)^2$

14. $x^2 - 8x \quad = \quad (.........)^2 - ......$ 15. $x^2 - 10x \quad = \quad (.........)^2 - ......$

$$(x + a)^2 = x^2 + 2ax + a^2 \quad \Rightarrow \quad x^2 + 2ax = (x + a)^2 - a^2$$

EXAMPLE   Write $x^2 - 6x$ in completed square form.

$$x^2 - 6x = \boxed{(x - 3)^2 - 9} \longleftarrow$$

$\boxed{\text{This is completed square form.}}$ *Taz*

Write in completed square form:

16. $x^2 - 2x$ 17. $x^2 + 30x$ 18. $x^2 - 50x$

EXAMPLE   Write $x^2 - 16x + 7$ in completed square form.

$$x^2 - 16x + 7 \quad = \quad [x^2 - 16x] + 7$$
$$= \quad [(x - 8)^2 - 64] + 7$$
$$= \boxed{(x - 8)^2 - 57}$$

Write in completed square form:

19. $x^2 - 4x + 3$ 20. $x^2 + 12x - 8$ 21. $x^2 - 14x + 50$

22. $x^2 - 18x + 14$ 23. $x^2 - 20x + 15$ 24. $x^2 - 6x + 1$

• *Check your answers.*

D1.2: When the coefficient of x is odd

EXAMPLE   Write $x^2 - 3x$ in completed square form.

$$x^2 - 3x = \left[x - \tfrac{3}{2}\right]^2 - \tfrac{9}{4}$$

It is much simpler if you use fractions rather than decimals.

$$\left[\tfrac{3}{2}\right]^2 = \tfrac{3 \times 3}{2 \times 2} = \tfrac{9}{4}$$

Driller

Write in completed square form:

1. $x^2 + 5x$ 2. $x^2 - 9x$ 3. $x^2 + 17x$

EXAMPLE   Write $x^2 - 5x + 7$ in completed square form.

$$
\begin{aligned}
x^2 - 5x + 7 &= [x^2 - 5x] + 7 \\
&= \left[x - \tfrac{5}{2}\right]^2 - \tfrac{25}{4} + 7 \\
&= \left[x - \tfrac{5}{2}\right]^2 - \tfrac{25}{4} + \tfrac{28}{4}
\end{aligned}
$$

It is easier if you write the integer in fraction form too !

$$\therefore \quad x^2 - 5x + 7 = \left[x - \tfrac{5}{2}\right]^2 + \tfrac{3}{4}$$

Write in completed square form:

4. $x^2 - 11x + 7$ 5. $x^2 + 15x + 6$ 6. $x^2 - 7x + 13$

7. $x^2 + x + 5$ 8. $x^2 + 21x - 3$ 9. $x^2 - 3x + 6$

• *Check your answers.*

D1.3: When the coefficient of x² is not 1

EXAMPLE   Write $2x^2 - 6x + 1$ in completed square form.

$$
\begin{aligned}
2x^2 - 6x + 1 &= 2[x^2 - 3x] + 1 \\
&= 2\left[\left[x - \tfrac{3}{2}\right]^2 - \tfrac{9}{4}\right] + 1 \\
&= 2\left[x - \tfrac{3}{2}\right]^2 - \tfrac{9}{2} + 1 \\
&= 2\left[x - \tfrac{3}{2}\right]^2 - \tfrac{9}{2} + \tfrac{2}{2}
\end{aligned}
$$

$$2x^2 - 6x + 1 = 2\left[x - \tfrac{3}{2}\right]^2 - \tfrac{7}{2}$$

Write in completed square form:

1. $2x^2 + 8x - 3$ 2. $3x^2 - 27x$ 3. $2x^2 + 16x + 3$

4. $4x^2 + 12x - 5$ 5. $2x^2 + 11x + 4$ 6. $5x^2 + 50x + 4$

7. $3x^2 + 11x - 8$ 8. $-2x^2 - 12x + 9$ 9. $-3x^2 + 7x + 1$

• *Check your answers.*

Section 2: Maximum and minimum values

In this section you will:
- find maximum and minimum values of quadratic functions
- sketch graphs of quadratic functions given in completed square form

DEVELOPMENT

D2.1: Maximum and minimum values

EXAMPLE For what value of x does $(x-3)^2 + 5$ have a minimum value and what is this minimum value ?

$(x-3)^2$ is positive or zero for all values of x ◄┈┈┈ This is the crux of the matter !

So, the minimum value of $(x-3)^2$ is zero

$\Rightarrow$ the minimum value occurs when $x = 3$

$\Rightarrow$ the minimum value of $(x-3)^2 + 5$ is $\boxed{5}$ *Frizzbang*

For what value of x does each expression have a minimum value and what is this minimum value ?

1. $(x-8)^2 - 3$ 2. $(x+1)^2 + 5$ 3. $2(x-15)^2$

For what value of x does each expression have a maximum value and what is this maximum value ?

4. $10 - (x-2)^2$ 5. $5 - (x-1)^2$ 6. $-2 - 4(x+3)^2$

• *Check your answers.*

D2.2: Sketching quadratic curves

EXAMPLE Sketch the graph of $y = (x-2)^2 + 1$

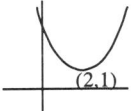

The curve is ∪ shaped since the coefficient of x^2 is positive.

The minumum value is 1 and this occurs when x = 2
Hence the vertex is (2,1)

(2,1)

Sketch the graph of each of the following.
Mark in the max/min point (the vertex).

1. $y = (x-5)^2 + 4$ 2. $y = (x+3)^2 - 4$ 3. $y = -2(x-7)^2 + 12$

Write each equation in completed square form.
Sketch the graph of the equation.
Mark in the max/min point (the vertex).

4. $y = x^2 - 4x + 4$ 5. $y = x^2 - 8x + 13$ 6. $y = x^2 - 5x + 10$

7. $y = x^2 + 12x + 27$ 8. $y = 2x^2 - 20x + 60$ 9. $y = 3x^2 + 6x - 5$

10. $y = -x^2 + 4x - 5$ 11. $y = 3 + 8x - 2x^2$

• *Check your answers.*

Section 3: Solving quadratic equations

In this section you will:
- solve quadratic equations by completing the square
- use completing the square to derive 'the formula'

DEVELOPMENT

D3.1: Solving equations in completed square form

EXAMPLE	Solve $(x + 2)^2 - 7 = 0$		
	$(x + 2)^2 - 7 = 0$		
$\Rightarrow$	$(x + 2)^2 = 7$		
$\Rightarrow$	$x + 2 = \pm\sqrt{7}$		
$\Rightarrow$	$x = -2 \pm \sqrt{7}$		
$\Rightarrow$	$x = -2 + \sqrt{7}$ and $-2 - \sqrt{7}$	(exact answers)	
or	$x = 0.65$ and -4.65	(to 2 d.p.)	

Find EXACT solutions to:

1. $(x - 3)^2 - 4 = 0$ 2. $(x + 5)^2 - 3 = 0$ 3. $(x - {}^3/_2)^2 - 4 = 0$

Put each equation into completed square form and solve it.
Give solutions to 2 d.p.

4. $x^2 - 2x - 5 = 0$ 5. $x^2 + 12x - 3 = 0$ 6. $x^2 + 8x + 11 = 0$

- *Check your answers.*

D3.2: More complex equations

EXAMPLE	Solve $3x^2 - 5x - 11 = 0$	
	$3x^2 - 5x - 11 = 0$	
$\Rightarrow$	$x^2 - {}^5/_3 x - {}^{11}/_3 = 0$	(dividing through by 3)
$\Rightarrow$	$(x - {}^5/_6)^2 - {}^{25}/_{36} - {}^{11}/_3 = 0$	
$\Rightarrow$	$(x - {}^5/_6)^2 - {}^{25}/_{36} - {}^{132}/_{36} = 0$	
$\Rightarrow$	$(x - {}^5/_6)^2 - {}^{157}/_{36} = 0$	
$\Rightarrow$	$(x - {}^5/_6)^2 = {}^{157}/_{36}$	
$\Rightarrow$	$x - {}^5/_6 = \pm\sqrt{({}^{157}/_{36})} \approx \pm^{12.53}/_6$	
$\Rightarrow$	$x \approx \pm^{12.53}/_6 + {}^5/_6$	
$\Rightarrow$	$x \approx 2.92$ and -1.255	

You can divide through by 3 here because you are dividing every term on both sides of the equation.

HOWEVER, you must not divide through by the coefficent of x^2 if you are working with an expression, not an equation.

Put each equation into completed square form and solve it. Give solutions to 2 d.p.

1. $2x^2 - 6x - 5 = 0$ 2. $3x^2 - 2x - 7 = 0$ 3. $5x^2 + 7x - 11 = 0$

4. $2x^2 + 7x - 9 = 0$ 5. $7x^2 - 3x - 8 = 0$ 6. $11x^2 - 2x - 3 = 0$

- *Check your answers.*

D3.3: Deriving the formula

EXAMPLE   Solve $x^2 + bx + c = 0$ by completing the square.

$$x^2 + bx + c = 0$$

$$\Rightarrow \quad \left[x + \frac{b}{2}\right]^2 - \frac{b^2}{4} + c = 0$$

$$\Rightarrow \quad \left[x + \frac{b}{2}\right]^2 = \frac{b^2}{4} - \frac{4c}{4} = \frac{b^2 - 4c}{4}$$

$$\Rightarrow \quad x + \frac{b}{2} = \frac{\pm\sqrt{(b^2 - 4c)}}{2}$$

$$\Rightarrow \quad x = \frac{\pm\sqrt{(b^2 - 4c)}}{2} - \frac{b}{2}$$

$$\Rightarrow \quad \boxed{x = \frac{-b \pm\sqrt{b^2 - 4c}}{2}}$$

1. Solve $ax^2 + bx + c = 0$ by completing the square.
   This should produce 'the formula' for solving quadratic equations.

If you cannot arrive at this formula,
ask your teacher to find out where you are going wrong.

EXTENSIONS

E3.4: Completed square challenges

1. The diagram show the graph of $y = x^2 - 2px + p$, where p is a positive constant. The
   point A is the lowest point on the graph and is given to lie above the x-axis.

   (i) By completing the square, express the
   coordinates of A in terms of p. Hence find the set of
   possible values of p.

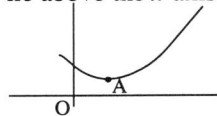

   (ii) Given that A lies on the straight line with equation $y = 2x - 1$, find the exact
   value of p.   *(OCR)*

2. The coordinates of the points A and B are $(p,2)$ and $(4,p)$ respectively. Show that
   $$AB^2 = 2p^2 - 12p + 20.$$
   Express AB^2 in the form $a(p - b)^2 + c$, where a, b and c are constants whose values
   are to be found.
   Hence write down   (i) the smallest possible value of AB, as p varies
                           (ii) the corresponding value of p.
   Using this value of p, show that the line through the points A and B meets the curve
   whose equation is $9x^2 - 10xy = 25$ at one point only.   *(OCR)*

• Check your answers.

Section 4: More quadratic inequalities

In this section you will:
- solve simple quadratic inequalities without factorising
- solve quadratic inequalities that cannot be factorised.

DEVELOPMENT

D4.1: Simple quadratic inequalities

Type 1:	$x^2 < -1$	No solution	
Type 2:	$x^2 > -1$	Solution is all values of x	
Type 3:	$x^2 < 25$	Solution is $-5 < x < 5$	
Type 4:	$x^2 > 25$	Solution is $x > 5$ and $x < -5$	

> Squares are always positive or zero
>
> *Gizmo*

Write down the solutions of :

1. $x^2 < 0$ 2. $x^2 > 4$ 3. $x^2 < 4$ 4. $x^2 > -4$

5. $x^2 > 9$ 6. $x^2 < 49$ 7. $x^2 < -2$ 8. $x^2 > 2$

EXAMPLE   Q: Find the solution of $(x-3)^2 > 16$

A: $(x-3)^2 > 16 \implies x-3 > 4$ and $x-3 < -4$

$\implies \boxed{x > 7 \text{ and } x < -1}$

$x^2 > 16$ is true for $x > 4$ & $x < -4$

Similarly, $(x-3)^2 > 16$ is true for $x - 3 > 4$ & $x - 3 < -4$

Find the solutions of :

9. $(x-2)^2 > -1$ 10. $(x+4)^2 < 25$ 11. $(x-1)^2 \le -9$ 12. $(x-7)^2 > 81$

13. Show that the solution of $(x-5)^2 > 2$ is $x > 5 + \sqrt{2}$ and $x < 5 - \sqrt{2}$

$x > 5 + \sqrt{2}$ and $x < 5 - \sqrt{2}$ are the <u>exact solutions</u> of $(x-5)^2 > 2$

14. Find the exact solutions of $(x-3)^2 < 5$

15. Solve $(x-1)^2 < 15$, giving your solutions to 3 d.p.

16. Solve $(x+2)^2 > -3$

17. Solve $(x-1)^2 < -4$

18. Solve $(x-6)^2 < 25$

19. Solve $(x-6)^2 < 20$, giving your solutions to 3 d.p.

• *Check your answers.*

D4.2: But what if the quadratic does not factorise ?

EXAMPLE   For what values of x is $2x^2 + 2 > 3x$

$2x^2 + 2 > 3x$

$2x^2 - 3x + 2 > 0$ This will not factorise.

Completing the square $\Rightarrow$ $x^2 - \frac{3}{2}x + 1 > 0$

$\Rightarrow$ $\left(x - \frac{3}{4}\right)^2 - \frac{9}{16} + 1 > 0$

$\Rightarrow$ $\left(x - \frac{3}{4}\right)^2 > -\frac{7}{16}$

Since squares are always +ve or zero, this expression is true for all values of x

ANS all values of x

EXAMPLE   For what values of x is $2x^2 - 4x + 1 \geq 0$

This will not factorise. So, we need to 'complete the square'

$2x^2 - 4x + 1 \geq 0$

$x^2 - 2x + \frac{1}{2} \geq 0$

$\Rightarrow$ $(x - 1)^2 - 1 + \frac{1}{2} \geq 0$

$\Rightarrow$ $(x - 1)^2 \geq \frac{1}{2}$

$\Rightarrow$ $x - 1 \geq +\frac{1}{\sqrt{2}}$ & $x - 1 \leq -\frac{1}{\sqrt{2}}$

$\Rightarrow$ $\boxed{x \geq 1 + {}^1/_{\sqrt{2}} \ \ \& \ \ x \leq 1 + {}^1/_{\sqrt{2}}}$

Remember:
You should show the same amount of working as in the example.

Solve these inequalities.
Some will factorise and some will not.

1. $(x + 3)^2 + 1 > 0$

2. $(x - 1)^2 < 0$

3. $(x - 2)^2 \leq 0$

4. $x^2 + x + 1 > 0$

5. $2x^2 + 7 \leq 4x$

6. $2x^2 - 8x + 7 \geq 0$

7. $2x^2 + 7x + 5 \geq 0$

8. $2x^2 + 7x + 5 \leq 0$

9. $3x^2 + 18x + 25 \leq 0$

10. $10x^2 - 10x + 1 < 0$

Reminder

EXAMPLE
Solve $(x + 2)(x - 4) < 0$

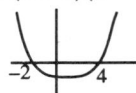

From the graph
$-2 < x < 4$

• *Check your answers.*

P1: Unit 6: Completing the square

Facts and formulae you need to know:

$(x + a)^2 = x^2 + 2ax + a^2 \implies x^2 + 2ax = (x + a)^2 - a^2$

$(x + a)^2$ is always positive or zero (it cannot be negative)

$(x + a)^2 \pm k$ has a minimum value when $x + a = 0$

<u>Simple quadratic inequalities</u>

Type 1:	$x^2 < -1$	No solution
Type 2:	$x^2 > -1$	Solution is all values of x
Type 3:	$x^2 < 25$	Solution is $-5 < x < 5$
Type 4:	$x^2 > 25$	Solution is $x > 5$ and $x < -5$

Competence Test P1.6

1. Write down the expansion of $(x + 7)^2$ (2A)

2. *Write each of these in completed square form:* (2M, 2A each = 16 marks)
   (a) $x^2 + 12x + 36$ (b) $x^2 - 6x + 7$
   (c) $x^2 - 5x + 1$ (d) $2x^2 + 7x - 5$

3. For what value of x does $(x - 3)^2 + 2.25$ have a minimum value and what is the minimum value ? (2A)

4. Sketch the graph of $y = (x + 5)^2 - 6$, (2M,2A)
   labelling the vertex with its coordinates.

5. (a) Write $x^2 + 3x - 5$ in completed square form. (3M,3A)
   (b) Sketch the graph of $y = x^2 + 3x - 5$, labelling the vertex.

6. *Solve these equations, using the completed square method:* (6M,6A)
   (a) $x^2 - 18x - 20 = 0$ (b) $2x^2 - 6x - 9 = 0$

7. *Solve these inequalities:* (1M, 2A each = 18 marks)
   (a) $x^2 < 25$ (b) $x^2 \geq 6$ (c) $(x + 4)^2 + 1 < 0$
   (d) $(x - 3)^2 > -2$ (e) $(x - 3)^2 \leq 9$ (f) $x^2 + 3x - 7 < 0$

Total	=	60

AIMING HIGH

Unit 7
Integral Calculus

CONTENTS
Section 1: Reverse differentiation
Section 2: Integration
Section 3: Definite integrals
Section 4: Areas under curves, the sign of the area and areas between curves
and lines
Section 5: Improper integrals **[OCR only]**

	OCR	AQA	Edexcel
Section 1	All	All	All
Section 2	All	All	All
Section 3	All	All	All
Section 4	All	All	All
Section 5	All	—	—

Unit 7: Integral Calculus
Section 1: Reverse differentiation

In this section you will:
• meet and use reverse differentiation;
• solve problems using reverse differentiation

DEVELOPMENT

D1.1: Differentiation in reverse

Copy and complete:

1. $y = x^2$ => $\frac{dy}{dx}$ = ...

2. y = ... => $\frac{dy}{dx}$ = $4x$

3. y = ... => $\frac{dy}{dx}$ = $10x$

4. y = ... => $\frac{dy}{dx}$ = x

5. $y = x^3$ => $\frac{dy}{dx}$ = ...

6. y = ... => $\frac{dy}{dx}$ = $12x^2$

7. y = ... => $\frac{dy}{dx}$ = $15x^2$

8. y = ... => $\frac{dy}{dx}$ = x^2

9. $y = x^4$ => $\frac{dy}{dx}$ = ...

10. y = ... => $\frac{dy}{dx}$ = $20x^3$

11. y = ... => $\frac{dy}{dx}$ = x^3

12. y = ... => $\frac{dy}{dx}$ = $5x^3$

13. y = ... => $\frac{dy}{dx}$ = $7x^6$

14. y = ... => $\frac{dy}{dx}$ = x^6

15. y = ... => $\frac{dy}{dx}$ = x^9

16. y = ... => $\frac{dy}{dx}$ = x^{12}

Find an expression for y in each of the following cases:

17. $\frac{dy}{dx} = 9x^8$

18. $\frac{dy}{dx} = x^8$

19. $\frac{dy}{dx} = 5x^8$

20. $\frac{dy}{dx} = \frac{1}{2}x^8$

21. $\frac{dy}{dx} = 6x$

22. $\frac{dy}{dx} = x$

23. $\frac{dy}{dx} = \frac{x}{2}$

24. $\frac{dy}{dx} = \frac{3x}{4}$

25. $\frac{dy}{dx} = 3x^{10}$

26. $\frac{dy}{dx} = 5x^6$

27. $\frac{dy}{dx} = \frac{1}{2}x^7$

28. $\frac{dy}{dx} = \frac{3}{4}x^5$

29. $\frac{dy}{dx} = x^n$

30. $\frac{dy}{dx} = ax^p$

31. $\frac{dy}{dx} = 3$

32. $\frac{dy}{dx} = k$

• *Check your answers*

D1.2: Applications of reverse differentiation

If $\frac{dy}{dx} = x^n$ then $y = \frac{x^{n+1}}{n+1} + c$

$n \neq -1$

> The general case is $+ c$ because the derivative of any constant $= 0$

EXAMPLE   Find the equation of the curve with gradient $6x^2 + 1$ which passes through the point $(1,4)$.

We know that $\frac{dy}{dx} = 6x^2 + 1$

$\Rightarrow \quad y = 2x^3 + x + c$

> c is a general constant and we will need to work out its value

The curve passes through $(1,4) \Rightarrow y = 4$ when $x = 1$

$$4 = 2 + 1 + c \Rightarrow c = 1$$

$\Rightarrow$ equation of curve is $\boxed{y = 2x^3 + x + 1}$

EXAMPLE   A body moves in a straight line.
Its speed is given by $v = 10t + t^2$
s is the distance in metres from a point 0 and $v = \frac{ds}{dt}$
Find the distance from O from 0 after $3s$.

$$v = \frac{ds}{dt} = 10t + t^2$$

$$\Rightarrow s = 5t^2 + \frac{1}{3}t^3 + c$$

when $t = 0$, $s = 0 \Rightarrow c = 0 \quad \Rightarrow s = 5t^2 + \frac{1}{3}t^3$

when $t = 3 \quad s = 45 + 9 = \boxed{54m}$

1. Find the equation of the curve, with gradient $4 - 3x^2$ which passes through the point $(0,2)$

2. If $\frac{dy}{dx} = 5x^3$, find y in terms of x, given that $y = -1$ when $x = 1$

3. If $\frac{dp}{dt} = 7 - 3t^2$, find p in terms of t, given that $p = 4$ when $t = 0$

4. A body moves in a straight line. s is the distance in mm from a point 0.
   The velocity of the body is given by $v = 20t - 3t^2$.
   Find the distance of the body from 0 when $t = 2$ seconds.

5. A can of paint is knocked over. The area of the paint after t s is given as A cm².

   The rate of increase of A is given by $\frac{dA}{dt} = 4 + t$. When $t = 0$, A $= 10$ cm².
   Work out the area after 3 s.

• *Check answers*

Section 2: Integration

In this section you will:
• meet integration as the inverse of differentiation;
• integrate products and quotients of powers of x

DEVELOPMENT

D2.1: Integrating powers of x

$\dfrac{d}{dx}(.....)$ is the instruction "differentiate with respect to x"

The reverse operation to differentiation is integration

The instruction "integrate with respect to x" is $\int ...... \, dx$

$$\frac{d}{dx}(x^2 + 3) = 2x$$ ← Read as "the derivative of $x^2 + 3$ is $2x$"

$$\int 2x \, dx = x^2 + c$$ ← Read as "the integral of $2x$ is $x^2 + c$"

c is called "the constant of integration"

$$\int x^n \, dx = \frac{x^{n+1}}{n+1} + c \qquad n \neq -1$$

Yerwat

EXAMPLE (a) $\int (5x + 4) \, dx$ $\qquad = \boxed{\,^5/_2 \, x^2 + 4x + c\,}$

(b) $\int 3x^{1/2} \, dx = \dfrac{3x^{3/2}}{^3/_2} + c \qquad = \boxed{2x^{3/2} + c}$

(c) $\int 7x^{-4/3} \, dx = \dfrac{7x^{-1/3}}{-^1/_3} + c \qquad = \boxed{-21x^{-1/3} + c}$

Evaluate:

1. $\int x^4 \, dx$
2. $\int x^{12} \, dx$
3. $\int x^{-4} \, dx$
4. $\int x^{5/2} \, dx$

5. $\int (4x^3 - x^2) \, dx$
6. $\int (4 - x^{-2}) \, dx$
7. $\int (5x^3 - 2x) \, dx$
8. $\int (2x^{3/2} - x^{-7/2}) \, dx$

9. $\int (4x^3 + x^{-2} - 3) \, dx$
10. $\int (5 - x^{5/2}) \, dx$

EXAMPLE

$$\int \left(x^3 + \frac{1}{x^2} - \sqrt{x}\right) dx = \int (x^3 + x^{-2} - x^{1/2}) \, dx = \frac{x^4}{4} + \frac{x^{-1}}{-1} - \frac{x^{3/2}}{^3/_2} + c$$

First, rewrite the expression with each term in the form x^n

$$= {}^1/_4 \, x^4 - \frac{1}{x} - {}^2/_3 \, x^{3/2} + c$$

Ruff

11. $\int \dfrac{1}{x^3} \, dx$
12. $\int \sqrt[3]{x} \, dx$
13. $\int \dfrac{2}{x^2} \, dx$
14. $\int \dfrac{3}{x^8} \, dx$

15. $\int \dfrac{1}{3x^4}\,dx$ 16. $\int \dfrac{3}{x^4}\,dx$ 17. $\int \sqrt{x}\,dx$ 18. $\int \dfrac{1}{\sqrt{x}}\,dx$

19. $\int \dfrac{1}{3\sqrt{x}}\,dx$ 20. $\int \dfrac{3}{\sqrt{x}}\,dx$ 21. $\int (5x^2 - \dfrac{1}{x^2} + 4x)\,dx$

22. $\int (\dfrac{3}{x^4} - \dfrac{1}{x^3} - x^3)\,dx$ 23. $\int (\sqrt{x} - (\sqrt{x})^3)\,dx$

• *Check your answers.*

D2.2: Integrating products and quotients of powers of *x*

EXAMPLE

(a) $\int x(x+4)\,dx = \int (x^2 + 4x)\,dx = \boxed{\dfrac{x^3}{3} + 2x^2 + c}$

↑ Rewrite the expression as a sum of powers of x

Spoton

(b) $\int \dfrac{x^2 + 5x + 3}{x^{1/2}}\,dx = \int (x^{3/2} + 5x^{1/2} + 3x^{-1/2})\,dx = \boxed{\dfrac{2x^{5/2}}{5} + \dfrac{10x^{3/2}}{3} + 6x^{1/2} + c}$

Evaluate each integral. Show all working.

1. $\int (3x-1)(x+1)\,dx$ 2. $\int x^4(x-3)\,dx$ 3. $\int \dfrac{x^4 - 1}{x^2}\,dx$

4. $\int (x+5)^2\,dx$ 5. $\int \left(x + \dfrac{1}{x}\right)^2$ 6. $\int \dfrac{x^4 + 3x^2 + 1}{2x^2}\,dx$

7. $\int x(x-3)(x+3)\,dx$ 8. $\int \dfrac{(x+2)(x-7)}{x^4}\,dx$ 9. $\int \dfrac{x^2 + 3x - 1}{\sqrt{x}}\,dx$

10. $\int \dfrac{(\sqrt{x} + 1)^2}{x}\,dx$ 11. $\int \dfrac{x(x+5)(x-1)}{\sqrt{x}}\,dx$ 12. $\int \dfrac{3x^2 + 2x - 5}{x\sqrt{x}}\,dx$

• *Check answers*

░░░░░░ PRACTICE ░░░░░░

P2.3: Miscellaneous practice exercise

Evaluate each integral. Show all working.

1: $\int x^2(x-3)\,dx$ 2. $\int (x^4 + \dfrac{5}{x^3} - 10)\,dx$ 3. $\int \dfrac{x\sqrt{x} + x + 1}{\sqrt{x}}\,dx$

4. $\int (x+4)(3x-2)\,dx$ 5. $\int \left[3x + \dfrac{3}{x}\right]^2\,dx$ 6. $\int \dfrac{(x+3)(x-2)}{x\sqrt{x}}\,dx$

7. $\int x(2x+5)^2\,dx$ 8. $\int \dfrac{(3\sqrt{x} + 1)^2}{\sqrt{x}}\,dx$ 9. $\int 5x^2 + \dfrac{3}{x^4} + \dfrac{4}{x\sqrt{x}}\,dx$

• *Check answers*

Section 3: Definite integrals

DEVELOPMENT

D3.1: Definite integrals

Indefinite integrals

$\int f(x)\,dx =$ as an expression in x is an indefinite integral

Definite integrals

$$\int_a^b f(x)\,dx = \left[\text{Value of } \int f(x)\,dx \text{ when } x = b\right] - \left[\text{value of } \int f(x)\,dx \text{ when } x = a\right]$$

$$= \text{a number}$$

$\int_a^b f(x)\,dx$ is a **definite integral**

EXAMPLE

$\int_2^3 (6x-2)dx = [3x^2 - 2x + c]_2^3 = [27 - 6 + c] - [12 - 4 + c] = \boxed{13}$

(value of integral when $x = 3$)   (value of integral when $x = 2$)

BUT - the constant of integration always disappears ,

so, in future, **for definite integrals we will leave out the constant.**

EXAMPLE

$\int_1^4 \left(x + \dfrac{1}{x^2}\right) dx = \int_1^4 (x + x^{-2})\,dx = \left[\dfrac{x^2}{2} + \dfrac{x^{-1}}{-1}\right]_1^4 = \left[\dfrac{x^2}{2} - \dfrac{1}{x}\right]_1^4$

$= \left[8 - \frac{1}{4}\right] - \left[\frac{1}{2} - 1\right] = \boxed{8\frac{1}{4}}$ (No c !)

Evaluate these definite integrals. Set out your working as in the example.

1. $\int_0^4 x^4\,dx$ 2. $\int_2^3 4x^5\,dx$ 3. $\int_1^{16} \sqrt{x}\,dx$ 4. $\int_{-2}^{-1} \dfrac{1}{x^3}\,dx$

5. $\int_{-1}^1 (3x^2 - 1)dx$ 6. $\int_0^2 (4x^2 - x)dx$ 7. $\int_1^2 \left[x^2 - \dfrac{3}{x^2}\right]dx$

8. $\int_{-1}^2 (3x-1)(x+2)dx$ 9. $\int_1^2 x(x-1)(x-3)dx$

10. $\int_1^9 \dfrac{x+1}{\sqrt{x}}dx$ 11. $\int_1^4 (t + \frac{1}{t})^2 dt$

• *Check answers.*

Some calculators can evaluate definite integrals which is very useful for checking answers.
However, all working out must be shown, for full marks.

Section 4: Areas under curves

In this section you will:
- use integration to calculate the area under a curve
- use integration to calculate the area between two graphs.

DEVELOPMENT

D4.1: Area under a curve

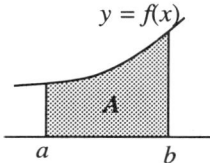

To find the shaded area, consider an element of the area of width δx. Call this element δA.

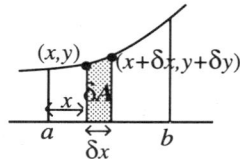

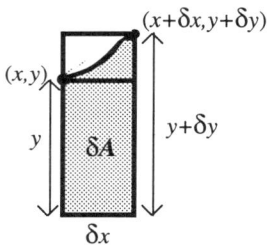

small rectangle $\leq \delta A \leq$ big rectangle

$$\Rightarrow \quad y\delta x \leq \quad \delta A \quad \leq \quad (y + \delta y)\delta x$$

$$\Rightarrow \quad y \leq \frac{\delta A}{\delta x} \leq \quad y + \delta y$$

As $\delta x \longrightarrow 0$, $\delta y \longrightarrow 0$ and $\dfrac{\delta A}{\delta x} \longrightarrow \dfrac{dA}{dx}$

$$\Rightarrow \quad \frac{dA}{dx} = y$$

$$\Rightarrow \quad A = \int y \, dx + c = \int f(x) \, dx + c$$

But, $A = 0$ when $x = a$ so $c = -$[value of $f(x) \, dx$ when $x = a$]

The required area is obtained by taking $x = b$

Hence, the area between the curve and the x-axis is given by

$$A = \left| \int_a^b y \, dx \right| = \int_a^b f(x) \, dx$$

Read this as "the integral of y with respect to x, between a and b"
The dx tells you that you must write the y as an expression in terms of x before you integrate.

EXAMPLE

$y = 3x^2$ Calculate the shaded area

$$\text{Area} = \int_1^3 3x^2 \, dx = \left[x^3 \right]_1^3$$

$$= 27 - 1 = \boxed{26 \text{ unit}^2}$$

1. Sketch the curve $y = 2x^2$ between $x = 0$ and $x = 4$
    Calculate the area between the curve, the x-axis, $x = 0$ and $x = 3$

Calculate each of the shaded areas:

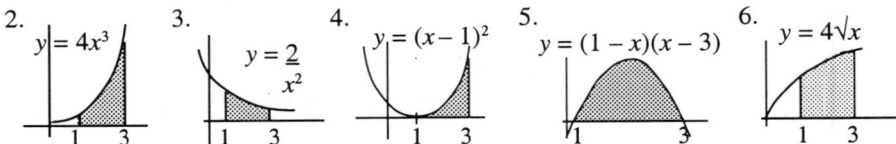

2.

$y = 4x^3$

1   3

3.

$y = 2$

x^2

1   3

4.

$y = (x - 1)^2$

1   3

5.

$y = (1 - x)(x - 3)$

1   3

6.

$y = 4\sqrt{x}$

1   3

7. (a) What are the coordinates of T ?

   (b) Work out the area between the curve
       and the x-axis that lies above the x-axis.

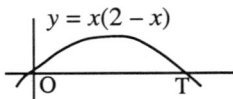

$y = x(2 - x)$

O   T

8. Sketch the curve $y = (1 - x)(4 + x)$.
    Calculate the area between the curve and the x-axis which lies above the x-axis.
                          • *Check your answers.*

D4.2: The sign of the area

1. Work out   (a) $\int_0^4 (4x - x^2)\, dx$

   (b) $\int_4^5 (4x - x^2)\, dx$ (c) $\int_0^5 (4x - x^2)\, dx$

$y = 4x - x^2$

A_1

0   4 A_2 5

   (d) Which integral gives the area of A_1 ?
   (e) Explain how you can work out the area of A_2 from one of these integrals.
   (f) $A_1 + A_2 \neq \int_0^5 (4x - x^2)\, dx$ Explain why.

$A_1 = \int_a^b f(x)\, dx$ = a positive value

For areas above the x-axis, the
integral gives a positive value.

$A_2 = \int_b^c f(x)\, dx$ = a negative value

For areas below the x-axis, the
integral gives a negative value.

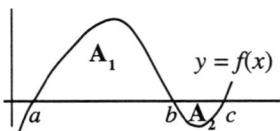

A_1 $y = f(x)$

a   b A_2 c

So: the area between a and b is A_1
      the area between b and c is $-A_2$
    & the total area is $A_1 - A_2$

2. For what values of x is y negative if $y = (2x - 1)(x - 4)$?
    Calculate the area of the curve below the x-axis.

3. Sketch the graph of $y = x(x - 1)(x - 3)$.
    Calculate the total area enclosed between the curve and the x-axis.

4. (a) Calculate the total shaded area.
   (b) Explain why this area is not given by $\int_0^5 (3x - x^2)\,dx$

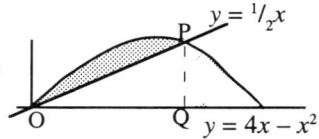

$y = 3x - x^2$

5. Calculate the total area enclosed by the curve $y = (x + 1)(x - 5)$, the x-axis and the lines $x = 1$ and $x = 7$.

• *Check your answers.*

D4.3: Areas between curves and lines

EXAMPLE   Calculate the area of the segment between the curve $y = 4x - x^2$ and the line $y = \frac{1}{2}x$

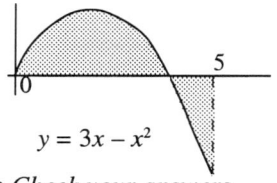

$y = \frac{1}{2}x$

P

O   Q $y = 4x - x^2$

Shaded area =

We need the coordinates of P: $4x - x^2 = \frac{1}{2}x$
$$\Rightarrow \quad x^2 - \frac{7}{2}x = 0$$
$$\Rightarrow \quad x(x - \frac{7}{2}) = 0$$
$$\Rightarrow \quad x = 0 \text{ or } x = \frac{7}{2} \qquad \Rightarrow \quad \text{P is } (\frac{7}{2}, \frac{7}{4})$$

Area under the curve = $\int_0^{7/2} (4x - x^2)\,dx = [2x^2 - \frac{1}{3}x^3]_0^{7/2} = \frac{49}{2} - \frac{343}{24} = \frac{245}{24}$

Area of $\triangle OPQ = \frac{1}{2} \times \frac{7}{2} \times \frac{7}{4} = \frac{49}{16}$ ◄── This could also have been worked out

Area of shaded segment = $\frac{245}{24} - \frac{49}{16}$ using $\int_0^{7/2} \frac{1}{2}x\,dx$

$= \frac{490}{48} - \frac{147}{48} = \boxed{\frac{343}{48}} \text{ units}^2$

Ruff

1. (a) Find the coordinates of the point of intersection, Q, of the curves $y = x^4$ and $y = x^3$

   (b) Show that the area enclosed between the two curves is $\frac{1}{20}$ units².

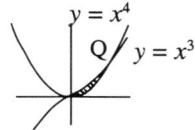

$y = x^4$

Q $y = x^3$

2. Calculate the total area enclosed between the curves $y = x^2$ and $y = x^4$.

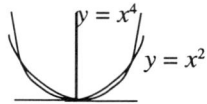

$y = x^4$

$y = x^2$

3. Calculate the area of the segment cut off on the curve $y = 6x - x^2$ by the line $y = 2x$.

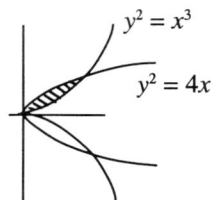

$y^2 = x^3$

$y^2 = 4x$

4. Calculate the area of the shaded segment between the curves $y^2 = 4x$ and $y^2 = x^3$

• *Check your answers.*

D4.4: Area between a curve and the y-axis

The area between the curve and the x-axis is given by

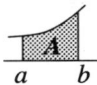

$$A = \int_a^b y \, dx = \int_a^b f(x) \, dx$$

Similarly, the area between the curve and the y–axis is given by

$$A = \int_{y_1}^{y_2} x \, dy$$

1. You are going to work out the area between the graph of $y = 3x^2$, the y-axis and the lines $y = 1$ and $y = 4$.

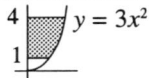

   Step 1: Rearrange $y = 3x^2$ to give x in terms of y.

   Step 2: Use the formula $\quad \text{Area} = \int_1^4 x \, dy$

   to show that the required area is $^{14}/_9\sqrt{3}$ units²

2. Sketch the curve $y = 2x^2$ between $x = -2$ and $x = 2$
   Calculate the area between the curve, the y-axis, $y = 1$ and $y = 4$

   • *Check your answers.*

E4.5: Miscellaneous areas

1. (a) Find the equation of the chord which joins the points A(–2,3) and B(0,15) on the curve $y = 15 - 3x^2$
   (b) Calculate the area enclosed by the curve and the chord AB.

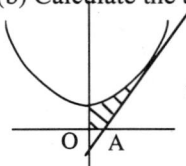

2. Calculate the area bounded by the curve $y = x^2 + 3$, the tangent to the curve at (2,7) and the x- and y-axes.

3. The curve $y = (x + 2)(x + 1)(x - 3)$ cuts the x-axis at A, B, C in that order.
   Calculate the total area enclosed by the curve from A to C and the x-axis.

4. **The ultimate challenge !**
   Show that the total area between the curve $y = 2x^3 + x^2$ and the line $y = x$ is $^{37}/_{96}$ units²

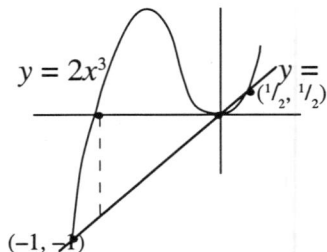

$y = 2x^3$

$y = x$

$(^1/_2, ^1/_2)$

$(-1, -1)$

   • *Check your answers.*

Section 5: Improper integrals

OCR only

In this section you will :
* meet and understand what is meant by an improper integral
* evaluate improper integrals.

DEVELOPMENT

D5.1: Introducing improper integrals

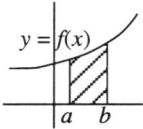

Shaded area $= \int_a^b f(x)\ dx$

Up to now, in calculating $\int_a^b f(x)\ dx$ we have assumed:

* that a and b are both finite
* $f(x)$ is defined (i.e. is finite) for all x in the interval $[a, b]$

Two new cases:

Case 1: Integrals of the form $\int_a^\infty f(x)\ dx$

∞ is infinity

We define $\int_a^\infty f(x)\ dx$ as $\lim_{t \to \infty} \int_a^t f(x)\ dx$

EXAMPLE   Investigate the existence of this integral:

$$\int_1^\infty \frac{1}{x^{3/2}}\ dx = \lim_{t \to \infty}\int_1^t \frac{1}{x^{3/2}}\ dx = \lim_{t \to \infty}\left[\frac{-2}{x^{1/2}}\right]_1^t = \lim_{t \to \infty}\left[\frac{-2}{t^{1/2}} + 2\right] = \boxed{2}$$

So, this integral does exist and its value is 2.

However, if the limit is infinite, we say that the integral does not exist.

Case 2: Integrals where the function is undefined (does not exist) at one of the limits, a or b.

EXAMPLE   Investigate the existence of $\int_0^1 x^{-2}\ dx$

x^{-2} does not exist for $x = 0$

$$\int_0^1 x^{-2}\ dx = \lim_{\varepsilon \to 0}\int_\varepsilon^1 x^{-2}\ dx = \lim_{\varepsilon \to 0}\left[\frac{x^{-1}}{-1}\right]_\varepsilon^1 = \lim_{\varepsilon \to 0}\left[-\frac{1}{1} - -\frac{1}{\varepsilon}\right]$$

As $\varepsilon \to 0$ $\frac{1}{\varepsilon} \to \infty$ so this integral is not finite

We say that $\int_0^1 x^{-2}\ dx$ $\boxed{\text{does not exist.}}$

ε = epsilon
Think of ε as 'a little bit'
or 'a very small number'

Find the value, if it exists, of each of the following integrals:

1. $\int_0^1 x^{-1/2}\ dx$ 2. $\int_{-3}^0 \frac{dx}{x^2}$ 3. $\int_1^\infty \frac{1}{x^3}\ dx$ 4. $\int_0^1 \frac{1}{x^3}\ dx$ 5. $\int_2^\infty x^{-1/2}\ dx$

• Check your answers.

P1: Unit 7: Integral Calculus

Facts and formulae you need to know:

$$\int x^n \, dx = \frac{x^{n+1}}{n+1}$$

Area between curve and the x-axis $= \int y \, dx$

Area between curve and the y-axis $= \int x \, dy$

Competence Test P1.7

Evaluate each of the following integrals: (1M, 2A each = 27 marks)

1. $\int (5x^2 + 3x - 1) \, dx$

2. $\int \left[\sqrt{x} + \frac{2}{\sqrt{x}} \right] dx$

3. $\int \left[\frac{1}{3x^2} + x + \frac{3}{x^4} \right] dx$

4. $\int (x-1)(2x+3) \, dx$

5. $\int \left[\frac{3x^4 - 2x + 5}{x^3} \right] dx$

6. $\int_1^9 \sqrt{x} \, dx$

7. $\int_1^3 (x^3 - 2x) \, dx$

8. $\int_{-3}^1 \left[x - \frac{5}{x^2} \right] dx$

9. $\int_a^b (a^2x + bx^2) \, dx$

10. If $\dfrac{dm}{dt} = 2 + 3t^2$, find m in terms of t, given that $m = 15$ when $t = 2$ (2M, 3A)

11. Calculate the shaded area.   (2M, 2A)

   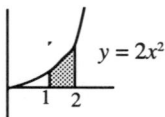
   $y = 2x^2$

12. (a) Sketch the graph of $y = (x+1)(2-x)$ (3M, 3A)
    (b) Work out the area between the curve and the x-axis, that lies above the x-axis.

13. Work out the area (shaded) between the line $y = \frac{1}{2}x$ and the curve $y = x(3-x)$ (4M, 5A)

> Total **(AQA & Edexcel)** = 51

14. Evaluate $\int_0^2 2x^{-1/3} \, dx$ **[OCR only]**   (2M, 2A)

> Total **(OCR)** = 55

AIMING HIGH

Unit 8
Trigonometry

CONTENTS
Section 1: Sin, cos, tan for angles of any size (solving simple trig equations)
Section 2: Graphs of sin x, cos x, tan x (coordinates of points on trig graphs, graph sketching and periods of trig graphs– using graphs to solve trig equations)
Section 3: Equations with complex angles (solving equations like $y = \sin kx$, $y = \cos (x - 30°)$, $y = \sin (3x - 90°)$
Section 4: Exact trig values [for 0°, 30°, 45°, 60°, 90°, 180°) **[OCR only]**
Section 5: Fundamental identities $\left(\tan \theta = \dfrac{\sin \theta}{\cos \theta}, \ \sin^2 \theta + \cos^2 \theta = 1\right)$

Section 6: Radians and trig equations **[Edexcel only]**

<table>
<thead>
<tr><th></th><th>OCR</th><th>AQA</th><th>Edexcel</th></tr>
</thead>
<tbody>
<tr><td>Section 1</td><td>All</td><td>All</td><td>All</td></tr>
<tr><td>Section 2</td><td>All</td><td>All</td><td>All</td></tr>
<tr><td>Section 3</td><td>All</td><td>All</td><td>All</td></tr>
<tr><td>Section 4</td><td>All</td><td>—</td><td>—</td></tr>
<tr><td>Section 5</td><td>All</td><td>All</td><td>All</td></tr>
<tr><td>Section 6</td><td>——</td><td>All</td><td>—</td></tr>
</tbody>
</table>

Unit 8: Trigonometry

Section 1: Sin, cos, tan for angles of any size

In this section you will:
- review the definition of sine and cosine for all angle sizes;
- review why calculators give the values they do for angles beyond 0°– 90°
- find all the angles in a given range for a given value of sin/cos/tan

The story so far ...

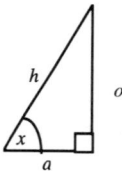

$$\sin x = \frac{o}{h}$$

$$\cos x = \frac{a}{h}$$

$$\tan x = \frac{o}{a}$$

Note:

$$\frac{\sin x}{\cos x} = \frac{{}^{o}/_{h}}{{}^{a}/_{h}} = {}^{o}/_{a}$$

So $\dfrac{\sin x}{\cos x} = \tan x$

However, with this definition of sin/cos/tan, x must lie between 0° and 90°. So, we need another definition of sin/cos/tan that will give values for angles of any size – BUT, it must also agree with the original values for 0° – 90°.

The new definition

Consider a circle of radius 1.

θ (theta) is the angle at the centre, measured from the x axis.

θ is positive in the anti-clockwise direction.

θ is negative in the clockwise direction.

θ can take all values.

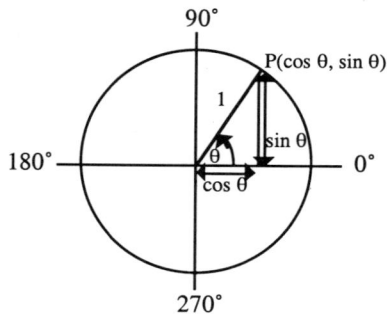

Definition:

The coordinates of the point P on the circle, where OP makes an angle θ with the x – axis, are $(\cos \theta, \sin \theta)$

This agrees with the original definition of values for 0° – 90°

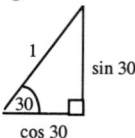

$$\sin 30 = \frac{o}{h} = \frac{\sin 30}{1} = \sin 30$$

$$\cos 30 = \frac{a}{h} = \frac{\cos 30}{1} = \cos 30$$

D1.1: Values for sin and cos without a calculator

EXAMPLE	Q: Find the value of cos 150° and sin 150° to 2 d.p.

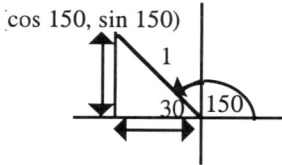

cos 150 $= x$–coord.
$= -\cos 30$
$= -0.87$

sin 150 $= y$–coord.
$= \sin 30$
$= 0.5$

Angle	cos	sin
0	1	0
10	0.98	0.17
20	0.93	0.34
30	0.87	0.5
40	0.77	0.64
50	0.64	0.77
60	0.5	0.87
70	0.34	0.93
80	0.17	0.98

EXAMPLE   Q: Find the value of cos 200° and sin 200° to 2 d.p.

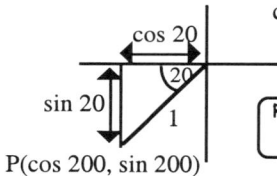

cos 200 $= x$–coord.   sin 200 $= y$–coord.
$= -\cos 20$ $= -\sin 20$
$= -0.93$ $= -0.34$

Remember:
the triangle is always drawn to the x–axis

P(cos 200, sin 200)

Use this method to calculate these values to 2 d.p. Show all working.

1. cos 160°, sin 160°   4. cos 230°, sin 230°   7. cos 260°, sin 260°

2. cos 210°, sin 210°   5. cos 340°, sin 340°   8. cos (–60°), sin (–60°)

3. cos 300°, sin 300°   6. cos 140°, sin 140°   9. cos 520°, sin 520°

10. Use the table of values and $\tan\theta = \dfrac{\sin\theta}{\cos\theta}$ to find the values of cos 180°, sin 180°, tan 180°

11. Explain how you could calculate the value of tan 300° from your answers to Q3.
* Check your answers.

D1.2: Calculating angles

By now you will probably have been asking "Why don't we just use a calculator ?"

210 sin = [–0.5]

From now on, to find sin, cos, tan of any angle, you will just put it into the calculator.

BUT, when finding angles, your calculator only gives one angle for each value. You need to understand the methods of D1 in order to calculate all the angles in a given range.

Summary of what we know

In each quadrant, except the first, two of the trig ratios are –ve and one is +ve. It is easier just to remember the positive value.

S+	A+
T+	C+

The acute angle used is always in the triangle that stands on the x–axis

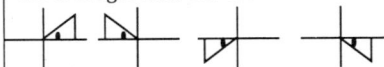

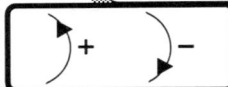

EXAMPLE : Find all solutions of (a) sin x = 0.5 (b) tan x = 1, for $0° \leq x \leq 360°$

(a) Step 1: Calculator gives x = 30°

Step 2:

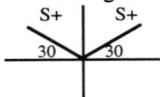

Step 3: Solutions are 30°, 180°– 30°

| Solutions are 30°, 150° |

(b) Step 1: Calculator gives x = 45°

Step 2:

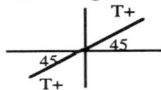

Step 3: Solutions are 45°, 180°+ 45

| Solutions are 45°, 225° |

Find all the solutions in the range $0 \leq x \leq 360°$. Show all working.

1. cos x = 0.5   2. tan x = 0.7   3. sin x = 0.951   4. cos x = 0.407

5. sin x = 0.259   6. cos x = 0.766   7. tan x = 2.75   8. sin x = 0.39

EXAMPLE : Find all solutions of tan x = 0.8, for $-180° \leq x \leq 180°$

(a) Step 1: Calculator gives x = 38.7°

Step 2:

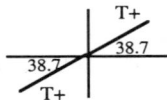

Step 3: only +ve value of x is 38.7°
only –ve value is – (180 – 38.7)

| Solutions are 38.7°, –141.3° |

Find all the solutions in the given range.   Show all working.

9. cos x = 0.5 $0 \leq x \leq 720°$ 10. tan x = 11.43 $-180° \leq x \leq 180°$

11. cos x = 0.407 $-360° \leq x \leq 360°$ 12. sin x = 0.53 $-360° \leq x \leq 360°$

EXAMPLE : Find all solutions of sin x = – 0.5, for $0° \leq x \leq 360°$

We need to know the ACUTE angle

(a) Step 1: Find calculator solution for sin x = 0.5 (not – 0.5)
Calculator gives x = 30°

Step 2:

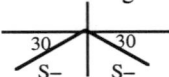

Step 3: Solutions are 180 + 30, 360 – 30

| Solutions are 210°, 330° |

Find all the solutions in the range $0 \leq x \leq 360°$:   *Show all working.*

13. cos x = – 0.5   14. tan x = – 1   15. sin x = 0.819   16. cos x = 0.208

17. sin x = – 0.866 18. cos x = –0.707 19. sin$x$ = – 0.819 20. sin x = –0.966

Section 2: Graphs of sinx, cosx and tanx

In this section you will:
- find coordinates of points on a variety of trigonometric graphs
- use trig graphs to solve equations
- sketch trig graphs
- determine the periods of various trig graphs.

DEVELOPMENT

D2.1: Graphs of sinx, cosx and tanx

1. (a) For the graph of $y = \sin x$,
   state the coordinates of
   the points A, B, C, D, E.
   (b) What is the maximum value of $\sin x$?
   (c) What is the minimum value of $\sin x$?

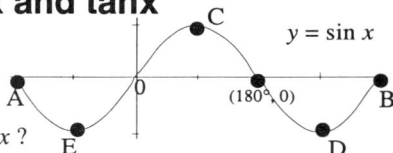

2. (a) For the graph of $y = \cos x$,
   state the coordinates of
   the points P, Q, R, S, T, U.
   (b) What is the maximum
   value of $\cos x$?
   (c) What is the minimum value of $\cos x$?

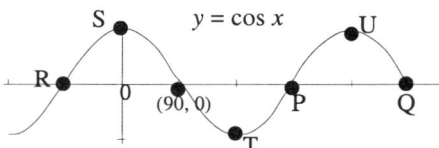

3. (a) For the graph of $y = \tan x$, state the
   coordinates of the three points where
   it crosses the x-axis.
   (b) If the graph were to be extended to
   the right, what would be the coordinates
   of the next point where it would cross the x axis ?

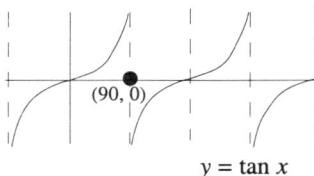

Each of these graphs repeats itself at regular intervals.
$y = \sin x$ repeats every 360°.
We say that the **period** of the sin x graph is 360°.

---

4. What is the period of the cos x graph ?

5. What is the period of the tan x graph ?

6. (a) Sketch the graph of $y = 2\sin x$ for $-180° < x < 360°$
   (b) What is the maximum value of $y = 2\sin x$?
   (c) What is the minimum value of $y = 2\sin x$?
   (d) What is the period of $y = 2\sin x$?

7. (a) Sketch the graph of $y = 1 + \frac{1}{2}\cos x$ for $-180° < x < 360°$
   (b) What is the maximum value of $y = 1 + \frac{1}{2}\cos x$?
   (c) What is the minimum value of $y = 1 + \frac{1}{2}\cos x$?   • *Check answers.*

D2.2: Using graphs to solve trig equations

EXAMPLE: Solve $\sin x = 0.342$ for $-180° \le x \le 360°$

Step 1 : Calculator gives one solution as 20°.

Step 2 : The graph tells us there are just two
solutions, both between 0° and 180°
Using the symmetry of the graph,
the solutions are 20° and $(180 - 20)°$

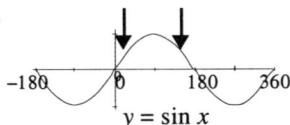

$y = \sin x$

| Solutions are 20° and 160° |

$y = \sin x$

$y = \cos x$

$y = \tan x$

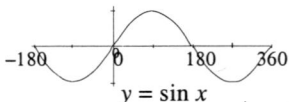

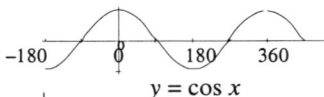

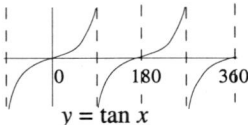

Use the graphs and a calculator to solve these for $-180° < x < 360°$
Give all answers to the nearest degree.

1. $\sin x = 0.5$ 2. $\sin x = -0.5$ 3. $\cos x = 0.5$

4. $\cos x = -0.5$ 5. $\sin x = 0.707$ 6. $\sin x = -0.707$

7. $\cos x = 0.707$ 8. $\cos x = -0.707$ 9. $\sin x = 0.26$

Use the graphs and a calculator to solve these for $0° < x < 360°$
Give all answers to the nearest degree.

10. $\tan x = 1$ 11. $\cos x = 0.643$ 12. $\sin x = 0.174$

13. $\tan x = -1.192$ 14. $\sin x = -0.342$ 15. $\tan x = -0.625$

16. $\cos x = 0.9063$ 17. $\cos x = -0.94$ 18. $\sin x = -0.9063$

19. The diagram shows part of the curve
    with equation $y = 2.5 + \sin x$.

    $y = 2.5 + \sin x$

    (a) State the coordinates of the point A,
        where the curve crosses the y axis ?

    (b) What is the maximum value of $2.5 + \sin x$?

    (c) What are the coordinates of the two lowest
        points of graph shown in this diagram ?

    (d) Use the graph to find the solutions of $2.5 + \sin x = 3$ for $-180° < x < 360°$

    (e) What is the first solution of $2.5 + \sin x = 3$ that is greater than $360°$?

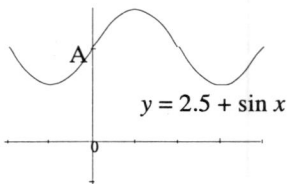

    • *Check your answers.*

D2.3: More sin, cos, tan graphs

EXAMPLE: Sketch $y = \sin 2x$

Method 1: We know that the graph of $\sin 2x$ is shaped like ⌒⌒
It crosses the x-axis where
$2x = ..., -180°, 0°, 180°, 360° ...$
$\Rightarrow\ x = ..., -90°, 0°, 90°, 180° ...$

Method 2: (Translations and stretches)
From $y = \sin x$, the x has been replaced by $2x$ or $x \div \frac{1}{2}$, so the graph has been stretched by a factor $\frac{1}{2}$ parallel to the x-axis.

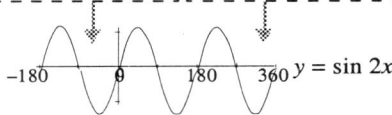
$-180 \qquad 0 \qquad 180 \qquad 360\ y = \sin 2x$

1. (a) Sketch the graph of $y = \cos 2x$ for $0° < x < 360°$
   (b) What is the period of $\cos 2x$?
2. (a) Sketch the graph of $y = \sin \frac{1}{2}x$ for $0° < x < 360°$
   (b) What is the period of $\sin \frac{1}{2}x$?
3. (a) Sketch the graph of $y = \tan 3x$ for $0° < x < 180°$
   (b) What is the period of $\tan 3x$?

EXAMPLE: Sketch $y = \sin (x - 30°)$

Method 1: $\sin (x - 30°)$ crosses the x-axis where
$x - 30° = -180°, 0°, 180°, 360°$
$\Rightarrow\ x = -150°, 30°, 210°, 390°$

Method 2: (Translations and stretches)
$y = \sin x$ has been translated 30° to the right.

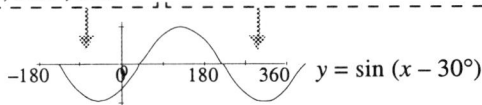
$-180 \qquad 0 \qquad 180 \qquad 360\ y = \sin (x - 30°)$

4. Sketch the graph of $y = \sin (x - 90°)$
5. Sketch the graph of $y = \cos(x + 30°)$
6. Sketch the graph of $y = 2\sin (x + 60°)$

7. The diagram shows part of the graph of $y = \sin (ax - b)$, where a and b are positive constants and b is less that $180°$. The curve cuts the x-axis at A, B(120,0), C(210,0) and D.

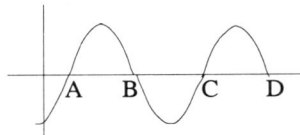

   (a) Write down the coordinates of A and D.
   (b) Find the values of a and b.

• *Check your answers.*

Section 3: Equations with complex angles

In this section you will solve equations with angles which are kx, $(x \pm k)$, $(px \pm q)$

D3.1: Solving equations with complex angles

EXAMPLE: Solve $\sin 2x = 0.5$ for $0° \leq x \leq 360°$

A: Step 1:   Calculator gives $2x = 30°$

Step 2: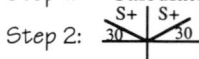

Step 3: $0 \leq 2x \leq 720°$

Step 4: $2x = 30, 180 - 30, 360 + 30, 540 - 30$

           $2x = 30, 150, 390, 510$

Step 5: $\boxed{x = 15°, 75°, 195°, 265°}$

> This stage is most important

Solve, for $0° \leq x \leq 360°$:

                                        Gizmo

1. $\cos 2x = 0.5$ 2. $\tan 2x = 1$

---

3. | Teacher set the question: "Solve $\cos 2x = 0.707$ for $0 \leq x \leq 360°$"

Youslas did the question like this:

     $\cos 2x = 0.707$

     $2x = 45°$

     $x = 22.5°$ & $360 - 22.5°$

     $\underline{x = 22.5° \ \& \ 337.5°}$

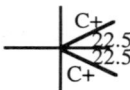 

                      Youslas

           Teacher marked it wrong.

(a) Explain what Youslas did wrong

(b) Solve the equation properly, showing all working.

4. If $\cos 2\theta = 0.699$ find all values of θ between $0°$ and $360°$

5. If $\tan 2\theta = -1$ find all values of θ between $0°$ and $180°$

6. If $\sin 3x = 0.5$, find all values of x between $0°$ and $180°$

7. The equation $\cos {}^{\theta}\!/_{2} = 0.5$ has two solutions between $0°$ and $720°$. Find them.

8. Solve $\tan {}^{\theta}\!/_{3} = 1$ for $0° \leq \theta \leq 720°$

EXAMPLE: Solve $\sin (2x - 30) = 0.5$ for $0° \leq x \leq 360°$

A: Step 1:   Calculator gives $2x - 30 = 30°$

Step 2: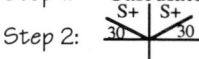

Step 3: $-30 \leq 2x - 30 \leq 690$

Step 4: $2x - 30 = 30, 180 - 30, 360 + 30, 540 - 30$ (rest are out of range)

           $2x - 30 = 30, 150, 390, 510$

Step 5: $2x = 60°, 180°, 420°, 540° \Rightarrow \boxed{x = 30°, 90°, 210°, 270°}$

Solve, for $0° \leq x \leq 360°$:

9. $\cos (x - 45) = 0.5$ 10. $\tan (x + 60°) = 1$ 11. $\sin (2x - 90)° = 0.707$

12. $\cos (3x + 20)° = 0.65$ 13. $\sin (2x - 40)° = 0.94$ • *Check answers.*

Section 4: Exact trig values

In this section you will meet and use the exact values ·for some trig ratios.

(but they will be met and used in Mechanics)

DEVELOPMENT

D4.1: Useful values

You will need to know these exact values for sine, cosine and tan of 30°, 45° and 60° It is probably easier to learn the two triangles and deduce the values from them.

$\sin 45° = \cos 45° = {}^1/_{\sqrt{2}}$

$\tan 45° = 1$

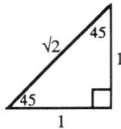

The 45° triangle is isosceles. If you let the two equal sides be 1 unit long, then Pythagoras' Theorem gives √2 for the hypotenuse.

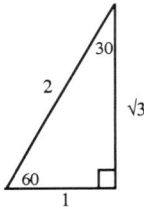

$\sin 30° = \cos 60° = {}^1/_2$

$\cos 30° = \sin 60° = {}^{\sqrt{3}}/_2$

$\tan 60° = \sqrt{3}$

$\tan 30° = {}^1/_{\sqrt{3}}$

The 30°, 60° triangle is half an equilateral triangle. If you let the sides of the equilateral Δ be 2 units long, then the short side is 1 unit long and Pythagoras' Theorem gives √3 for the third side.

$\sin 0° = 0$	$\sin 90° = 1$	$\sin 180° = 0$
$\cos 0° = 1$	$\cos 90° = 0$	$\cos 180° = -1$

Find the exact values of:

1. $\sin 45° + \cos 45°$

2. $\tan 45° - \cos 60°$

3. $\cos 90° + 2\sin 45°$

4. $\cos 30° + \sin 60°$

5. $\tan 60° - 2\cos 30°$

6. $\cos 0° - \cos 180°$

7. $\tan 45° + \sqrt{3}\tan 30°$

8. $\sin 0° + \sqrt{2}\sin 45°$

9. $\sin 90° + \sin 30°$

10. $3\cos 60° - \sin 30° + \sin 90°$

Solve, for $0° \leq x \leq 360°$:

11. $\sin x = 0.5$

12. $\tan x = -1$

13. $\cos x = {}^1/_{\sqrt{2}}$

14. $\sin x = {}^{\sqrt{3}}/_2$

15. $\tan x = \sqrt{3}$

16. $\sin 2x = 1$

17. $\tan x = -{}^1/_{\sqrt{3}}$

18. $\cos {}^1/_2 x = 1$

19. $\sin(x - 30°) = 0.5$

20. $\tan 2x = 1$

• *Check your answers.*

Section 5: Fundamental identities

In this section you will:
- understand the difference between an equation and an identity
- meet fundamental trigonometric identities
- use trigonometric identities to simplify expressions and solve equations

DEVELOPMENT

D5.1: Trigonometric identities

$x^2 + 3x + 2 = 0$ is **an equation**
It is true when $x = 2$ or $x = 1$
An equation either has no solution
or a finite number of solutions.
It is <u>not</u> true for all values of x

$x(x + 3) \equiv x^2 + 3x$ is **an identity**
It is true for all values of x.
Strictly, an identity should be written
using $\equiv$ rather than $=$.
$\equiv$ means 'is identical to'

Fundamental identities

$$\tan \theta \equiv \frac{\sin \theta}{\cos \theta}$$

$$\sin^2 \theta + \cos^2 \theta \equiv 1$$

Note: Writing $(\sin x)^2$ as $\sin x^2$
could be confusing. So, $(\sin x)^2$
is usually written as $\sin^2 x$. It
is read as 'sine squared x'

1. Use the basic definitions of sin, cos and tan
   to prove that $\tan \theta \equiv \dfrac{\sin \theta}{\cos \theta}$ for all values of θ.

2. Use the basic definitions of sin, cos and tan
   to prove that $\sin^2 \theta + \cos^2 \theta \equiv 1$ for all values of θ.
   - *Check your answers.*

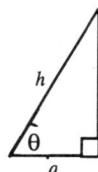

$$\sin \theta = \frac{o}{h}$$
$$\cos \theta = \frac{a}{h}$$
$$\tan \theta = \frac{o}{a}$$

D5.2: Simplifying trigonometric expressions

EXAMPLE   Express $5 \cos^2\theta + 2 \sin^2\theta$ in terms of $\cos \theta$

$5 \cos^2\theta + 2 \sin^2\theta$
$= 5 \cos^2\theta + 2(1 - \cos^2\theta)$
$= 5 \cos^2\theta + 2 - 2\cos^2\theta$
$= \boxed{3 \cos^2\theta + 2}$

Ruff

$\sin^2 \theta + \cos^2 \theta \equiv 1$
$\Rightarrow \sin^2 \theta \equiv 1 - \cos^2 \theta$

Express in terms of sinθ only:
1. $2 \cos^2\theta - \sin^2\theta$

2. $5 \sin\theta - \cos^2\theta$

Simplify: 3. $\dfrac{\sin^2\theta \cos\theta + \cos^3\theta}{\cos \theta}$

4. $\dfrac{2\sin^2\theta + 2\cos^2\theta}{\cos^2\theta}$

5. $\dfrac{\sin \theta}{\sqrt{(1 - \cos^2\theta)}}$

6. $\dfrac{4 - \sin^2\theta - \cos^2\theta}{3}$

- *Check answers.*

D5.3: Solving quadratic trig equations

EXAMPLE   Solve $5 \sin^2 x + 3 \sin x - 2 = 0$ for $0° \le x \le 360°$

$5 \sin^2 x + 3 \sin x - 2 = 0$

$\Rightarrow$ $(5\sin x - 2)(\sin x + 1) = 0$

$\Rightarrow$ $\sin x = 0.4$ & $\sin x = -1$ $\Rightarrow$ $\boxed{x = 23.6°, \ 156.4°, \ 270°}$

Solve, for $0° \le x \le 360°$:

1. $3 \tan^2 x - 10 \tan x + 3 = 0$ 2. $6 \sin^2 x - 7\sin x + 2 = 0$

3. $15 \cos^2 x + 4 \cos x - 4 = 0$ 4. $20\sin^2 x + 3\sin x - 2 = 0$

        • *Check your answers.*

D5.4: Using fundamental identities to solve equations

EXAMPLE   Q: Solve $2 \cos^2 \theta + \sin \theta = 1$ for $0° \le \theta \le 360°$

A: $2 \cos^2 \theta + \sin \theta = 1$ $\boxed{\text{Use } \sin^2 \theta + \cos^2 \theta = 1}$

$2(1 - \sin^2 \theta) + \sin \theta = 1$

$2 \sin^2 \theta - \sin \theta - 1 = 0$

$(2 \sin \theta + 1)(\sin \theta - 1) = 0$

$\sin \theta = -\frac{1}{2}$ and $\sin \theta = 1$

$\boxed{\theta = 90°, 210°, 330°}$

> Rearrange to give a quadratic in the form $ax^2 + bx + c = 0$, where a is positive.
> x is a variable
> – but it could be sinθ or …

Solve each equation for $0° \le \theta \le 360°$:

1. $\cos^2 \theta + \cos\theta = \sin^2 \theta$ 2. $2 \sin^2 \theta + \cos\theta = 1$

3. $4 \cos^2 \theta + 5 \sin\theta = 5$ 4. $1 + \sin\theta \cos^2 \theta = \sin\theta$

EXAMPLE   Solve $\cos \theta + \sin \theta = 0$ for $0° \le \theta \le 360°$

$\cos \theta + \sin \theta = 0$

$\Rightarrow \sin \theta = - \cos \theta$

$\Rightarrow \dfrac{\sin \theta}{\cos \theta} = -1$

$\Rightarrow \tan \theta = -1$ $\Rightarrow$ $\boxed{\theta = 135° \text{ and } 315°}$

5. Solve $2 \cos\theta = 3 \sin\theta$ for $0° \le \theta \le 360°$

6. Solve $\sin 2\theta + 2 \cos 2\theta = 0$ for $-90° \le \theta \le 90°$

        • *Check your answers.*

Section 6: Radians and trig equations

In this section you will:
• find solutions to trig equations in radians.

Edexcel only

DEVELOPMENT

D6.1: Working in radians

EXAMPLE   Find all solutions of $\sin x = 0.2588$ for $0 \leq x \leq 3\pi$

Step 1:   Calculator gives $x = 15° = {}^\pi/_{12}$

Step 2:

Step 3:   Solutions are ${}^\pi/_{12}$, $\pi - {}^\pi/_{12}$, $2\pi + {}^\pi/_{12}$, $3\pi - {}^\pi/_{12}$

Solutions are ${}^\pi/_{12}$, ${}^{11\pi}/_{12}$, ${}^{25\pi}/_{12}$, ${}^{35\pi}/_{12}$

If the range is given in radians then you must find answers in radians.

Find all the solutions in the range $0 \leq x \leq 2\pi$. Show all working.

1. $\cos x = 0.866$

2. $\sin x = 0.309$

3. $\tan x = 1$

4. $\cos x = 0.707$

5. $\sin x = -0.5$

6. $\tan x = 1.732$

7. $\cos x = 0.9397$

8. $\tan x = 0.839$

Find all the solutions in the given range.   Show all working.

9. $\cos x = -0.5$ $0 \leq x \leq 4\pi$

12. $\tan x = -0.5774$ $0 \leq x \leq 3\pi$

10. $\cos x = 0.866$ $-\pi \leq x \leq \pi$

13. $\sin x = -0.866$ $-2\pi \leq x \leq 2\pi$

11. $\sin x = 0.5877$ $-2\pi \leq x \leq 2\pi$

14. $\tan x = 3.078$ $-2\pi \leq x \leq 2\pi$

• *Check your answers.*

D6.2: Trig equations with complex angles in radians

Find all the solutions in the range $0 \leq x \leq 2\pi$. Show all working.

1. $\cos 2x = 0.5$

2. $\sin 3x = 0.707$

3. $\tan {}^1/_2 x = -1$

4. $\cos (x - {}^\pi/_6) = 0.866$

5. $\sin (2x + {}^\pi/_5) = 0.309$

6. $\tan (2x - {}^\pi/_6) = 1.732$

• *Check your answers.*

P1: Unit 8: Trigonometry

Facts and formulae you need to know:
Solving trig equations

The acute angle used is always in the triangle that stands on the x–axis

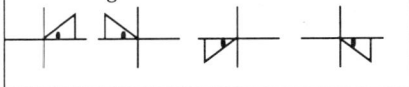

$$\sin^2 \theta + \cos^2 \theta \equiv 1 \qquad \tan \theta = \frac{\sin \theta}{\cos \theta}$$

If the given range is $0° < x < 360°$, say, and you are solving an equation in $(kx - p)$, then you must start by finding the range for $(kx - p)$

S^+	A^+
T^+	C^+

Competence Test P1.8

1. *Find all solutions for $0° \le x \le 360°$:*   (2M, 2A each = 12 marks)
    (a) $\sin x = 0.77$ (b) $\cos x = 0.5$ (c) $\tan x = -1$

2. (a) Sketch a graph of $y = \sin x$ for $0° \le x \le 540°$ (3A)
    (b) Use your calculator and the graph to find all solutions to $\sin x = 0.34$
          for $0° \le x \le 540°$ (2M, 4A)

3. (a) Sketch the graph of $y = 1 + 2 \sin x$ for $0° \le x \le 360°$ (2M, 6A)
    (b) What is the maximum value of $1 + 2 \sin x$ in $0° \le x \le 360°$?
    (c) What is the minimum value of $1 + 2 \sin x$ in $0° \le x \le 360°$?
    (d) Give the coordinates of two points on the graph which lie on the x-axis.

4. *Sketch these graphs for $0° \le x \le 360°$:*   (2A each = 6 marks)
    (a) $y = \cos 2x$ (b) $y = \sin (x + 60)°$ (c) $y = \sin \frac{1}{2}x$

5. Solve $2 \cos^2\theta + 3 \sin \theta = 3$ for $0° \le x \le 360°$

6. *Find all solutions for $0° \le x \le 360°$:*   (2M, 3A each = 15 marks)
    (a) $\sin (x + 60) = 0.707$ (b) $\cos 3x = 0.578$ (c) $\tan (2x - 45°) = 1$

Total = 57

[Edexcel only]

7   *Find all solutions for $0 \le x \le 2\pi$:*   (2M, 3A each = 15 marks)
    (a) $\cos x = 0.707$ (b) $\sin 2x = 0.866$ (c) $\tan (x - {}^\pi/_3) = \sqrt{3}$

Total 57 + 15 = 72

AIMING HIGH

Unit 9
Sequences and Series

CONTENTS
[AQA and Edexcel only]
Section 1: Introducing sequences and series (finding rules)
Section 2: Generating sequences (rules and notation; finding the general term)
Section 3: Arithmetic Progressions (formula for general term, two formulae for sum of APs, sums of natural numbers)
Section 4: The Σ notation for series (working with Σ and evaluating sums)
[Edexcel only]
Section 5: Geometric progressions (general term, sum of n terms, sum to infinity)
[AQA only]
Section 6: Sums of powers of natural numbers (iusing the standard formulae)

	OCR	**AQA**	**Edexcel**
Section 1	——	All	All
Section 2	——	All	All
Section 3	——	All	All
Section 4	——	All	All
Section 5	——	—	All
Section 6	——	All	—

Unit 9: Sequences and Series

Section 1: Introducing sequences and series

In this section you will:
- work with sequences and series;
- meet some of the associated terminology;
- find rules for forming some sequences.

**Edexcel
and AQA
only**

DEVELOPMENT

D1.1: What is a sequence ? What is a series ?

Rule: Draw a square. Shade half of the square. Then, shade half of the unshaded part. Repeat the last instruction until told to stop.

Step 1   Step 2   Step 3   ... **This is a sequence.**

          ... **This is a series.**

The sequence is $^1/_2$, $^1/_4$, $^1/_8$ ...

The series is $^1/_2 + ^1/_4 + ^1/_8$ ...

$^1/_2 + ^1/_4 + ^1/_8$ is a finite series of 3 terms

$^1/_2 + ^1/_4 + ^1/_8 + ...$ is an infinite series

1. 5c   10c   15c 50c

The value of each stamp in this sequence is 5c more than the value of the stamp before it.

(a) How many stamps are there in the set ?

(b) How many terms are there in the sequence 5, 10, 15, ... 40 ?

(c) Write down the series that gives the total value of the first five stamps – but do not find its sum.

(d) What is the total value of all the stamps in the set ?

2. This is the side view of a pyramid of snooker balls.

These are the plans of the layers   O   ...

The numbers of balls in each of the layers forms a sequence.

(a) Find the first six terms in this sequence.

(b) Write down the series that gives the total number of balls in the top 3 layers.

(c) Write down the total number of balls in the top 3 layers.

(d) Find the total number of balls in the top six layers.

• *Check answers.*

D1.2: Rules for sequences

1.

	Bridge 1	Bridge 2	Bridge 3
Number of spars	7	11	15

Here we have two sequences: • a sequence of bridges
                          and • a sequence of numbers

(a) Draw the next bridge in the sequence.

(b) Write down the first six terms in the sequence of numbers.

(c) Explain the rule for finding the next number in the number sequence.

2.

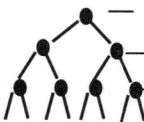

 — — — — At the first level there is 1 node

— — — — At the second level there are 2 nodes

— — — At the third level there are 4 nodes

(a) Write down the first 5 terms in the sequence of numbers of nodes in this network.

(b) Explain the rule for finding the next number in the sequence.

3.

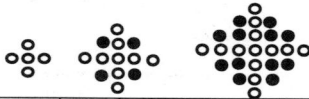

Pattern number	1	2	3	4	5	6
Number of ○	5					
Number of ●	0					

(a) Copy and complete this table.

(b) Explain the rule for each of the two sequences.   • *Check answers.*

EXTENSIONS

E1.3: Extending the idea

For each of the sequences of patterns in question 1–3:

   (a) find the first seven terms in the associated sequence of numbers;

   (b) explain the rule for the number sequence.

1. diamond numbers

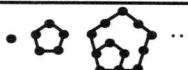

2. pentagonal numbers

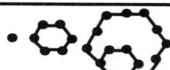

3. hexagonal numbers

4. The first three octagonal numbers are 1, 8, 21
   Find the next three octagonal numbers.

5. 2, 3, 5, 7, 11, 13 …
   This sequence has no obvious geometrical significance.
   What are the next two terms in this sequence ?
                                    • *Check answers.*

Section 2: Generating sequences

In this section you will:
- review using algebraic rules to generate sequences
- deduce the formula for a sequence.

DEVELOPMENT

D2.1: Using functions to generate sequences

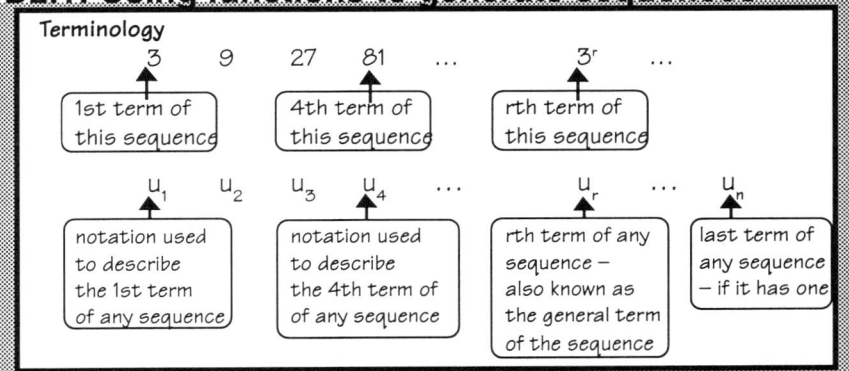

Terminology

| 3 | 9 | 27 | 81 | ... | | 3^r | ... |

| 1st term of this sequence | 4th term of this sequence | rth term of this sequence |

| u_1 | u_2 | u_3 | u_4 | ... | | u_r | ... | | u_n |

| notation used to describe the 1st term of any sequence | notation used to describe the 4th term of any sequence | rth term of any sequence – also known as the general term of the sequence | last term of any sequence – if it has one |

EXAMPLE $u_r = 2^r$ is a **generating rule** for a sequence. What sequence does it generate ?

1st term $= u_1 = 2^1 = 2$
2nd term $= u_2 = 2^2 = 4$ => $\boxed{u_r = 2^r \text{ generates the sequence } 2, 4, 8, ...}$
3rd term $= u_3 = 2^3 = 8$

1. Write down the first four terms generated by the rule $u_r = 2r$

2. $u_r = 2r + 1$ Find: (a) the 10th term in the sequence   (b) u_{25}
                     (c) the 200th term in the sequence   (d) u_{150}

Given	Find
3. $u_r = r^2 - 3$	first four terms
4. $u_r = 3r - 1$	u_7 and u_{10}
5. $u_r = 6 - 2r$	third term and fifth term
6. $u_r = 2r^2 - 2$	first term and u_6
7. $u_r = {}^{15}/_r$	first five terms
8. $u_r = r(r - 1)$	first three terms and u_9
9. $u_r = (-1)^r$	first five terms and u_{11}
10. $u_r = (-1)^{r-1}$	first five terms and u_{11}
11. $u_r = (-1)^r \, 3^r$	u_1, u_2, u_3, u_4

• *Check your answers.*

D2.2: Finding the general term of a sequence

$$u_1, \quad u_2, \quad u_3, \quad \ldots \quad u_r \quad \ldots \quad u_n$$

The rth term is the general term

A possible point of confusion – at GCSE, the general term is often called the nth term.

At A–Level (and beyond), we call the general term the rth term. The nth term is the label usually given to the last term of the sequence.

Type 1: The terms have a common difference

1	2	3	4	
4	7	10	13	...

$+3 \quad +3 \quad +3$

Here, the common difference is 3.

Hence the general term is $3r +$ something.

We find the value of 'something' by looking at the first term.

$\Rightarrow u_r = 3r + 1$

Type 2: The terms do not have a common difference. In these cases, you need to look for patterns in the structure of the numbers.

1	2	3	4	
3	6	12	24	...
3	3×2^1	3×2^2	3×2^3	

$\Rightarrow u_r = 3 \times 2^{r-1}$

For each of these sequences:
- *(a) Write down the first 6 terms*
- *(b) find the general term*
- *(c) find the specified term*

1. $5, 7, 9, 11, \ldots$: 42nd term
2. $1, 4, 7, \ldots$: 15th term
3. $8, 13, 18, \ldots$: 20th term
4. $-4, 0, 4, \ldots$: 18th term
5. $1, -1, -3, \ldots$: 31st term
6. $3, 9, 27, \ldots$: 9th term
7. $5, 15, 45, \ldots$: 11th term
8. $6, 26, 126, \ldots$: 8th term
9. $-1, 1, -1, 1, \ldots$: 391st term
10. $1, 4, 9, \ldots$: 11th term
11. $3, 6, 11, \ldots$: 12th term
12. $2, 6, 12, 20, \ldots$: 20th term
13. $4, 16, 64, \ldots$: 8th term
14. $1, 4, 16, 64, \ldots$: 10th term
15. $1, 2, 4, 8, \ldots$: 9th term

• *Check your answers.*

EXTENSION

E2.3: *n*th term challenge

1. The nth term of a sequence is defined by $t_n = \tfrac{1}{2}n(n+1)$ for all positive integers n.

   (i) Find the value of $t_1 + t_2$ and of $t_2 + t_3$

   (ii) By simplifying an expression for $t_n + t_{n+1}$, show that the sum of any two consecutive numbers is a perfect square.   *(OCR)*

• *Check your answers.*

Section 3: Arithmetic Progressions

Edexcel and AQA only

In this section you will:
- meet and work with arithmetic progressions (A.P.s);
- meet and use two formulae for the sum of an A.P.;
- use the general term and the sum of an A.P. to solve problems.

DEVELOPMENT

D3.1: Arithmetic progressions

One of the most common types of sequences is an Arithmetic Progression (usually called an A.P.), where each term is obtained from the previous term by adding a fixed number.

Number of term	1	2	3	4	...	r	...	n
Term	a	$a+d$	$a+2d$	$a+3d$		$a+(r-1)d$		$a+(n-1)d$

first term   common difference   general term or rth term   last term

1. *In each case, state whether the sequence is an A.P.:*
   (a) 27, 29, 31, 33, ...   (b) 31, 33, 36, 40, 45, ...   (c) 4, 1, –2, –5, ...
   (d) 2, 4, 6, 8, ...   (e) 2, 4, 8, 16, ...

2. An arithmetic progression has first term –5 and common difference 3.
   (a) Find the first four terms   (b) Find the rth term (general term)
   (c) Show how the rth term can be simplified to $3r - 8$ (d) Find the 10th term

3. *For each sequence:*   • *work out and simplify the general term.*
                        • *use the general term to work out the 10th term*
   (a) $a = 3$, $d = 4$ (b) first term = 4, common difference = –3

4. An A.P. is 2, 7, 12, 17, ...(a) Write down the first term and common difference
   (b) find and simplify the general term   (c) work out the 20th term

5. The rth term of an A.P. is $20 - 5r$.
   Find the first term, second term and hence, the common difference.

6. How many terms are there in each of the following A.P.s ?
   (a) 12, 15, 18, ...90   (b) 10, 8, 6, 4, ... –10   (c) 161, 165, 169, ... 301

7. Find the 100th term in the sequence ab, $3ab$, $5ab$, ...

8. The fifth term of an A.P. is 28. The tenth term is 58.
   Find the first term and the common difference.

9. The sixth term of an A.P. is twice the third term. The first term is 3.
   Find the common difference and the eighth term.

• *Check your answers.*

D3.2: The sum of an A.P. given the first and last terms

Let an A.P. be

$$a, \quad a + d, \quad a + 2d, \quad \dots \qquad \dots (l - d), \quad l$$

first term n terms   last term

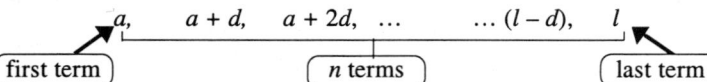

For Edexcel, you need to be able to derive this formula

Let S_n = the sum of the first n terms of this A.P.

$$S_n = a + (a + d) + (a + 2d) + \dots + (l - 2d) + (l - d) + l$$

Also $\quad S_n = l + (l - d) + (l - 2d) + \dots + (a + 2d) + (a + d) + a$

Adding $\quad 2S_n = (a + l) + (a + l) + (a + l) + \dots + (a + l) + (a + l)$

$\Rightarrow \quad 2S_n = n (a + l)$

$\Rightarrow \quad \boxed{S_n = \frac{1}{2} n (a + l) \text{ for the sum of terms of an A.P.}}$

Note: 1,2,3, ... 100 is an Arithmetic Progression (a sequence) but $1 + 2 + 3 + \dots + 100$ is an Arithmetic Series.

1. In ten pin bowling, the pins are set up in four rows as shown. To make a strike, all the pins must be knocked over.
   The number of pins is $1 + 2 + 3 + 4 = 10$

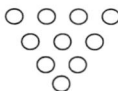

   (a) Show that the formula for the sum of n terms, given above, gives the same total number of pins.

   (b) A giant set of pins is set up with 20 rows. Work out the number of pins.

2. Find the sum of the series $51 + 53 + 55 + \dots + 99$.

EXAMPLE   Find the sum of the series $20 + 23 + 26 + 29 + \dots + 83$

To find n, the number of terms, use the formula for the last term (met in D3.1).

$$\text{last term} = a + (n-1)d$$

$a = 20$ and $d = 3 \quad \Rightarrow \quad 83 = 20 + (n - 1)3$

$\Rightarrow \quad 63 = (n - 1)3$

$\Rightarrow \quad 21 = n - 1 \qquad \Rightarrow \quad n = 22$

$S_n = \frac{1}{2} n (a + l) \quad \Rightarrow \quad S_{22} = \frac{1}{2} \times 22(20 + 83) = \boxed{1133}$

For each of the following A.P.s:
- *work out how many terms there are in the sequence;*
- *use the formula to work out the sum of all the terms;*
- *show all working.*

3. $11, 14, 17, \dots , 95$ 4. $45, 50, 55, \dots 220$ 5. $13, 11, 9, \dots -5$

6. Find the sum of all the numbers between 50 and 150.

7. Find the sum of the even numbers between 3 and 75.

8. The first term of an A.P. is 2. The sum of the first 76 terms is 4484.
   Work out the last term.

• *Check your answers.*

D3.3: The sum of an A.P. when the last term is unknown

An alternative formula for the sum of an A.P.

For an A.P. $S_n = \frac{1}{2} n (a + l)$ —— (1)

 last term = $l = a + (n-1)d$

Substituting for l in (1) $\Rightarrow$ $S_n = \frac{1}{2} n [a + a + (n-1)d]$

$\Rightarrow$ $\boxed{S_n = \frac{1}{2} n [2a + (n-1)d]}$

For Edexcel, you need to be able to derive this formula

EXAMPLE   Find the sum of the first 16 terms of the A.P.   11, 15, 19, …

$a = 11, d = 4, n = 16$

$S_n = \frac{1}{2} n [2a + (n-1)d]$ $\Rightarrow$ $S_{16} = 8[22 + 15 \times 4] = \boxed{656}$

Find the sum of each of the following A.P.s:

1.   20, 25, 30, …   to 15 terms

2.   40, 36, 32, …   to 10 terms

3.   −7, −4, …   to 20 terms

4.   The first term of an A.P. is 4. The sum of the first 8 terms is 256.
     Find the common difference.

5.   How many terms of the A.P. 8, 12, 16, … must be taken for the sum of the
     terms to equal 140 ?

• *Check your answers.*

D3.4: A mixture of problems

1. A jogger is training for a 5 km charity run. He starts with a distance of 400m
   and increases the distance by 100m every day.
   (a) How many days does it take him to reach the distance of 5 km in his training ?
   (b) What total distance will he have run in training in that time ?

2. When a parachutist falls from an aeroplane, the distance in feet that he falls in
   successive seconds before he pulls the ripcord are   16 48   80 112   …
   (a) How far does he fall in the tenth second, provided he has not yet pulled
       the ripcord ?
   (b) What is the total distance that he falls in the first eight seconds ?

3. Find five numbers in arithmetic progression whose sum is 155 and whose last
   term is 47.

4. The sum of the first n terms of an A.P. 3 + 7 + 11 + … is equal to the sum of the
   first n terms of the A.P. 5 + 8 + 11 + …. Find the value of n.

5. A trades telephone directory is published every year. This year it has 1244 pages.
   Every printing it has about 90 pages more than the previous edition.
   (a) When is it likely to have more than 2000 pages ?
   (b) What is the likely number of pages in 25 years time ?

• *Check your answers.*

D3.5: Sums of natural numbers

> Natural numbers (also called counting numbers) are 1, 2, 3, 4, ...
>
> Sequences of natural numbers are Arithmetic Progressions

1. Calculate the sum of the first 100 natural numbers.

2. Calculate the sum $51 + 52 + 53 + ... + 100$

3. The sum of the first n natural numbers is $1 + 2 + 3 + ... + n$.
   By considering this an an arithmetic series, show that the sum of the first n
   natural numbers is given by $\frac{1}{2}n(n + 1)$

> The sum of the first n natural numbers is given by the formula
> $$S_n = \tfrac{1}{2}n(n + 1)$$

4. Use this formula to calculate the sum of the first 150 natural numbers.

5. Use the formula to calculate the sum of the series $71 + 72 + ... + 120$

> • *Check your answers.*

EXTENSIONS

E3.6: A.P. challenges

1. For an A.P., the sum of the first 16 terms is 304 and the seventh term is twice the
   third term. Find the common difference, the first term and the sum of the first 20
   terms.

2. The sixth term of an A.P. is 7 and the seventh term is 4. Find the sum of the first
   25 terms of the sequence.

3. In Cornwall, there are many disused mines. It is common to find mineshafts with just a
   fence round the top. It is possible to estimate the depth of the mineshaft by dropping a
   stone down it. The time is measured, to the nearest half second, until a splash is heard.
   The stone falls 1.25m in the first half second, 3.75m in the second half second, 6.25m in
   the third half second ... At one mineshaft head, a stone is dropped from one metre above
   ground level and took 6 seconds to reach the bottom.

   How deep was the shaft ?

4. A company wishes to give a young executive a five year contract, starting at
   £20 000 per year and with a 12% rise each year.
   (a) Work out how much she would receive over the five years.

   After considering the offer, the executive says that she would prefer a fixed
   rise in salary each year, with the same starting salary.

   (b) Work out the fixed annual raise that would give the same total income
   over the five years.

> • *Check your answers.*

Section 4: The sigma (Σ) notation for series

In this section you will meet and use a shorthand notation for series.

D4.1: Meet Σ

Edexcel and AQA only

The general term for the sequence 1, 4, 9, 16, ... is r^2

There is a shorthand notation used for the sum of a series.

$r = 10$ gives the last term

$r = 1$ gives the first term

$$\sum_{r=1}^{r=10} r^2 = 1 + 4 + 9 + \dots + 100$$

the general term of the series

Σ is read as 'sigma' and means 'the sum of'

Read this as 'sigma from 1 to 10 of r^2'
or 'the sum from 1 to 10 of r^2'

There is generally more than one way of describing any series:

$$\sum_{r=5}^{r=10} r \quad = \quad 5 + 6 + 7 + 8 + 9 + 10 \quad = \quad \sum_{r=1}^{r=6}(r+4)$$

$$\sum_{r=1}^{r=9}(2r+1) \quad = \quad 3 + 5 + 7 + \dots + 19 \quad = \quad \sum_{r=2}^{r=10}(2r-1)$$

$$\sum_{r=1}^{r=2n}(r-1) \quad = \quad 0 + 1 + 2 + \dots + (2n-1) \quad = \quad \sum_{r=0}^{r=2n-1} r$$

Write out each of the following series in full:

1. $\displaystyle\sum_{r=1}^{r=6}(2r+1)$ 2. $\displaystyle\sum_{r=2}^{r=8}(8-3r)$ 3. $\displaystyle\sum_{r=10}^{r=n}(3+4r)$

4. $\displaystyle\sum_{r=2}^{r=5}\frac{3r+2}{2r-3}$ 5. $\displaystyle\sum_{r=1}^{r=3}2$ 6. $\displaystyle\sum_{r=-1}^{r=2n}(r^2 - r)$

Sometimes, i or j is used instead of r

Slight variations in this notation are often used.

$$2 + 3 + 4 + 5 \quad = \quad \sum_{r=2}^{r=5} r \quad = \quad \sum_{r=2}^{5} r \quad = \quad \sum_{2}^{5} r \quad = \quad \sum_{2}^{5} i$$

Write out the series given by each of these:

7. $\displaystyle\sum_{r=8}^{r=15} 3r$ 8. $\displaystyle\sum_{r=2}^{7} r(r-1)$ 9. $\displaystyle\sum_{4}^{6}\frac{1}{r}$ 10. $\displaystyle\sum_{2}^{n} 2i^3$ 11. $\displaystyle\sum_{3}^{2n}\frac{r}{r+1}$ 12. $\displaystyle\sum_{1}^{n-1}(i+1)$

Use Σ notation to describe each of these series:

13. $3 + 6 + 9 + \dots + 30$

14. $1 + \frac{1}{2} + \frac{1}{3} + \frac{1}{4} + \dots + \frac{1}{n}$

15. $1^4 + 3^4 + 5^4 + \ldots$ 15 terms

16. $\dfrac{2}{5} + \dfrac{4}{7} + \dfrac{6}{9} + \dfrac{8}{11} + \ldots + \dfrac{2n}{2n + 3}$

17. State whether each of the expressions written under the series represents the series correctly (Y) or not (N) [3 answers].

> $1 + 4 + 7 + \ldots + 19$
>
> A: $\displaystyle\sum_{1}^{7} (3r - 2)$ B: $\displaystyle\sum_{0}^{6} (3r + 1)$ C: $\displaystyle\sum_{1}^{6} (3r - 2)$

• Check your answers.

D4.2: Alternating positive and negative terms

Write down the first five terms in the sequence whose general term is:

1. r 2. $-r$ 3. $(-1)^r$ 4. $(-1)^{r+1}$ 5. $(-1)^{r-1}$ 6. $(-1)^r r$

7. Consider the sequences generated by r and $(-1)^r r$.
    What effect does the term $(-1)^r$ have ?

8. What effect do you think that the term $(-1)^{r+1}$ would have on a sequence.
    Check with two sequences.

• Check your answers.

D4.3: Evaluating sums given in Σ form

Type 1: Simple sums

   EXAMPLE   Evaluate $\displaystyle\sum_{r=1}^{4} (2r + 1)$

   $\displaystyle\sum_{r=1}^{4} (2r + 1) = 3 + 5 + 7 + 9 = 24$

Type 2: More complex sums

   EXAMPLE   Evaluate $\displaystyle\sum_{r=15}^{40} (2r + 1)$

   $\displaystyle\sum_{r=15}^{40} (2r + 1) = 31 + 33 + 35 + \ldots + 81$

                This is an A.P., where $a = 31$, $d = 2$ and $n = 26$

   Sum $= S_{26} = {}^{26}/_2 [62 + 25 \times 2] = \boxed{1456}$

Evaluate:

1. $\displaystyle\sum_{1}^{4} (r^2 + 1)$ 2. $\displaystyle\sum_{1}^{35} (5r - 1)$ 3. $\displaystyle\sum_{15}^{18} (3r + 5)$ 4. $\displaystyle\sum_{16}^{40} (2r - 3)$

5. $\displaystyle\sum_{1}^{6} (-1)^r r$ 6. $\displaystyle\sum_{1}^{7} (-1)^{r-1} r(r+1)$ • Check answers.

Section 5: Geometric Progressions

Edexcel only

In this section you will:
- meet and work with geometric progressions (G.P.s);
- derive and use the formula for the sum of a G.P.;
- use the general term and the sum of an G.P. to solve problems;
- find the sum of an infinite G.P. .

DEVELOPMENT

D5.1: Geometric progressions

An even more common type of sequence is a Geometric Progression (usually called a G.P.), where each term is obtained from the previous term by multiplying it by a fixed number.

Number of term	1	2	3	4	...	q	...	n
Term	a	ar	ar^2	ar^3		ar^{q-1}		ar^{n-1}

first term   common ratio   general term – we can't call it the rth term as r = common ratio   last term

1. All living things grow in the same way. They start as a single cell, which divides into two. These cells divide to make four, which divide to make eight ...

   For this sequence, write down:

   (a) the sixth term   (b) the tenth term   (c) the qth term

   (d) the 25th term (use a calculator and give the answer in standard form, to 3s.f.

2. Write down the common ratio, the sixth term and the nth term of each G.P.:

   (a) 3, 12, 48, ...   (b) 64, 32, 16, ...   (c) 5, 10, 20, ...

3. Fill in the missing terms in these G.P.s

   (a) 4, __, 36, __ ...   (b) 81, __, 9, __, ... (c) 5, –10, __, __

4. A tank is filled with 20 litres of water. Half the water is removed and replaced with antifreeze and thoroughly mixed. Half this mixture is then removed and replaced with antifreeze. This process is continued ...

   (a) Find the first 5 terms of the sequence of amounts of water in the tank at each stage.

   (b) Find the first 5 terms of the sequence of amounts of antifreeze in the tank at each stage.

   (c) Are either, or both, of these G.P.s ? Explain why or why not.

5. Use the formula for the nth term to work out how many terms there are in each of these G.P.s:

   (a) 8, 16, ... 256   (b) 3, 15, ... 9375   (c) 5, 10, ... 1280

   • *Check your answers.*

D5.2: The sum of a G.P.

Let S_n = the sum of the first n terms of a G.P.

$$S_n = a + ar + ar^2 + \ldots + ar^{n-1}$$

Also $\qquad rS_n = \qquad ar + ar^2 + \ldots + ar^{n-1} + ar^n$

Subtracting $\quad (1 - r)S_n = a - ar^n$

$$\Rightarrow \qquad \boxed{S_n = \frac{a(1 - r^n)}{1 - r}} \qquad or \qquad \boxed{S_n = \frac{a(r^n - 1)}{r - 1}}$$

It is easier to use this formula when $r < 1$

It is easier to use this formula when $r > 1$

EXAMPLE Find the sum of the first ten terms of the GP 3, 4.5, 6.75, ...

$a = 3$ $r = 1.5$ and $n = 10$ $\qquad \Rightarrow \quad S_{10} = \dfrac{3(1.5^{10} - 1)}{(1.5 - 1)} \approx \boxed{340}$

Find the sum of each of these G.P.s:

1. 2, 6, 18, ..., 6 terms
2. 1024, 512, 256, ..., 10 terms
3. 16, −24, 36, ... 5 terms
4. 1000, 250, 62.5 ... 8 terms

5. Start with an equilateral triangle with sides each 8 units long. Form another equilateral triangle by joining the midpoints of the sides of the first triangle. Continue to make a sequence of triangles in the same way.

   (a) Write down the first four terms of the sequence formed by the perimeters of these triangles. Calculate the tenth term of this sequence.

   (b) Write down the series whose sum is the total length of the lines in the diagram at any stage. Calculate the total length of the lines after the tenth triangle has been drawn.

6. A pendulum is set swinging. Its first oscillation is through 30°, and each succeeding oscillation is 90% of the one before it.
   What is the total angle it has swung through at the end of the 12th oscillation ?

7. The sum of the first two terms of a G.P. is 5 and the sum of the first four terms is 16.25. Find the first term and the common ratio.

8. How many terms of the geometric series $3 + 9 + 27 + \ldots$ must be taken for the sum to exceed 400 ?

9. A G.P. has first term 8 and the sum of the first three terms is 38. Find two possible values for the common ratio.

10. Sara invests £5 000 in a Building Society which pays 8% interest, which is added to the account each year.
    (a) How much would be in the account at the end of 5 years ?
    (b) How much more would Sara have been paid if the interest had been added to the account every six months ?   • *Check your answers.*

D5.3: The sum of an infinite G.P.

The sum of an infinite G.P. is $\quad S_n = a + ar + ar^2 + \ldots$
$$= a(1 + r + r^2 + \ldots)$$
This sum only exists if $1 + r + r^2 + \ldots$ converges to a limit.
The condition for this limit to exist is $-1 < r < 1$, which is $|r| < 1$
If $|r| < 1$, then $r^2, r^3, r^4, \ldots$ get smaller and smaller and $r^n \longrightarrow 0$

$$S_n = \frac{a(1 - r^n)}{1 - r} \qquad \text{and this gives} \qquad \boxed{S_\infty = \frac{a}{1 - r} \quad \text{provided} \quad |r| < 1,}$$

1. (a) Show that the geometric series $50 + 25 + 12.5 + \ldots$ converges.
   (b) Calculate the sum to infinity of this series.

2. Work out the sum to infinity of each of these series. Give each answer as a fraction.
   (a) $1 - \frac{1}{3} + \frac{1}{9} - \frac{1}{27} + \ldots$ (b) $5 + 1 + \frac{1}{5} + \frac{1}{25} + \ldots$
   (c) $1 + 0.1 + 0.01 + 0.001 + \ldots$ (d) $0.6 + 0.06 + 0.006 + \ldots$
   (e) $1 + x + x^2 + x^3 + \ldots$ where $|x| < 1$

3. Find the range of values of y for which each series converges:
   (a) $1 + y + y^2 + y^3 + \ldots$ (b) $1 + 2y + 4y^2 + 8y^3 + \ldots$ (c) $y + \dfrac{1}{y} + \dfrac{1}{y^3} + \ldots$

4. The sum to infinity of a G.P. is three times the first term.
   Find the common ratio.

5. After an undetected leak at a Nuclear Power Station, some of the staff were exposed to radiation :
   • on the first day 450 curie hours;
   • on the second day 360 curie–hours;
   • on the third day 288 curie-hours.
   (a) How many curie-hours were they exposed to on the ninth day ?
   (b) What was the total radiation after 15 days ?
   (c) If the leak had gone on undetected, what would have been the total exposure ?

6. A ball is thrown vertically up from the ground. It rises to a height of 10 m and then falls and bounces. After each bounce, it rises vertically to $\frac{2}{3}$ of the height of the previous bounce.
   (a) Find the height to which it will rise after the nth bounce.
   (b) Find the total distance travelled by the ball from the first throw to the 10th impact with the ground.
   (c) Calculate the total distance travelled by the ball, by the time it has come to rest.

7. Work out the sum to infinity of each of the following:
   (a) $p + p^2 + p^3 + \ldots$ where $|p| < 1$ (b) $q - q^2 + q^3 + \ldots$ where $|q| < 1$
                                          • *Check your answers.*

Section 6: Sums of powers of natural numbers

In this section you will meet and use standard formulae for sums of powers of natural numbers.

DEVELOPMENT

AQA only

D6.1: Standard formulae

$$\sum_1^n r = \tfrac{1}{2}\, n(n+1) \qquad \sum_1^n r^2 = \tfrac{1}{6}\, n(n+1)(2n+1) \qquad \sum_1^n r^3 = \tfrac{1}{4}\, n^2(n+1)^2$$

EXAMPLE   Find the sum of the squares of the numbers 10 to 20 inclusive.

$$\begin{aligned} \text{Sum} &= 10^2 + 11^2 + 12^2 + \ldots \\ &= \sum_1^{20} r^2 - \sum_1^9 r^2 \\ &= \tfrac{1}{6}\, 20 \times 21 \times 41 - \tfrac{1}{6}\, 9 \times 10 \times 19 \qquad = \boxed{2585} \end{aligned}$$

EXAMPLE   Find the sum of the series $2^2 + 4^2 + 6^2 + \ldots + 50^2$

$$\begin{aligned} 2^2 + 4^2 + 6^2 + \ldots + 50^2 &= 2^2(1^2 + 2^2 + 3^2 + \ldots + 25^2) \\ &= 2^2 \sum_1^{25} r^2 \\ &= 2^2 \times \tfrac{1}{6}\, 25 \times 26 \times 51 \qquad = \boxed{22100} \end{aligned}$$

Find the sums of the following series:

1. $1^2 + 2^2 + 3^2 + \ldots + 24^2$

2. $2 + 3 + 4 + \ldots 28$

3. $15 + 16 + 17 + \ldots + 40$

4. $6^3 + 7^3 + \ldots + 15^3$

5. Find the sum of the even numbers between 11 and 121

6. Find the sum of the cubes of natural numbers from 10 to 20 inclusive.

7. Evaluate : (a) $2 + 4 + 6 + \ldots + 50$ (b) $2^3 + 4^3 + 6^3 + \ldots 50^3$

    (c) $3^2 + 6^2 + 9^2 + \ldots + 90^2$ (d) $5^3 + 10^3 + 15^3 + \ldots + 75^3$

8.   Evaluate $101 + 103 + 105 + \ldots + 199$

9.   Show that the sum of the series $1 - 2 + 3 - 4 + 5 - \ldots - 100$ is -50

10.   Work out the sum of the squares of the first $2n$ natural numbers.

11.   Show that the sum of the series

$$n^2 + (n + 1)^2 + (n + 2)^2 + \ldots (2n)^2$$

is $\tfrac{1}{6}\, n(n + 1)(14n + 1)$

• *Check your answers.*

D6.2: Sums of series with rth terms ar³ + br² + cr + d

$$rth\ term\ =\ ar^3\ +\ br^2\ +\ cr\ +\ d$$

Sum of first n terms $=\quad a\,1^3\ +\ b\,1^2\ +\ c1\ +\ d$

$+\quad a\,2^3\ +\ b\,2^2\ +\ c2\ +\ d$

$+\quad a\,3^3\ +\ b\,3^2\ +\ c3\ +\ d$

$+\quad ...$

$\vdots$

$\vdots$

$+\quad \underline{a n^3\ +\ b n^2\quad +\ cn\ +\ d}$

$\Rightarrow\quad$ Sum $\quad=\quad a\sum_1^n r^3 + b\sum_1^n r^2\ + c\sum_1^n r + nd$

EXAMPLE   Evaluate $\sum_1^n (3r^2 + r - 1)$

$\sum_1^n (3r^2 + r - 1)\ =\ 3\sum_1^n r^2 + \sum r - n$

$=\ 3 \times \frac{1}{6} n(n + 1) + \frac{1}{2} n(n + 1) - n$

$=\ \frac{1}{2} n \left[(n + 1)(2n + 1) + (n + 1) - 2\right]$

$=\ \frac{1}{2} n \left[2n^2 + 4n\right]$

$=\ \boxed{n^2\,(n + 2)}$

> Factorise :
> take out any
> common
> factors
> and any
> fractions
> (makes the
> algebra simpler)

EXAMPLE   Find (a) the rth term and (b) the sum to n terms
of the series $1^2 + 3^2 + 5^2 + ...$

(a) rth term $\ =\ (2r - 1)^2\ =\ 4r^2 - 4r + 1$

(b) $\quad S_n\ =\ \sum_1^n (4r^2 - 4r + 1)$

$=\ 4\sum_1^n r^2\ - 4\sum_1^n r + n$

$=\ 4 \times \frac{1}{6} n(n + 1)(2n + 1)\ - 4 \times \frac{1}{2} n(n + 1) + n$

$=\ \frac{1}{3}n[2(n + 1)(2n + 1) - 6(n + 1) + 3]$

$=\ \boxed{\frac{1}{3}n(4n^2 - 1)}$

Evaluate:

1. $\Sigma(2r + 1)$ 2. $\Sigma r(r + 1)$ 3. $\Sigma(r - 2)^2$ 4. $\Sigma(4r^3 + 1)$

In each of the following series, find the rth term and the sum to n terms:

5. $4 + 8 + 12 + ...$ 6. $1^2 + 3^2 + 5^2 + ...$ 7. $2\times3 + 3\times4 + 4\times5 + ...$

8. $1^2 + 4^2 + 7^2 + ...$ 9. $3^3 + 6^3 + 9^3 + ...$ 10. $3\times5 + 7\times9 + 11\times13 + ...$

11. The sum to n terms of a series is $2n^2 + n$.
By putting $n = 1$, find the first term. Find the second and third terms.
Deduce the rth term.

• *Check your answers.*

P1: Unit 9: Sequences and Series

Facts and formulae you need to know:

general term of an AP is $\quad a + (r - 1)d$

last term of an AP is $\qquad a + (n - 1)d$

sum of an AP: $S_n = \frac{1}{2} n(a + l)$ or $\quad S_n = \frac{1}{2} n(2a + (n - 1)d)$

general term of a GP is $\quad ar^{n-1}$

last term of a GP is $\quad ar^{n-1}$

sum of a GP: $S_n = \frac{a(1 - r^n)}{1 - r}$ or $\quad S_n = \frac{a(r^n - 1)}{r - 1}$

sum of an infinite GP: $S_\infty = \frac{a}{1 - r}$ provided $|r| < 1$

$\sum_1^n r = \frac{1}{2} n(n+1)$

$\sum_1^n r^2 = \frac{1}{6} n(n+1)(2n + 1)$

$\sum_1^n r^3 = \frac{1}{4} n^2(n+1)^2$

Competence Test P1.9

1. Work out the first four terms of each of these sequences: $\hspace{2cm}$ (4A)

   (a) $u_r = r(r + 2)$ $\qquad$ (b) $u_r = (-1)^r (2r + 1)$

2. Evaluate: (a) $\sum_2^5 (3r - 1)$ (b) $\sum_1^{30} (2r + 3)$ (c) $\sum_1^4 (-1)^{r-1} r$ $\qquad$ (2M, 6A)

3. The first term of an A.P. is -2. The common difference is 3.
   Work out the 10th term and the sum of the first 8 terms. $\qquad$ (3M,3A)

4. The 11th term of an A.P. is 20 more than the 6th term and the second term is 11.
   Work out the first term and the common difference. $\qquad$ (3M,3A)

5. How many terms of the A.P. -4, -1, 2, 5, ... must be taken for the sum to
   equal 217 ? $\qquad$ (3M,3A)

6. Use the formula for the sum of natural numbers to evaluate $\qquad$ (3M,3A)

   $\qquad 50 + 52 + 54 + ... 124$

   | Total A & E = 36 |

7. The seventh term of a G.P. is 32 and the third term is 2.
   Find the first term and the common ratio. $\qquad$ (3M,3A)

8. The first term of a G.P. is 0.5 and the fifth term is 0.0008. $\qquad$ (3M,3A)
   Calculate the sum to infinity.

9. What is the value of the first term of the series 5, 20, 80, ...which (3M,3A)
   exceeds 5000 ?

10. How many terms of the G.P. 5, $2\frac{1}{2}$, $1\frac{1}{4}$ ... must be taken so that the sum
    may differ from the sum to infinity by less than 0.01 ? $\qquad$ (3M,3A)

    | Total E = 36 + 24 = 60 |

11. Evaluate : $\sum_1^n (2r^2 + 3r + 5)$

    $\hspace{8cm}$ (2M,4A)

    | Total A = 36 + 4 = 40 |

AIMING HIGH

Unit 10
Functions

CONTENTS

[AQA only]

Section 1: Function notation, composite functions, combining functions
Section 2: Inverse functions (conditions for and finding inverse functions)
Section 3: Graphs and functions (domain, range, graphs of inverse functions
Section 4: Odd and even functions
Section 5: Locating roots by change of sign

	OCR	AQA	Edexcel
Section 1	——	All	——
Section 2	——	All	——
Section 3	——	All	——

Unit 10: Functions

Section 1: Function notation

> In this section you will :
> * become familiar with the terminology and notation for functions
> * form composite functions.

DEVELOPMENT

D1.1: Notation and terminology

A **function** is a one–one or many–one mapping.

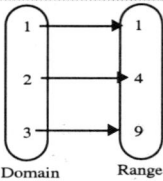

Domain   Range

Domain   Range

Read one–one as "one to one" and many–one as "many to one".

This is a one–one mapping
It is a function

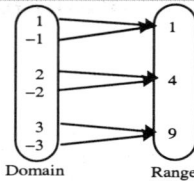

This is a many–one mapping
It is a function

Headbanger

In a function, every element has one, and only one, image.

The **domain** is the set of elements that is being mapped (transformed).

The **image set** or **range** is the set of mapped elements.

The **rule** is the connection between the domain and the image set.

For the first function :
* the domain is $\{1, 2, 3\}$
* the image set is $\{1, 4, 9\}$
* the rule is $f(x) = x^2$

For the second function :
* the domain is $\{\pm1, \pm2, \pm3\}$
* the image set is $\{1, 4, 9\}$
* the rule is $f(x) = x^2$

$\{................\}$ is shorthand for "the set"

$f(x)$ is the image of the element x under the function f
$f(x)$ is read as "f of x"

If you are working with two (or more) functions they are given different labels.
$g(x)$ is the image of the element x under the function g, $h(x)$ is ...

EXAMPLE : $f(x) = 2x + 1$ for the domain $\{3, 4, 6\}$ Find the range of f
A: The domain is $\{3, 4, 6, 8\}$. We need to find the image of each element.
$f(3) = 2(3) + 1 \qquad = 7$
$f(4) = 2(4) + 1 \qquad = 9 \qquad$ The range is
$f(6) = 2(6) + 1 \qquad = 13 \qquad \{7, 9, 13\}$

Think of it like this:

If $f(x) = x^2 + 3x$

then $f(5) = 5^2 + 3 \times 5$

If, in $f(x)$, x is replaced by 5, then every x in the expression is replaced by 5

Crumbl

EXAMPLE : If $g(x) = x^2 + 2$ find g(3) g(−2) g(y) g(x^3) g(cos x)

A: $g(x) = x^2 + 2$

$cos^2 x$ is the usual notation for $(\cos x)^2$

Read it as "cos squared x"

$g(3) = 3^2 + 2 \Rightarrow g(3) = 11$

$g(-2) = (-2)^2 + 2 \Rightarrow g(-2) = 6$

$g(y) = y^2 + 2$

$g(x^3) = (x^3)^2 + 2 \Rightarrow g(x^3) = x^6 + 2$

$g(\cos x) = (\cos x)^2 + 2 \Rightarrow g(\cos x) = \cos^2 x + 2$

Yusu Al

1. If $f(x) = x + 5$ find $f(4), f(-3), f(0), f(t^2), f(\sin x)$

2. If $g(y) = \frac{24}{y}$ find $g(1), g(8), g(-4), g(x)$

3. If $h(t) = 6 - 2t$ find $h(0), h(3), h(-2), h(-7), h(x), h(2x), h(3x), h(5t)$

4. If $p(x) = \sqrt{[(x-1)(x-4)]}$ find $p(4), p(6), p(0), p(-2)$

5. $f(x) = \sqrt{[(x-2)(x-5)]}$
   (a) Find $f(2), f(5)$
   (b) Explain why f is many–one.

Alternative function notations

$f : x \longmapsto x^2$

f is the function such that x maps to x^2

and

$f(x) = x^2$

The image of x under f is x^2

: means 'such that' $\longmapsto$ means 'maps to'

6. $g : x \longmapsto x^2 + 2$
   (a) Find $g(2), g(-2), g(7), g(-7)$
   (b) Find the range if the domain is $\{1, 2, 3, 4\}$
   (c) Find the range if the domain is $\{-2, -1, 0, 1, 2, 3\}$
   (d) If the domain is $\{1, 2, 3, 4\}$ is g one–one or many–one ?
   (e) If the domain is $\{-2, -1, 0, 1, 2, 3\}$ is g one–one or many–one ?
   (f) If the domain is $\{\pm 5, \pm 4, 3, 2\}$ is g one–one or many–one ?

In questions, functions may be defined in either of these ways, BUT, it is easier to work with the f(x) = ... format.

7. $k : t \longmapsto 3t^2 - 1$
   (a) If the domain is $\{-3, -2, -0.75\}$ is k many–one or one–one ?
   (b) The domain is $\{3, \pm 2, \pm 1\}$. What is the image set of k ?
   (c) Find the value of t if $k(t) = 74$

Big Edd

8. $h : x \longmapsto 2^x - 1$
   (a) Find $h(0), h(3), h(-1) \ h(6)$
   (b) Find the value of x if $h(x) = 31$

• Check your answers.

D1.2: Composite functions (functions of functions)

EXAMPLE $f(x) = 2x + 1$ $g(x) = x^2$ $h(x) = \sin x$
Find $fg(x)$, $gf(x)$, $fh(x)$, $hf(x)$, $f^2(x)$, $ghf(x)$

$$fg(x) = f(g(x)) = f(x^2) = 2x^2 + 1$$
$$gf(x) = g(f(x)) = g(2x + 1) = (2x + 1)^2$$
$$fh(x) = f(h(x)) = f(\sin x) = 2\sin x + 1$$
$$hf(x) = h(f(x)) = h(2x + 1) = \sin(2x + 1)$$
$$f^2(x) = f(f(x)) = f(2x + 1) = 2(2x + 1) + 1 = 4x + 3$$
$$ghf(x) = g(h(f(x))) = g(h(2x + 1)) = g(\sin(2x + 1)) = \sin^2(2x + 1)$$

Note: The right hand function is always applied first.

1. $f(x) = \cos x$ $g(x) = 3x - 1$
   Find (a) $fg(x)$ (b) $gf(x)$ (c) $g^2(x)$

2. $f(x) = x + 1$ $h(x) = x^2$
   Find (a) $fh(x)$ (b) $hf(x)$ (c) $h^2(x)$ (d) $f^2(x)$

3. $k(x) = 2x$ $f(x) = x - 3$ $p(x) = \sin x$
   Find (a) $fk(x)$ (b) $kf(x)$ (c) $k^2(x)$ (d) $f^2(x)$
   (e) $fp(x)$ (f) $pf(x)$ (g) $fpk(x)$ (h) $pkf(x)$
   (i) $kfp(x)$ (j) $fkf(x)$ (k) $kfk(x)$ (l) $k^2f(x)$

4. $f(x) = x + 5$ $g(x) = x^2$ $h(x) = \cos x$
   Find (a) $fg(x)$ (b) $gf(x)$ (c) $h^2(x)$ (d) $f^2(x)$
   (e) $fh(x)$ (f) $hf(x)$ (g) $fgh(x)$ (h) $ghf(x)$
   (i) $gfh(x)$ (j) $g^2h(x)$ (k) $hf^2(x)$ (l) $fgf(x)$

• *Check your answers.*

D1.3: Combining functions

EXAMPLE $f(x) = x - 4$ $g(x) = x^2$
Find (a) $f(x) + g(x)$ (b) $f(x) \times g(x)$ (c) $f(g(x))$

(a) $f(x) + g(x) = x^2 + x - 4$
(b) $f(x) \times g(x) = x^2(x - 4)$
(c) $f(g(x)) = f(x^2) = x^2 - 4$

$f(x) = x + 3$	$g(x) = 3x$	$h(x) = x^3$	$j(x) = \cos x$

Find 1. $f(x) + g(x)$ 2. $f(x) \times g(x)$ 3. $h(x) \times h(x)$ 4. $fg(x)$
5. $fh(x)$ 6. $f^2(x)$ 7. $g(x) - f(x)$ 8. $fj(x)$
9. $g(x) \times h(x)$ 10. $gh(x)$ 11. $j(x) + f(x)$ 12. $jf(x)$
13. $fgh(x)$ 14. $ghj(x)$ 15. $g^2j(x)$ • *Check answers.*

Section 2 : Inverse functions

In this section you will :
- find inverse functions, when they exist
- understand the conditions for an inverse function to exist
- understand the relationship between a function and its inverse.

//////DEVELOPMENT//////

D2.1 : Inverse functions

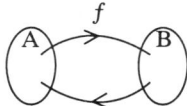

f

A → B

The inverse function f^{-1} only exists if f is one–one for the given domain

domain of f f^{-1} range of f
= range of f^{-1} = domain of f^{-1}

read f^{-1} as "ef to the minus 1"

EXAMPLE : Find the inverse function of the following one–one functions
   (a) $f(x) = x + 2$ (b) $g(x) = 2x$ (c) $h(x) = {}^1/3x$

A : (a) $f(x) = x + 2 => f^{-1}(x) = x - 2$
   (b) $g(x) = 2x   => g^{-1}(x) = {}^1/2x$
   (c) $h(x) = {}^1/3x => h^{-1}(x) = 3x$

The inverse of "add 2 to a number" is "take 2 from a number"

---

1. State the inverse functions of :
   (a) $f(x) = x - 7$ (b) $g(x) = {}^1/4x$ (c) $h(x) = 15x$ (d) $k(x) = {}^2/3x$

EXAMPLE :(a) Find the inverse function of $f(x) = x^2$ for the domain $\{1,2,3\}$
         (b) State the domain and range of f^{-1}
         (c) Why does $f^{-1}(x)$ not exist for f with domain $\{-1,0,1,2\}$

A :   (a) $f(x) = x^2$ f => $f^{-1}(x) = \sqrt{x}$

$\sqrt{x}$ implies the positive square root only

      (b)   1 → 1
            2   4
            3 f^{-1} 9
                              domain of $f^{-1} = \{1,4,9\}$
                              range of f^{-1} $= \{1,2,3\}$

         range of f^{-1} domain of f^{-1}
      (c) $f(-1) = f(1)$ so f is not one–one for this domain $\Rightarrow f^{-1}$ does not exist

---

2. If $f : x \longmapsto x + 3$ for the domain $\{-1,0,3\}$
   (a)   state the range of f
   (b)   write down the inverse function $f^{-1}(x)$
   (c)   state the domain and range of $f^{-1}(x)$

The inverse function f^{-1} only exists if f is one–one for the given domain

3. $k(x) = x^2 - 1$
   (a)   If the domain is $\{-1,0,3,6\}$ state the range of k
   (b)   State the range of k if the domain is $\{-2, 0, 2, 4\}$
   (c)   For which of these domains does $k^{-1}(x)$ exist?
   (d)   When $k^{-1}(x)$ exists, state the domain and range of $k^{-1}(x)$
   (e)   What is the function $k^{-1}(x)$

Blurbl

• *Check answers*

D2.2 : Inverses of more complex functions

Method 1 : using flow charts

EXAMPLE : Find $f^{-1}(x)$ if $f(x) = \dfrac{5x-1}{3}$

A :

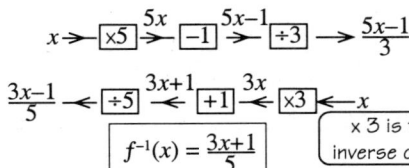

$$x \rightarrow \boxed{\times 5} \xrightarrow{5x} \boxed{-1} \xrightarrow{5x-1} \boxed{\div 3} \rightarrow \dfrac{5x-1}{3}$$

$$\dfrac{3x-1}{5} \xleftarrow{} \boxed{\div 5} \xleftarrow{3x+1} \boxed{+1} \xleftarrow{3x} \boxed{\times 3} \xleftarrow{} x$$

> ×3 is the inverse of ÷3

$$\boxed{f^{-1}(x) = \dfrac{3x+1}{5}}$$

Icee

Use the flow chart method to find the inverse function if :

1. $f(x) = 2x + 1$ 2. $f(x) = 3(x - 2)$ 3. $f(x) = \frac{1}{3}(3x - 2)$

Method 2 : using algebraic techniques

EXAMPLE : Find $f^{-1}(x)$ if $f(x) = \dfrac{3(x-4)}{2}$

> The method is to put
> $y = f(x)$
> and then rearrange the equation to get
> $x = f^{-1}(y)$

$$\begin{aligned}
\text{Let } y &= \dfrac{3(x-4)}{2} \\
\Rightarrow 2y &= 3x - 12 \\
\Rightarrow 3x &= 2y + 12 \\
\Rightarrow x &= \tfrac{1}{3}(2y + 12) \\
\Rightarrow f^{-1}(y) &= \tfrac{1}{3}(2y + 12) \quad \text{or} \quad \boxed{f^{-1}(x) = \tfrac{1}{3}(2x + 12)}
\end{aligned}$$

Use algebraic techniques to find the inverse function if:

4. $f(x) = \frac{1}{3}(2x - 1)$ 5. $f(x) = 10 - x$ 6. $f(x) = \frac{7}{5}x + 3$

Choose either method to find $f^{-1}(x)$ if:

7. $f(x) = 6 - 2x$ 8. $f(x) = \dfrac{x+1}{x-3}$ 9. $f(x) = \dfrac{7+2x}{3}$ • Check answers.

D2.3: Inverses of quadratic functions

EXAMPLE 4 : Find $f^{-1}(x)$ if   (a) $f(x) = x^2 - 1$ (b) $f(x) = x^2 - 2x + 5$

(a) $f(x) = x^2 - 1$ Let $y = x^2 - 1$

$$\begin{aligned}
\Rightarrow \quad x^2 &= y + 1 \qquad \Rightarrow x = \sqrt{(y+1)} \\
\Rightarrow \quad \boxed{f^{-1}(x) = \sqrt{(x+1)}}
\end{aligned}$$

> For $f^{-1}(x)$ to exist $f(x)$ must be 1-1, so √ must mean 'the positive square root'.

(b) $f(x) = x^2 - 2x + 5$ Let $y = x^2 - 2x + 5$
$$= (x-1)^2 - 1 + 5 = (x-1)^2 + 4$$

$$\begin{aligned}
\Rightarrow \quad (x-1)^2 &= y - 4 \\
\Rightarrow \quad x - 1 &= \sqrt{(y-4)} \qquad \Rightarrow x = \sqrt{(y-4)} + 1 \\
\Rightarrow \quad \boxed{f^{-1}(x) = \sqrt{(x-4)} + 1}
\end{aligned}$$

Fission

Find the inverse function if :

1. $f(x) = 2x^2 + 3$ 2. $\quad f(x) = x^2 + 6x - 3$ 3. $\quad f(x) = x^2 - 14x + 5$
4. $f(x) = x^2 + 12x$ 5. $\quad f(x) = 2x^2 - 20x + 5$ • Check answers.

Section 3: Graphs and functions

In this section you will:
- meet and use interval notation;
- represent functions graphically
- work with graphs of inverse functions.

DEVELOPMENT

D3.1: Interval notation for continuous functions

{1,2,3} is a set containing just three values

$1 \leq x \leq 3$ is the set of all values between 1 & 3 inclusive

We now meet a new form of notation

$[a,b]$ is equivalent to $a \leq x \leq b$ $]a,b[$ is equivalent to $a < x < b$

$]a,b]$ is equivalent to $a < x \leq b$ $[a,b[$ is equivalent to $a \leq x < b$

$[a,\infty[$ is equivalent to $x \geq a$

Write in interval notation :

1. $x \geq 0$ 2. $2 \leq x \leq 5$ 3. $-1 < x \leq 1$

4. $3 < x < 21$ 5. $x < 7$ 6. $x \leq -3$

• *Check answers*

D3.2: Representing functions graphically

Functions may be represented graphically by putting $y = f(x)$

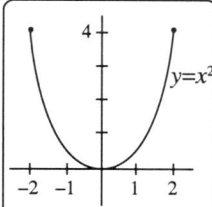

Domain = $[-2,2]$
Range = $[0,4]$
This is *not* 1–1
It has no inverse.

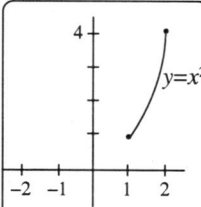

Domain = $[1,2]$
Range = $[1,4]$
This is 1–1
It has an inverse.

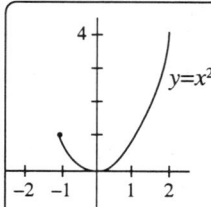

Domain = $[-1,\infty[$
Range = $[1,\infty[$
This is *not* 1–1
It has no inverse.

The domain is the set of values of

The range (or image set) is the set of values of y

If the end of a graph is not marked with a dot, it is assumed to continue indefinitely.

1. (a) What is the equation of the axis of
      symmetry of $y = x^2 - 2$?
   (b) What is the minimum value of $x^2 - 2$?
   (c) The domain of $x^2 - 2$ is $[-2,2]$
      What is the range?

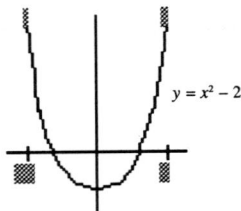

$y = x^2 - 2$

2.

$y = (x + 1)(3 - x)$

   (a) What is the equation of the axis of
       symmetry of $f(x) = (x + 1)(3 - x)$?
   (b) What are the coordinates of its vertex ?
   (c) What is the maximum value of $(x + 1)(3 - x)$?
   (d) What is the domain of $f(x)$?
       What is the range?

3.

$f(x)=(x+1)(x-2)$

   (a) What is the domain of f?
   (b) What is the range of f?

Graphs of 1–1 functions

If a mapping is 1– 1, then any line drawn —— or | across its graph will
cut the graph only once. Therefore the inverse function exists.

If any —— or | line cuts the graph more than once the mapping is not
1– 1 and hence the inverse function does not exist.

For each of these mappings:
   • *sketch a graph for the given domain*
   • *state the image set (or range) of the mapping*
   • *state whether the mapping is 1– 1*
   • *state whether an inverse function exists*

4. $f(x) = x^2$ Domain = $[0,3]$

5. $f(x) = x^2$ $x \in [-1,3]$

6. $f(x) = x^2$ $x \in [1,\infty[$

7. $f(x) = (x - 1)(x + 3)$ $x \in [1,5]$

8. $f(x) = (x - 1)(x + 3)$ $x \in [-4,5]$

9. $f(x) = x(x - 6)$ $x \in [0,7]$

10. $f(x) = x(x - 6)$ $x \in [4,9]$

> $x \in [-1,3]$ means domain is $[-1,3]$.
> Read as "x belongs to $[-1,3]$"

• *Check your answers.*

D3.3: Graphs of inverse functions

$f^{-1}(x)$ only exists if $f(x)$ is 1– 1

The graph of $f^{-1}(x)$ is the reflection of the graph of $f(x)$ in the line $y = x$

Sketch the graph of the function and the graph of its inverse on the same diagram.
State the range of the given function.

1. $y = x+3$ $x \in [0,\infty[$ 2. $y = x^3$ $x \in \Re$
3. $y = 1/x$ $x \in [1,\infty[$ 4. $y = \sin x$ $x \in [0,\pi/2]$
5. $y = \cos x$ $x \in [0,\pi]$

> $\Re$ = the set of all real numbers
> $x \in \Re \Rightarrow$ takes all real values

In the following questions:
- *Sketch & label the graph of the function for the given domain.*
- *State whether the inverse exists.*
- *If it does not exist, explain why.*
- *If it does exist, sketch the inverse function on the graph of the original function.*
- *State the domain and range of each inverse function.*

6. $f(x) = x^2$ $x \in [0,\infty[$ 7. $g(x) = x^2$ $x \in \Re$
8. $h(x) = x^2 + 1$ $x \in [0,3]$ 9. $k(x) = x^2 - 1$ $x \in [0,3]$

10.
    (a) Work out the coordinates of A and B
    (b) $f(x) = 6 - x^2$
        State the domain and range of $f(x)$
    (c) Write down the inverse function $f^{-1}(x)$
    (d) State the domain & range of $f^{-1}(x)$
    (e) Copy the graph & put on it the graph of $f^{-1}(x)$
    (f) Hence find the value of x for which $f(x) = f^{-1}(x)$

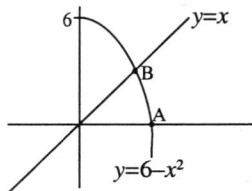

- *Check answers.*

E3.4: Function challenges

1. If $f(x) = x^3$, $g(x) = 2x + 1$, $h(x) = \cos x$
   find $fg(x)$, $gf(x)$, $hg(x)$, $gh(x)$, $fgf(x)$, $g^{-1}(x)$, $gg(x)$

2. If $f(x) = \dfrac{x+2}{x+1}$, show that $f(f(x)) = \dfrac{3x+4}{2x+3}$ and find $f^{-1}(x)$

3. (a) Work out the coordinates
   of A and B

   (b) What is the range of f

   (c) Work out an expression
   for $f(f(x))$

   (d) Work out $f^{-1}(x)$

   (e) State the domain and range of $f^{-1}(x)$

   This is the graph of
   $f(x) = \dfrac{x+3}{x-1}$ $x \neq 1$

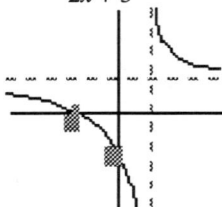

4. The function f is defined by $f : x \longmapsto \dfrac{2x+3}{x-2}$, $x \in \Re$, $x \neq 2$

   $\boxed{f \circ f \equiv f^2}$

   (a) Calculate $f \circ f(x)$, simplifying your answer as much as possible.

   (b) The inverse of f is f^{-1}. Write down $f^{-1}(x)$.

   (c) Determine the values of x for which $f(x) = x$, expressing your answers in
   the form $m \pm \sqrt{n}$ where m and n are integers.   (AQA)

5. (i) Express $x^2 - 6x + 10$ in the form $(x - a)^2 + b$, where a and b are constants.
   (ii) The one-one function f is defined by $f : x \longmapsto x^2 - 6x + 10$, $x \leq c$,
   where c is a constant. Explain why the greatest possible value of c is 3.
   Given that c is 3,
   (iii) sketch on a single diagram the graphs of f and f^{-1}, making clear the
   relationship between the two graphs.
   (iv) find the value of x that satisfies the equation $f(x) = f^{-1}(x)$ (OCR)

6. The diagram shows the graph of $y = f(x)$,
   where the function f is defined by
   $$f : x \longmapsto \frac{1}{6x + 5} \qquad x \geq 0$$

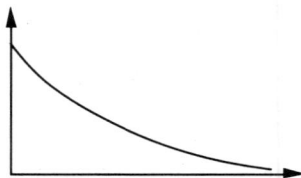

   (i) Copy the sketch and show on the same
   diagram the graph of the function f^{-1}, making
   clear the relation between the two graphs.

   (ii) Find an expression, in terms of x, for $f^{-1}(x)$, and state the domain and range of f^{-1}.

   (iii) Given that the function g is defined by $g : x \longmapsto \dfrac{1}{2x + 1}$ $x \geq 0$

   show that the equation $fg(x) = \frac{1}{5}$ has no roots.   (OCR)

Section 4: Odd and even functions

In this section you will recognise and sketch odd and even functions

DEVELOPMENT

D4.1: Odd and even functions

A function is **even** if $f(x) = f(-x)$ for all values of x.
Graphs of even functions are symmetrical about the y-axis.

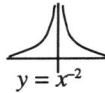

$y = x^{-2}$

A function is **odd** if $f(x) = -f(-x)$ for all values of x.
Graphs of odd functions are symmetrical about the origin.
The graph is unchanged by a half turn about the origin.

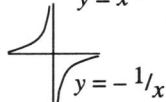

$y = -\frac{1}{x}$

For each of these graphs, state whether these functions are odd, even or neither:
1. $y = \sin^2 x$ 2. $y = x^2 + 1$ 3. $y = \cos x$ 4. $y = \tan x$

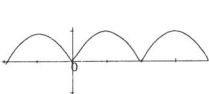

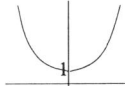

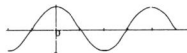

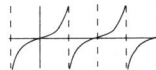

Sketch the graph for each function and state whether these functions are odd, even or neither:
5. $y = \sin x$ 6. $y = 5 - x^2$ 7. $y = x^3$ 8. $y = 3x$
9   $y = x^3 - 2$ 10. $y = (x - 2)^2$

• *Check your answers.*

D4.2: Odd, even and periodic functions

A function is **periodic** if the graph repeats at regular intervals.
The width of the repeated part is the **period**.
If $f(x + a) = f(x)$ for all values of x, then a is the period of f.

1. A function f is defined by $f(x) = x^2$ for $0 < x \le 2$
   $f(x) = 12 - 4x$ for $2 < x \le 3$
   and f is periodic with $f(x + 3) = f(x)$.
   Sketch f for $-3 < x < 9$ and evaluate $f(11)$.

2. An *even* function g is defined by $g(x) = x^2$ for $0 < x \le 2$
   $g(x) = 12 - 4x$ for $2 < x \le 3$
   and $g(x + 6) = g(x)$.
   Sketch g for $-3 < x < 9$ and evaluate $g(20)$.

• *Check your answers.*

Section 5 : Locating roots of equations

> In this section you will meet a method for locating roots of equations

DEVELOPMENT

D5.1: Location of roots by change of sign

If $f(a)$ is positive and $f(b)$ is negative, and f is
continuous between a and b then $f(x) = 0$ for some
value of x between a and b.
Hence there is at least one root between $x = a$ and $x = b$

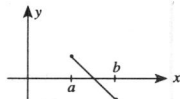

EXAMPLE : Q : Find the value of $f(x) = x^3 - 12$ for integral values of x from 0
to 4. Hence deduce the two consecutive integers between
which the real root of $x^3 = 12$ lies.

A : The root of $x^3 = 12$ is the root of $f(x) = 0$

> Integers are
> ...–3, –2, –1, 0, 1, 2, 3...

x	0	1	2	3	4
$f(x)$	–12	–11	–4	9	52

> f(x) changes sign
> between x = 2 and x = 3

Since $f(2)$ is negative and $f(3)$ is positive, $f(x)$ must be zero for a value of
x between 2 and 3

> So the real root of $x^3 = 12$ lies between $x = 2$ and $x = 3$

Important note : Before considering changes of sign, an equation must
first be put in the form $f(x) = 0$

1. The equation $x^4 - 2x = 1$ has two real roots.
   Find two pairs of consecutive integers
   between which these two roots lie.

   > Integers are
   > ...–3, –2, –1, 0, 1, 2, 3...

2. Find the value of k such that the three roots of
   $$x^3 - x^2 = 5x - 3$$
   lie in the intervals $]k, k +1[$ where k is an integer

3. Show that the equation
   $$x^3 + 2x^2 = 5x + 7$$
   has a root in the interval $[2, 3]$
   Use trial and improvement methods to find this root to 2 d.p.

4. Between which two integers does the smallest positive root
   of $x^3 + 2x^2 + 2x = 1$ lie ?

• *Check answers*

P1: Unit 10: Functions

Facts and formulae you need to know:

A function is a one-one or many-one mapping.

The domain is the set of elements that is being mapped

The image set or range is the set of mapped elements

> An inverse can only exist if the function is 1-1

The rule is the connection between the domain and the image set.

$[a,b]$ is equivalent to $a \leq x \leq b$ $]a,b[$ is equivalent to $a < x < b$

$[a,b[$ is equivalent to $a \leq x < b$ $]a,b]$ is equivalent to $a < x \leq b$

The graph of $y = f^{-1}(x)$ is the reflection of the graph of $y = f(x)$ in the line $y = x$

Competence Test P1.10

$$f(x) = 2x - 1 \qquad g(x) = x + 3 \qquad h(x) = x^2 + 5x + 1$$

Find: (2A for each = 20 marks)

1. $f(x) + g(x)$
2. $h(x) - g(x)$
3. $f(x) \times h(x)$
4. $fg(x)$
5. $gf(x)$
6. $gh(x)$
7. $hg(x)$
8. $f^2(x)$
9. $g^{-1}(x)$
10. $h^{-1}(x)$

Find the values of: (1A for each = 4 marks)

11. $f(5)$
12. $g^{-1}(6)$
13. $fg(2)$
14. $hf(5)$

15. (a) Sketch the graph of $y = \cos x$ for $-360° \leq x \leq 540°$ (4A)
    (b) State whether the graph is odd, even, or neither.
    (c) State the period of the graph.

16. $h(x) = x^2 - 2x - 3$ Domain of h is $[1,4]$
    (a) Sketch the graph of $y = h(x)$ (2A)
    (b) Is h one-one ? (1cao)
    (c) Can $h^{-1}(x)$ be formed? Explain why or why not ? (2A)
    (d) On the same graph as $y = h(x)$, sketch $y = x$ and the graph of $y = h^{-1}(x)$. (2A)
    (e) Hence find an approximate value of x for which $h(x) = h^{-1}(x)$. (1M,2A)

17. $h(x) = x^2 - 2x - 3$ Domain of h is $[2,4]$ (6A)
    State (a) the range of h (b) the domain of h^{-1}
            (c) the range of h^{-1}

18. $x^3 = 13x + 10$ has three real roots. (2M, 3A)
    Use an algebraic method to find the three intervals $[k, k + 1]$, where k is an integer, that contains these roots.

Total =	/49

AIMING HIGH

Unit 11
Polynomials and the Factor Theorem

CONTENTS **[All Edexcel]**
Section 1: Polynomials (add, subtract, multiply and divide polynomials)
Section 2: The Factor Theorem
Section 3: Identities (equating coefficients)

	OCR	AQA	Edexcel
Section 1	——	——	All
Section 2	——	——	All
Section 3	——	——	All

Unit 11: Polynomials and ...

Section 1 : Polynomials

In this section you will:
  • understand what is meant by a polynomial
  • add, subtract, multiply & divide polynomials

DEVELOPMENT

D1.1: Working with polynomials – good habits

Terminology

A function of the form $\quad P(x) = a_n x^n + a_{n-1} x^{n-1} + \dots + a_0 \quad (a_n \neq 0)$
where n is a positive integer and $a_n, a_{n-1} \dots$ are constants
is called **a polynomial of degree n**

a_n is **the coefficient of x^n**
a_{n-1} is **the coefficient of x^{n-1}**

For example :

$x^4 - 4x^3 + 2x$	is a polynomial of degree 4
$3x + 5$	is a polynomial of degree 1 (also called a linear function)
$2x^2 - 3x + 1$	is a polynomial of degree 2 (also called a quadratic function)
$3x^3 - 5$	is a polynomial of degree 3 (or a cubic)

Addition :

EXAMPLE : Q : Add $3x^3 + 2x + 6$ and $2x^4 + x^3 - 2x^2 + 5$

$$
\begin{array}{llll}
A: & 3x^3 & +2x & +6 \\
+ & 2x^4 + x^3 & - 2x^2 & +5 \\
\hline
& 2x^4 + 4x^3 & - 2x^2 +2x & +11 \longleftarrow \text{Answer}
\end{array}
$$

Stacking terms like this minimises errors.
Take care to leave gaps for missing terms.

Subtraction :

EXAMPLE : Q : Subtract $3x^2 - 4x + 7$ from $5x^3 - 3x^2 + 2x$

$$
\begin{aligned}
A: \quad & 5x^3 - 3x^2 + 2x - (3x^2 - 4x + 7) \\
= \quad & 5x^3 - 3x^2 + 2x \\
& \quad\quad\quad - 3x^2 + 4x - 7 \\
\hline
= \quad & 5x^3 - 6x^2 + 6x - 7 \longleftarrow \text{Answer}
\end{aligned}
$$

multiply brackets through by −1 and then ADD terms
− LESS ERRORS WHEN ADDING !

Multiplication :

EXAMPLE: Q : Multiply $3x^2 - x + 7$ by $5x^3 + 2x^2 + 1$

$$
\begin{aligned}
A: (3x^2 - x + 7)(5x^3 + 2x^2 + 1) \quad &= 15x^5 + 6x^4 \quad\quad\quad\quad +3x^2 \quad\quad \longleftarrow \boxed{\text{x } 3x^2} \\
& \quad\quad\quad -5x^4 - 2x^3 \quad\quad -x \quad \longleftarrow \boxed{\text{x } -x} \\
& \quad\quad\quad\quad\quad\quad + 35x^3 + 14x^2 \quad +7 \longleftarrow \boxed{\text{x } 7} \\
\hline
&= 15x^5 + x^4 + 33x^3 + 17x^2 - x + 7
\end{aligned}
$$

$$f(x) = 3x^2 - 5x + 4 \qquad g(x) = 7x^3 - 2x + 5$$
$$h(x) = 2x^4 + 3x^2$$

Find:

1. $f(x) + g(x)$ 2. $h(x) - g(x)$ 3. $f(x) - g(x)$

4. $f(x) \times g(x)$ 5. $g(x) \times h(x)$ 6. $f(x) + h(x) - g(x)$

Find the product of :

7. $3x^3 - 2x^2 + 5x - 2$ and $2x - 1$

8. $5x^3 - 3x + 7$ and $x^2 - 1$

9. $x^5 + x^4 + x^3 + x^2 + x + 1$ and $x - 1$

Finding single terms in a product

EXAMPLE : Find the coefficient of x^4 in the product of
$x^3 - 3x^2 + x - 5$ and $3x^3 + x^2 - 5x + 1$

$$(x^3 - 3x^2 + x - 5)(3x^3 + x^2 - 5x + 1)$$

Term in x^4 $= x^3(-5x) + (-3x^2)(x^2) + x(3x^3)$
$= -5x^4 - 3x^4 + 3x^4$
$= -5x^4$
$\therefore$ coefficient of $x^4 = \boxed{-5}$

Find the coefficients of the given terms in the following products :

10. $(3x - 5)(x^3 - 5x^2 + x - 3)$ find coefficients of x and x^3

11. $(x^2 - 2x + 1)(3x^2 - 5x - 2)$ find coefficients of x and x^2

12. $(7x^3 + x - 3)(2x^2 - 5x + 4)$ find coefficients of x^2 and x^4

13. $(3x^3 - 2x^2 + 5x + 3)(x^3 + 2x^2 - x - 9)$ find coefficients of x^2 and x^5

• *Check answers*

D1.2: Division of polynomials

Dividing a polynomial by a linear expression is similar to the method of long-division.

$$374 \longleftarrow \boxed{\text{quotient} = 374}$$

$$23\,\overline{)8602}$$

working out the remainder when dividing 86 by 23 $\longrightarrow$ 69

(170) $\longleftarrow$ instead of putting the 17 up next to the 0, bring the 0 down to the 17

161

92 $\longleftarrow$ working out the remainder when dividing 170 by 23

92

3 $\longleftarrow$ $\boxed{\text{remainder} = 3}$

$$\boxed{\text{So, } 8605 \div 23 = 374 + {}^{3}/_{23}}$$

EXAMPLE

$5x \times (x-2) = 5x^2 + \ldots$

$5x + 13 \longleftarrow \boxed{\text{quotient}}$

$x-2\,\overline{)\,5x^2 + 3x - 6}$

$\underline{5x^2 - 10x}$ $\quad$ bring down the 6

working out the remainder when dividing $5x^2 + 3x$ by $x-2$ $\longrightarrow$ $13x - 6 \longleftarrow$ working out the remainder when dividing $13x - 6$ by $x - 2$

$\underline{13x - 26} \longleftarrow$

$20 \longleftarrow \boxed{\text{remainder}}$

$$\boxed{\begin{array}{l}\text{So, } 5x^2 + 3x - 6 \div (x - 2) \\ \quad = 5x + 13 + \dfrac{20}{x-2}\end{array}}$$

EXAMPLE

$\boxed{\text{gap because no term in } x^2}$

$x^2 + x - 6$

$x-1\,\overline{)\,x^3 \qquad - 7x + 6}$

$\underline{x^3 - x^2}$

$x^2 - 7x$

$\underline{x^2 - x}$

$-6x + 6$

$\underline{-6x + 6}$

0

$$\text{So, } \boxed{(x^3 - 7x + 6) \div (x - 1) = x^2 + x - 6}$$

$$\text{or } \boxed{x^3 - 7x + 6 = (x - 1) \times (x^2 + x - 6)}$$

Find the remainder when :

1. $5x^2 + 2x - 1$ is divided by $x - 2$
2. $x^3 - 2x^2 + 6x - 2$ is divided by $x - 5$
3. $x^4 - 3x + 10$ is divided by $x - 2$
4. $x^5 + 11$ is divided by $x + 1$

Find the quotient and remainder when :

5. $3x^2 - 2x + 1$ is divided by $x - 1$
6. $4x^3 - 4x^2 + 5x - 3$ is divided by $2x - 3$
7. $x^3 + 16$ is divided by $x + 4$
8. $x^4 - 2x^2 + 3x - 1$ is divided by $x + 1$
9. $x^2 - 2x + 5$ is divided by $x - 5$
10. $x^4 - 3x^3 + 3x$ is divided by $2x - 1$
11. $x^3 + 5x^2 + 7x + 3$ is divided by $x^2 + 3x + 1$
12. $2x^4 + 5x^3 - 8x^2 + 5x + 2$ is divided by $2x^2 - 3x + 2$ $\qquad$ • *Check your answers.*

Section 2 : The Factor Theorem

In this section you will :
- meet the Factor Theorem
- use the Factor Theorem to find factors
- use the Factor Theorem to evaluate unknown coefficients

DEVELOPMENT

D2.1: Meet the Factor Theorem

> **The Factor Theorem**
> If, for a given function $f(x)$,
> $$f(a) = 0$$
> then $x - a$ is a factor of $f(x)$

EXAMPLE   Q : Show that $x - 4$ is a factor of $x^3 - 6x^2 + 11x - 12$
A: Let $f(x) \equiv x^3 - 6x^2 + 11x - 12$
$f(4) = 4^3 - 6 \times 4^2 + 11 \times 4 - 12 = 64 - 96 + 44 - 12 = 0$
Since $f(4) = 0$, $x - 4$ is a factor of $f(x)$

Determine whether the linear function is a factor of the given polynomial :

1. $x^3 - 7x + 6$: $x - 1$
2. $2x^2 + 3x - 5$: $x + 1$
3. $x^3 - 5x^2 + 3x + 6$: $x - 3$
4. $x^3 - 8$: $x - 2$
5. $6x^3 + x^2 - 4x + 1$: $3x - 1$
6. $x^3 + ax^2 + a^2x - a^3$: $x + a$

• *Check your answers*

D2.2: Factorising using the Factor Theorem

EXAMPLE   Q: Factorise $x^3 - 2x^2 - 15x + 36$ completely
A: Let $f(x) = x^3 - 2x^2 - 15x + 36$
$f(1) = 1 - 2 - 15 + 36 \neq 0 \Rightarrow x - 1$ is <u>not</u> a factor
$f(-1) = -1 - 2 + 15 + 3 \neq 0 \Rightarrow x + 1$ is <u>not</u> a factor
$f(3) = 27 - 18 - 45 + 36 = 0 \Rightarrow x - 3$ <u>is</u> a factor

$$
\begin{array}{r}
x^2 + x - 12 \\
x-3 \overline{\smash{\big)}\, x^3 - 2x^2 - 15x + 36} \\
\underline{x^3 - 3x^2} \\
x^2 - 15x \\
\underline{x^2 - 3x} \\
-12x + 36 \\
\underline{-12x + 36} \\
0
\end{array}
$$

So $x^3 - 2x^2 - 15x + 36 = (x - 3)(x^2 + x - 12)$

& since $x^2 + x - 12$ factorises
to give $(x - 3)(x + 4)$

$$\boxed{x^3 - 2x^2 - 15x + 36 = (x - 3)^2(x + 4)}$$

Factorise completely :

1. $x^3 + x^2 - 5x + 3$ 2. $x^4 - 3x^3 + 4x^2 - 8$

3. $x^4 + x^3 - 8x^2 - 9x - 9$ 4. $x^4 - 3x^3 + 6x^2 - 12x + 8$

> Quadratic factors should be factorised where possible

5. Show that $2x - 1$ is a factor of $2x^3 - 3x^2 - 3x + 2$.
   Hence factorise the expression completely.

6. Factorise $3x^4 - 2x^3 + 5x^2 - 4x - 2$ • *Check answers.*

D2.3: Using the factor theorem to determine unknown coefficients

EXAMPLE	Q: If $x^2 - x + a = 0$ has a root $x = 2$, find a
A : When $x = 2$,	$x^2 - x + a = 0$
	$\Rightarrow 4 - 2 + a = 0$
	$\Rightarrow \quad \boxed{a = -2}$

1. If $x^2 - 3x + a = 0$ has a root $x = 1$, find a

2. If $x^2 + 6x + p$ has a factor $x + 2$, find p and hence find the other factor

3. If $x - 3$ is a factor of $x^2 + tx - 6$, find t

4. One root of $x^2 - 5x + k = 0$ is 2. Find k and the other root

5. $x = 2$ is a root of $x^3 + 2x^2 - kx - 2$. Find k

6. $x - 2$ and $x + 3$ are factors of $x^3 + 6x^2 + mx + n$
   Find m and n. Hence find the third factor.   • *Check answers.*

EXTENSION

E2.4: Factor challenges

1. (a) Use the Factor Theorem to factorise $x^3 - 7x^2 + 4x + 12$
   (b) Sketch the curve $y = x^3 - 7x^2 + 4x + 12$
   (c) Use the graph to solve $x^3 - 7x^2 + 4x \leq -12$

2. If $x - p$ is a factor of $px^3 - 3x^2 - 5px - 9$ find the two possible values of p.
   Factorise the expression for each of these values.
   • *Check answers.*

Section 3: Identities

In this section you will :
- distinguish between equations and identities
- work out the values of constants in identities
- factorise cubics

DEVELOPMENT
D3.1: Polynomial identities

What is an identity?

Equations

$x^2 + 2x = -1$ *is an equation*
It can be solved
Its solution is $x = -1$

Identities

$x^2 + 2x \equiv x(x + 2)$ *is an identity*
It cannot be solved
It is true for all value of x
$\equiv$ *means 'is identical to'*
However $\equiv$ is often written as $=$

EXAMPLE   Find the values of a and b in the identity
$$(3x + a)^2 \equiv 9x^2 + 30x + b$$

A : This is equivalent to
$9x^2 + 6ax + a^2 \equiv 9x^2 + 30x + b$

This identity is true for all x, so :
- the terms in x^2 must be the same
- the terms in x must be the same
- the constant terms must be the same

Baggy

$\therefore$ $6ax \equiv 30x$ $\Rightarrow$ $\boxed{a = 5}$

Also $a^2 \equiv b$ $\Rightarrow$ $\boxed{b = 25}$

1. Find the values of p and q in the identity
$(2x + p)^2 \equiv 4x^2 - 28x + q$

2. Find the values of u and v in the identity
$(3x + u)(2x + 9) \equiv 6x^2 + vx - 45$

3. (a) Solve the equation $x^2 - 5x + 6 = 0$

   (b) Find the values of a and b in the identity
$$x^2 + ax + b \equiv (x - 3)(x + 1)$$

• *Check your answers.*

D3.2: Equating coefficients

EXAMPLE : Q : Express the function $4x^2 + x - 1$ in the form
$A + B(x + 1) + Cx(x + 1)$ where A, B, C are constants

A : Let $4x^2 + x - 1 \equiv A + B(x + 1) + Cx(x + 1)$
$\equiv A + B + (B + C)x + Cx^2$

Equating coefficients of x^2 : $C = 4$

Equating coefficients of x : $B + C = 1$ $\therefore B = -3$

Equating coefficients of x^0 : $A + B = -1$ $\therefore A = 2$

Hence $4x^2 + x - 1 \equiv \boxed{2 - 3(x + 1) + 4x(x + 1)}$

Remember:
You should show the same amount of working as in the example.

1. Find the values of the constants A and B in each of the following :
   (a) $2(x - 1)^2 \equiv A(x^2 + 1) + Bx$
   (b) $3x - 1 \equiv A(x - 1) + B(x + 1)$

2. Express $6 - 8x + 6x^2$ in the form $A(1 - x)^2 + B(1 + x)^2$ where A & B are constants.

3. If $x^4 + 40x - 96 \equiv (x^2 - ax + 12)(x^2 + 2x - b)$ find a and b

4. If $x^4 + x^3 - 3x^2 + 7x - 6 \equiv (x^2 - x + 2)(x^2 + ax + b)$ find a and b and hence completely factorise the expression.

5. Express $5x^2 - 18x + 17$ in the form
   $a(x - 1)(x - 2) + b(x - 3)(x - 1) + c(x - 2)(x - 3)$

   • *Check answers.*

D3.3: Perfect squares & cubics

EXAMPLE : Q: Find p and q so that $9x^4 - 6x^3 + 13x^2 + px + q$ may be a perfect square

Let $9x^4 - 6x^3 + 13x^2 + px + q \equiv (3x^2 + Ax + B)(3x^2 + Ax + B)$
$\equiv 9x^4 + 3Ax^3 + 3Bx^2 + 3Ax^3 + A^2x^2 + ABx$
$+ 3Bx^2 + Abx + AB$

Equating coefficients of x^3 : $6A = -6$ $\therefore A = -1$

Equating coefficients of x^2 : $6B + A^2 = 13$ $\therefore B = 2$

Equating coefficients of x : $2AB = p$ $\boxed{\therefore p = -4}$

Equating coefficients of x^0 : $B^2 = q$ $\boxed{\therefore q = 4}$

Remember:
You should show the same amount of working as in the example.

1. If $4x^4 - 4x^3 + 5x^2 + ax + b$ is a perfect square, find a & b

2. If $(ax + y)^2 \equiv a^2x^2 + 10xy + y^2$ find a

3. Express $x^3 + 8$ in the form $(x + 2)(x^2 + Bx + C)$ where B & C are constants

4. Express $x^3 + y^3$ in the form $(x + y)(x^2 + Qxy + Ry^2)$ where P, Q, R are constants

5. $x^3 - y^3 \equiv (x - y)(x^2 + Axy + By^2)$ Find the constants A & B

• *Check your answers*

P1: Unit 11: Polynomials and The Factor Theorem

Facts and formulae you need to know:
  The Factor Theorem: If, for a given function $f(x)$, $f(a) = 0$,
  then $x - a$ is a factor of $f(x)$

Competence Test P1.11

$f(x) = 3x + 2$ $\qquad$ $g(x) = x - 2$ $\qquad$ $h(x) = x^2 - 2x + 1$

Find: $\hfill$ (1M, 2A for each = 12 marks)

1. $f(x) + g(x)$ $\qquad$ 2. $h(x) - g(x)$ $\qquad$ 3. $f(x) \times h(x)$ $\qquad$ 4. $h(x) \div g(x)$

5. If $x^2 - 2x + a$ has a root $x = 2$, find a $\hfill$ (2M, 1A)

6. Express $4x^2 + x - 1$ in the form $A + B(x + 1) + Cx(x + 1)$ $\hfill$ (2M, 3A)

7. $4x^4 + 12x^3 - 11x^2 + ax + b$ is a perfect square. Find a and b. $\hfill$ (3M, 4A)

8. $f(x) = x^3 - 2x^2 - 16x + 32$
   (a) Show that $(x - 4)$ is a factor of $f(x)$ $\hfill$ (2M)
   (b) Factorise $f(x)$ completely $\hfill$ (1M, 2A)
   (c) Sketch the graph of $y = f(x)$ $\hfill$ (2A)
   (d) Solve $x^3 - 2x^2 - 16x + 32 \leq 0$ $\hfill$ (1M, 2A)

9. $g(x) = 2x^3 + Ax^2 - 8x + B$ $\quad$ $(2x - 1)$ and $(x + 3)$ are both factors of $g(x)$
   (a) Work out the values of A and B $\hfill$ (1M, 2A)
   (b) Factorise $g(x)$ completely. $\hfill$ (1M, 2A)

Total	/43

AIMING HIGH

AS/A-Level Questions *(Revision for P1 Exam)*

Students should do all questions, regardless of board, unless specifically told not to.

Unit 2: Quadratic Equations and Expressions

1. The specification for a new rectangular car park states that its length, x m, is to be 5 m more than its width. The perimeter of the car park is to be greater than 32 m.
   (a) Form a linear inequality in x.
   The area of the car park is to be less than 104 m².
   (b) Form a quadratic inequality in x.
   (c) By solving your inequalities, determine the possible range of values of the length of the car park. *(Edexcel)*

2. Factorise $x^3 - 16x$ completely. *(OCR)*

3. Factorise $(x + 3)^2 - 16$ *(OCR)*

4. The quadratic equation $x^2 + kx + 36 = 0$ has two different real roots. Find the set of possible values of k. *(OCR)*

5. Solve the inequality $3x^2 + x - 2 > 0$ *(OCR)*

6. Find the set of values of a for which the equation $ax^2 - 6x + a$ has two distinct real roots. *(OCR)*

7. A biologist claims that the average height, h metres, of trees of a certain species after t months growth is given by $h = \frac{1}{5}t^{2/3} + \frac{1}{8}t^{1/3}$
   For this model,
   (i) find the average height of trees of this species after 64 months
   (ii) find the number of months that the trees have been growing when the average height is 10 metres.   **[OCR students only]** *(OCR)*

Unit 3: Coordinate Geometry and Graphs

1. The diagram, not drawn to scale, shows a trapezium OABC with OA parallel to CB. Given that B is the point (4,3), C is the point (0,2) and the diagonal CA is parallel to the x axis, calculate the coordinates of A. *(OCR)*

2. (a) Find an equation of a straight line passing through the points with coordinates (–1,5) and (4,–2), giving your answer in the form $ax + by + c = 0$, where a, b and c are integers.
   The line crosses the x-axis at the point A and the y-axis at the point B, and O is the origin. (b) Find the area of $\triangle OAB$ *(Edexcel)*

3. The points A and B have coordinates (1,5) and (3,1) respectively. Find the equation of the perpendicular bisector of the line AB. *(OCR)*

4. The diagram shows the points A(–2,4), B(6,–2) and C(5,5).

(a) Find the equation of the line passing through the points A and B, giving your answer in the form $y = mx + c$, where the values of m and c are to be found.

× A(–2,4)   × C(5,5)

Not to scale

× B(6,–2)

(b) The point D is the midpoint of AB. Prove that CD is perpendicular to AB.

(c) Show that the line through C parallel to AB has equation $3x + 4y = 35$. *(AQA)*

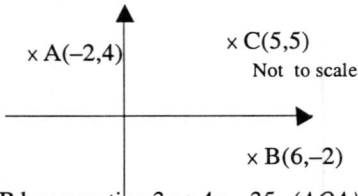

5. The diagram shows a sketch of the graph of $y = kx^n$, which passes through the point (1,3). Find the value of k.

By considering the form of the graph, write down possible values for n.

Given further that the point $(2, {}^3/_8)$ also lies on this graph, find the value of n. *(OCR)*

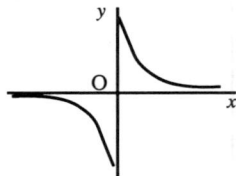

6. The straight line $y = 10 – 3x$ is denoted by L. Show, by means of an appropriate sketch, that the curve $y = x^{1/2}$ and the line L have only one point of intersection.

This point of intersection is denoted by P. Calculate the exact coordinates of P.

A second straight has gradient m and passes through the point P. Given that m is an integer and that this second line meets the y-axis at a point between (0,20) and (0,23), find the value of m.   **[OCR students only]**   *(OCR)*

7. The graph of $y = f(x)$ is sketched below, where a is a positive constant.

[Not Edexcel students]

(a) On separate sets of axes sketch the graphs of the following, indicating clearly the intercepts with the x axis:

–2a   a   a   2a

(i) $y = f(x + a)$ (ii) $y = f(–x)$ (iii) $y = f(2x)$

(b) The function g is an even function and $g(x) = f(x)$ for $x \geq 0$.
Sketch the graph of g for $–2a \leq x \leq 2a$.   **[(b) is in Unit 8]**   *(AQA)*
[(b) AQA students only]

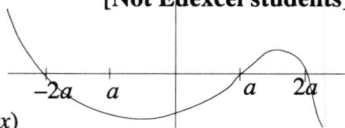

Unit 4: Surds, Powers, Simultaneous Equations and Radians

1. (a) Given that $8^y = 4^{2x+1}$, find y in the form $y = px + q$, where p and q are exact fractions.

(b) Solve, giving your answers as exact fractions, the simultaneous equations
$$8^y = 4^{2x+1}, \qquad 27^{2y} = 9^{x-3}$$ *(Edexcel)*

2. (i) Write down the exact value of 7^{-2} *(OCR)*

(ii) Simplify $\dfrac{(x\sqrt{x})^3}{2x^4}$

3. (i) Solve the simultaneous equations $y = x^2 - 3x + 2$, $y = 3x - 7$
   (ii) Interpret your solution to part (i) geometrically. *(OCR)*

4. A manufacturer needs to make a thin metal plate in the shape of a circular sector with perimeter 20 cm. Figure 1 shows such a sector with radius r cm, angle θ radians and area A cm². **[Edexcel students only]**

   (a) Prove that $A = 25 - (r - 5)^2$

   Given that r can vary,

   (b) deduce the value of r for which A is a maximum and state the maximum value of A. *(Edexcel)*

   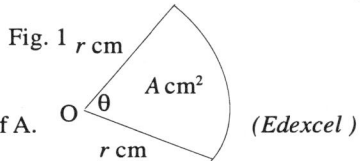

   Fig. 1

Unit 5: Differential Calculus

1. A curve has equation $y = (x^2 + 3)(2x - 1)$.

   (a) Find $\dfrac{dy}{dx}$

   (b) Determine the coordinates of the points on the curve where the gradient is equal to 6. *(AQA)*

2. The equation of a curve is $y = 6x^2 - x^3$. Find the coordinates of the two stationary points on the curve and determine the nature of these stationary points.

   State the set of values of x for which $6x^2 - x^3$ is a decreasing function of x.

   The gradient at the point M on the curve is 12. Find the equation of the tangent to the curve at M. *(OCR)*

3. A piece of wire, of length 20 cm, is to be cut into two parts. One of the parts, of length x cm, is to be formed into a circle and the other part into a square.

   (a) Show that the sum, A cm², of the areas of the circle and the square is given by

   $$A = \frac{x^2}{4\pi} + \frac{1}{16}(20 - x)^2.$$

   (b) Show that A has a stationary value when $x = \dfrac{20\pi}{4 + \pi}$ *(AQA)*

4. An architect is drawing up plans for a mini-theatre. Figure 3 shows the plan of the base which consists of a rectangle of length $2y$ metres and width $2x$ metres and a semicircle of radius x metres which is placed with one side of the rectangle as diameter.

   Find in terms of x and y, expressions for
   (a) the perimeter of the base
   (b) the area of the base

   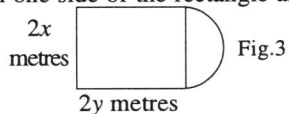

   Fig.3

   The architect decides the base should have a perimeter of 100 metres.

   (c) Show that the area A square metres of the base is given by
   $$A = 100x - 2x^2 - \tfrac{1}{2}\pi x^2.$$
   (Edexcel)

   (d) Given that x can vary, find the value of x for which $dA/dx = 0$ and determine the corresponding value of y, giving your answers to 2 s.f.

   (e) Find the maximum value of A and explain why this value is a maximum.

Unit 6: Completing the Square

1. A curve has equation $y = x^2 + kx + 9$
   (a) Given that the curve does not cross or touch the x-axis, find the set of values that k can take.
   (b) In the case when $k = 8$, express the equation of the curve in the form
   $$y = (x + a)^2 + b,$$ finding the values of a and b.
   (c) In the case when $k = -7$, prove that the curve crosses the x-axis at a point $(\alpha, 0)$, where $1.6 < \alpha < 1.7$ (AQA)

2. The coordinates of the points A and B are $(p, 2)$ and $(4, p)$ respectively.
   Show that $AB^2 = 2p^2 - 12 p + 20$.
   Express AB^2 in the form $a(p - b)^2 + c$, where a, b and c are constants whose values are to be found.
   Hence write down   (i) the smallest possible value of AB, as p varies
                            (ii) the corresponding value of p.
   Using this value for p, show that the line through the points A and B meets the curve whose equation is $9x^2 - 10xy = 25$ at one point only.   (OCR)

Unit 7: Integral Calculus

1. The diagram shows sketches of the line with equation $x + y = 4$ and the curve with equation $y = x^2 - 2x + 2$ intersecting at points P and Q. The minimum point of the curve is M. The shaded region R is bounded by the line and the curve.

   (a) Show that the coordinates of M are $(1, 1)$.
   (b) Find the coordinates of the points P and Q.
   (c) Prove that the triangle PMQ is right-angled and hence show that the area of the triangle PMQ is 3 square units.
   (d) Show that the area of the region R is $1\frac{1}{2}$ times that of the triangle PMQ. (AQA)

3. $$y = 3x^{1/2} - 4x^{-1/2}, \; x > 0$$
   (a) Find $\dfrac{dy}{dx}$ (b) Find $\int y \, dx$ (Edexcel)
   (c) Hence show that $\int_1^3 y \, dx = A + B\sqrt{3}$, where A and B are integers to be found.

4. Find $\displaystyle\int_0^3 \frac{1}{\sqrt{x}} \, dx$ (OCR)
                                                                      [OCR students only]

Unit 8: Trigonometry

1. Find all solutions of the equation $\cos(3x + 40°) = 0.2$
    in the interval $0° \leq x \leq 180°$, giving your answers correct to the nearest $0.1°$.
    (You may use your graphics calculator to check your answers but no credit will be given for simply reading values from a graph.) *(AQA)*

2. Sketch the graph of $y = \cos x°$, for values of x from 0 to $360°$. **[Not Edexcel**
    Sketch on the same diagram, the graph of $y = \cos (x - 60)°$. **students]**
    Use your diagram to solve the equation $\cos x° = \cos (x - 60)°$
    for value of x between 0 and 360. Indicate clearly on your diagram how the solutions relate to the graphs.
    State how many values of x satisfying the equation
    $$\cos (10x)° = \cos (10x - 60)°$$
    lie between 0 and 360. (You should explain your reasoning briefly, but no further detailed working or sketching is necessary.) *(OCR)*

3. Show that the equation $15 \cos^2\theta = 13 + \sin \theta$
    may be written as a quadratic equation in $\sin \theta$.
    Hence solve the equation, giving all values of θ such that $0° \leq \theta \leq 360°$ *(OCR)*

4. (i) Determine the solutions of the equation $\cos (2x - 30°) = 0$ for which $0 \leq x \leq 360$.
    (ii) Figure 2 shows part of the curve with equation $y = \cos(px - q)°$, where p and q are positive constants and $q < 180$. The curve cuts the x-axis at points A, B and C, as shown. Given that the coordinates of A and B are $(100,0)$ and $(220,0)$ respectively,
    (a) write down the coordinates of C
    (b) find the value of p and the value of q. *(Edexcel)*

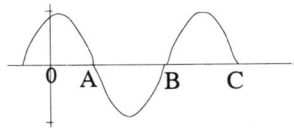

Unit 9: Sequences and Series   [Edexcel and AQA students only]

1. Evaluate $\sum\limits_{r=1}^{40} (5r + 7)$ *(OCR)*

2. The first term of an arithmetic series is 3. The seventh term is twice the third term.
    (a) Find the common difference.
    (b) Calculate the sum of the first 20 terms of the series. *(AQA)*

3. An arithmetic progression has first term a and common difference 3. The Nth term is 128 and the sum of the first $2N$ terms is 9842. Find N and a. *(OCR)*

4. The second term of a geometric series is 80 and the fifth term of the series is 5.12
    (a) Find the common ratio and the first term of the series.
    (b) Find the sum to infinity of the series, giving your answer as an exact fraction.

(c) Find the difference between the sum to infinity of the series and the sum of the first 14 terms of the series, giving your answer in the form $a \times 10^n$. where a is $1 \le a < 10$ and n is an integer. *(Edexcel)*

Unit 10: Functions and Numerical Methods   **[AQA students only]**

1. The functions f and g are defined with their respective domains by

   $$f: x \longmapsto \frac{5}{x-2} \qquad x \, \varepsilon \, \Re$$

   $$g: x \longmapsto x^2 + 3 \qquad x \, \varepsilon \, \Re$$

   (a) Calculate the exact values of x for which $f(x) = x$.

   (b) Find the range of g.

   (c) The domain of the composite function fg is $\Re$. Find $fg(x)$ and state the range of fg.

   (d) State whether the inverse of g exists, giving a reason for your answer. *(AQA)*

2. Express $x^2 + 4x$ in the form $(x + a)^2 + b$, stating the numerical values of a and b.

   The functions f and g are defined by $\quad f: x \longmapsto x^2 + 4x \qquad x \ge -2$

   $$g: x \longmapsto x + 6 \qquad x \, \varepsilon \, \Re$$

   (i)   Show that the equation $gf(x) = 0$ has no real roots.

   (ii) State the domain of f^{-1}

   (iii) Find an expression in terms of x for $f^{-1}(x)$.

   (iv) Sketch, on a single diagram, the graphs of $y = f(x)$ and $y = f^{-1}(x)$.

   (OCR)

Unit 11: Polynomials and the Factor Theorem   **[Edexcel students only]**

1. $f(x) \equiv 2x^3 + 5x^2 - 8x - 15$

   (a) Show that $(x + 3)$ is a factor of $f(x)$.

   (b) Hence, factorise $f(x)$ as the product of a linear factor and a quadratic factor.

   (c) Find, to 2 d.p., the two other values of x for which $f(x) = 0$ *(Edexcel)*

2. It is given that $f(x) = 2x^3 - 3x^2 - 56x - 27$. Show that $(2x + 1)$ is a factor of $f(x)$ and find the corresponding quadratic factor of f.

   Hence find the positive root of the equation $f(x) = 0$, giving your answer in the form $a + b\sqrt{7}$, where a and b are integers.   *(OCR)*

3. It is given that $(x^2 + ax + 2)(x^2 + bx + 3) \equiv x^4 + cx^3 + x^2 - 5x + 6$ where a and b are constants.

   (i)   Show that $ab = -4$ and find another equation connecting a and b only.

   (ii) Find the possible values of a and b.

   (iii) Given that a and b are integers, find the value of c.

   (OCR)

Unit 1: The Bridge

Section 1: Equation solving techniques p 9

D1.1: Basic linear equations
1. A, B, E   2. $6^1/_2$ 3. $^5/_3$ 4. -2
5. 2   6. 10   7. $^5/_3$

D1.2: Equations with brackets
1. $2^1/_2$ 2. $^{26}/_{17}$ 3. 3   4. $^{17}/_{12}$
5. 1   6. 2   7. $^9/_{16}$

D1.3 : Equations with square roots
1. 121   2. 83   3. 16   4. 36
5. 0   6. 9   7. 24   8. 48

D1.4 : Working with fractions
1. 17   2. $^{14}/_5$ 3. $^{15}/_2$ 4. 8
5. $^{16}/_3$ 6. $^{65}/_8$ 7. $^{40}/_9$ 8. $^{23}/_6$
9. $^{10}/_{11}$ 10. 6   11. -1 12. $^{23}/_8$

D1.5 : The cross-multiplication shortcut
1. $^7/_5$ 2. $-^1/_2$ 3. $^{47}/_3$ 4. $^{-6}/_{11}$ 5. -7

P1.6 : Solving miscellaneous equations

Batch A:
1. 1   2. 11   3. 12   4. $^{37}/_3$
5. $^5/_{24}$ 6. $^{-15}/_7$ 7. 49   8. $^{-7}/_3$

Batch B:
1. $-^1/_6$ 2. $-10^1/_2$ 3. $^1/_2$ 4. 8
5. $^{105}/_{11}$ 6. $-^5/_8$ 7. 41   8. -4

Section 2 : Changing the subject... p13

D2.1 : Simple formulae
1. $x = ^{11}/_3$ 2. $x = ^n/m$ 3. $x = ^{q^2}/p$
4. $x = \dfrac{K+L}{5}$ 5. $x = \dfrac{y+nz}{n}$ 6. $x = w - v$
7. $x = 3 - K$ 8. $x = m + n$ 9. $x = \dfrac{k-5}{3}$
10. $x = T^2 - v$ 11. $x = \dfrac{3t-z}{P}$ 12. $x = 11$
13. $x = \dfrac{5n+p}{5}$ 14. $x = \dfrac{z-Ny}{N}$ 15. $x = \dfrac{v+3p}{m}$

D2.2 : Formulae with fractions
1. $n = \dfrac{ct-b}{a}$ 2. $n = ey + 2x$ 3. $n = a + bk$
4. $n = -^1/_2$ 5. $n = \dfrac{aq-k}{p}$ 6. $n = \dfrac{5-k}{A}$

D2.3 : Squares and square roots
1. $x = a^2$ 2. $x = b^2 - a$ 3. $x = z^2 - 2y$
4. $x = (k + m)^2$ 5. $x = a - b^2$ 6. $x = \sqrt{a-c}$
7. $x = \sqrt{5t}$ 8. $x = \sqrt{d-n}$ 9. $x = ^1/_4 c^4$ 10. $x = \sqrt{3c+p}$

D2.4 : Equivalent formulae
1. $n = 3$ 2. $n = \dfrac{b-a}{-1}$ or $\boxed{\dfrac{a-b}{}}$ 3. $n = 3$
4. $n = \dfrac{y-x}{-2}$ or $\boxed{\dfrac{x-y}{2}}$ 5. $n = \dfrac{C-3A}{-B}$ or $\dfrac{3A-C}{B}$
6. $n = \dfrac{s-f}{m}$ or $\boxed{\dfrac{f-s}{-m}}$ 7. $n = 1$

$\boxed{\text{denotes preferred answer}}$

8. $n = \dfrac{5r-x}{-1}$ or $x - 5r$ 9. $n = \dfrac{ct-mx}{-m}$ or $\boxed{\dfrac{mx-ct}{m}}$

D2.5 : Using Cross Multiplication
1. $x = ^6/_5$ 2. $x = \dfrac{m}{q}$ 3. $x = \dfrac{c}{a+b}$ 4. $x = \dfrac{a}{10t}$
5. $x = 9$ 6. $x = \dfrac{30}{n}$ 7. $x = \dfrac{55-5n}{a}$ 8. $x = \dfrac{5g+35}{h}$
9. $x = \dfrac{pt+qt}{3}$ 10. $x = \dfrac{ea}{4}$ 11. $x = \dfrac{ct+cs}{7}$
12. $x = \dfrac{p+mg}{n}$

Section 3: An important technique p ?16

D3.1: You must master this
1. $x = -6^1/_2$ 2. $x = \dfrac{q}{4p}$ 3. $x = \dfrac{q-p}{2m}$ 4. $x = \dfrac{u+v}{3r}$
5. $x = \dfrac{q-p}{a+b}$ 6. $x = \dfrac{3z+y}{3a-b}$ 7. $x = \dfrac{z+w}{y-1}$ 8. $x = \dfrac{3b}{a-c}$
9. $x = \dfrac{t+d}{r+e}$ 10. $x = \dfrac{1-a}{1+a}$ 11. $x = \dfrac{d-pc}{c}$ 12. $x = \dfrac{5t}{3}$

P3.2 : Miscellaneous rearrangement exercise
1. $x = \dfrac{k-y}{3}$ 2. $x = \dfrac{a-3b}{2}$ 3. $x = \dfrac{a-5b}{m}$ 4. $x = \dfrac{16}{3a}$
5. $x = \dfrac{6}{y-u}$ 6. $x = \sqrt{m-n}$ 7. $x = \dfrac{a}{m+2a}$ 8. $x = \dfrac{2-ba}{a-1}$
9. $x = \dfrac{2d}{2-a}$ 10. $n = \dfrac{6}{\sqrt{a}}$ 11. $n = \sqrt{(p-e)}$ 12. $n = \dfrac{t}{12uc}$
13. $n = \sqrt{\dfrac{p-7k}{2}}$ 14. $n = \dfrac{6p-3a}{x}$ 15. $n = 17$

Section 4: Expansions p 17

D4.1: Multiplying out brackets
1. $x^2 + 7x + 10$ 2. $x^2 - x - 6$
3. $x^2 - 5x + 4$ 4. $x^2 + 4x - 12$
5. $2x^2 + 7x + 3$ 6. $3x^2 - 10x - 8$

D4.2 : Writing out expansions directly
1. $x^2 + 6x + 5$ 2. $x^2 + 5x - 14$
3. $x^2 + x - 12$ 4. $x^2 - 12x + 20$
5. $x^2 + 2x - 15$ 6. $x^2 + 8x - 33$
7. $2x^2 + 11x + 5$ 8. $2x^2 + 13x - 7$
9. $6x^2 - 5x - 4$ 10. $7x^2 + 33x - 10$

D4.3 : The difference of two squares
1. $x^2 - 9$ 2. $a^2 - 1$
3. $c^2 - 49$ 4. $4x^2 - 9$
5. $(p - q)(p + q)$ 6. $(x - 2)(x + 2)$
7. $(m - 5)(m + 5)$ 8. $(2p - q)(2p + q)$
9. $(7x - 3y)(7x + 3y)$ 10. $(6y - 10)(6y + 10)$
11. $(u - 2v)(u + 2v)$ 12. $(mn - p)(mn + p)$

D4.4 : Squaring brackets
1. $x^2 + 6x + 9$ 2. $x^2 - 12x + 36$
3. $x^2 - 2x + 1$ 4. $x^2 + 2xy + y^2$
5. $a^2 - 2ab + b^2$ 6. $x^2 + 14x + 49$
7. $4x^2 + 4x + 1$ 8. $n^2 - 6n + 9$
9. $4x^2 + 12xy + 9y^2$ 10. $4t^2 + 20tu + 25u^2$
11. $x^2 - 8x + 16$ 12. $m^2 + 16m + 64$
13. $4x^2 - 20x + 25$ 14. $16x^2 - 8xy + y^2$
15. $9a^2 - 6ab + b^2$

D4.5 : Perfect squares
1. $x^2 + 2x + 1 = (x + 1)^2$ 2. $x^2 + 10x + 25 = (x + 5)^2$
3. $x^2 - 8x + 16 = (x + 4)^2$ 4. $x^2 - 20x + 100 = (x - 10)^2$
5. $x^2 + 6x + 9 = (x + 3)^2$ 6. $x^2 - 14x + 49 = (x - 7)^2$
7. $x^2 - 4x + 4 = (x - 2)^2$ 8. $x^2 + 24x + 144 = (x + 12)^2$
9. $x^2 + 30x + 225 = (x + 15)^2$ 10. $x^2 - 12x + 36 = (x - 6)^2$

Section 5: Properties of a circle — p 19

D5.1: Working with circles
1. $a = 58°$ 2. $x = 30°$ 3. $b = 40°$ $c = 70°$ $d = 45°$
4. $h = 4.9$ 5. $x = 36.9°$ 6. $d = 72.8$ cm
7. $c = 65°$ $d = 25°$ $e = 40°$ 8. $i = 80°$ $j = 40°$ 9. 13.1cm

Section 6: Cosine Rule and Sine Rule — p 20

D6.1: The Cosine Rule
1. 8.3 2. 3.4 3. 4.9 4. 41° 5. 107° 6. 127°

D6.2: The Sine Rule
1. 8.6° 2. 31.9° 3. 19.8° 4. 36.5° 5. 92.5° 6. 15.4

Section 7: Applications of ratio — p 22

D7.1: Dividing in ratio
1. 16 cm 2. 10 cm 3. 4 m 4. 15 cm 5. (3,5) 6.(1,4)

D7.2: Similar triangles
1. 12 ; 5 2. 7 ; 12 3. 6 ; $2^2/_3$ 4. 10 ; 12 5. $4^1/_2$; 4

D7.3: Areas of similar shapes
1. 50 2. 9.375 3. 303.75 4. 4 5. 6 cm 6. 7.5

D7.4: Volumes of similar shapes
1. 400 2. 405 3. 264 4. 0.8 5. 632.8 cm^3
6. 0.2 kg 7. (a) 2 : 5 (b) 4 : 9 8. 80 kg

Section 8: Proportion — p 26

D8.1: Direct proportion
1. 8.8 h 2. 2.098 s 3. 603 cm^3

D8.2: Direct and inverse proportion
1. (a) 12 (b) 20 2. 7.5 h 3. $k = 3$; $^{75}/_{144}$ 4. 24

Section 9: Miscellaneous Techniques — p 28

D9.1: Lowest common multiples (LCMs)
1. 12 2. 12 3. 40 4. $\dfrac{5x + 4}{6}$ 5. $\dfrac{5x + 7}{6}$

6. $\dfrac{5 - 3x}{10}$ 7. $\dfrac{5x - 2}{x(x - 1)}$ 8. $\dfrac{7x - 5}{x(2x - 1)}$ 9. $\dfrac{7x + 1}{(x-2)(x+3)}$

10. $\dfrac{5 + x}{x(x + 2)}$ 11. $\dfrac{1 - x}{x(x - 1)}$ 12. $\dfrac{5 + 3x}{x(x + 3)}$

D9.2: Highest common factors (HCFs)
1. 6 2. 7 3. 9 4. $x^2(x - y)$
5. $2a(b - 2c)$ 6. $pqr(1 + p)$ 7. $n(5n - 2n^2 + 1)$
8. $3mn(n - 3m)$ 9. $ac(b^2 + a + cd)$

D9.3: Volumes of cones and spheres
1. 382 cm^3 2. 503 cm^3 3. 4.29 cm
4. 15.0 cm 5. 1060 m^3 6. 13 cm

D9.4: Areas of triangles
1. 7.7 cm^2 2. 12.4 cm^2

Unit 2: Quadratics

Section 1: Factorising quadratics — p 32

D1.1: Systematic factorisation - type 1 quadratics
1. $(x - 1)(x - 6)$ 2. $(x - 3)(x - 8)$
3. $(x + 1)(x + 5)$ 4. $(x - 1)(x - 5)$

D1.2: Systematic factorisation - type 2 quadratics
1. $(x + 9)(x - 2)$ 2. $(x + 4)(x - 5)$ 3. $(x + 3)(x - 4)$
4. $(x - 5)(x + 3)$ 5. $(x + 2)(x - 7)$ 6. $(x + 3)(x - 10)$
7. $(x - 1)(x - 6)$ 8. $(x - 2)(x - 9)$ 9. $(x - 3)(x + 5)$
10. $(x + 2)(x - 9)$ 11. $(x - 2)(x - 3)$ 12. $(x - 4)(x + 5)$

D1.3 : More complex quadratics
1. $(2x + 3)(x + 2)$ 2. $(2x + 3)(x + 1)$ 3. $(3x + 1)(x + 2)$
4. $(3x + 1)(5x + 2)$ 5. $(4x - 5)(x - 5)$ 6. $(3x - 7)(2x + 5)$
7. $(3x + 1)(8x - 7)$ 8. $(2x - 1)(x + 3)$ 9. $(5x - 4)(6x - 5)$
10. $(12x - 5)(x + 1)$ 11.$(10x - 1)(x + 1)$ 12.$(2x - 3)(6x + 7)$

Section 2: Solving equations by factorisation p 34

D2.1: Solving factorised equations
1. 1, 9 2. $-5, 6$ 3. 0, 2 4. 4, -4
5. $-3, -^1/_2$ 6. 0, 2, $-^2/_3$

D2.2: Solving quadratic equations by factorisation
1. 1 2. $-1, -2$ 3. 3, 5 4. 1, -4
5. 2, -12 6. $^1/_2$, 1 7. $-^1/_2$, -2 8. $2^1/_2$, 2
9. $^1/_3$, -4

D2.3: Solving quadratics & cubics with x as a factor
1. 0, 5 2. 0, -2 3. 0, 4 4. 0, 2, 4
5. 0, -3, -7 6. 0, 5, -5 7. 0, 3, -3 8. 0, -1, -4
9. 0, 7, -7

P2.4: Mixed factorisation practice
1. $^1/_6$, -5 2. 1, 8 3. 0, 5 4. 5, -4
5. 0, 6, -6 6. -5, -9 7. $^1/_3$, $^5/_4$ 8. 0, 1, 7
9. $^1/_2$ 10. $^1/_7$, -4 11. $^3/_8$, -2 12. 0, 49

E2.5: Factorisation challenge
1. 0, $^1/_2$, -10 2. -1, $-^2/_5$ 3. 3, -5 4. 3, -3
5. $-^3/_2$, $^3/_2$ 6. $^3/_5$, -1

Section 3: Quadratic inequalities — p 36

D3.1: Solving quadratic inequalities
1. $1 < x < 3$ 2. $x > -3 \, \& \, x < -5$ 3. $2 < x < 5$
4. (a) 2, -2 (b) $x < -2 \, \& \, x > 2$
5. (a) $\pm\sqrt{5}$ (b) $x < -\sqrt{5} \, \& \, x > \sqrt{5}$ 6. $2 < x < 4$
7. $x \le -1 \, \& \, x \ge 6$ 8. $-5 < x < 0.5$ 9. $x < 0 \, \& \, x > 3$

Section 4: Linear inequalities — p 37

D4.1: Review of linear inequalities
1. $x > ^4/_3$ 2. $x > ^7/_3$ 3. $x < -^1/_4$
4. $x \ge ^3/_7$ 5. $x > -2$ 6. $x \ge ^{15}/_{17}$
7. $x < ^{17}/_7$

Section 5: 'The formula' — p 38

D5.1: Solving quadratic equations by formula
1. 0.275 & -7.275 2. 1 & $^1/_3$ 3. 4.16 & 0.84
4. 2.21 & 0.38 5. $2^1/_2$ & 1 6. -4.56 & -0.44
7. 2.65 & -0.82 8. 0.44 & -1.69 9. 1.11 & 0.09

D5.2: Choosing which method to use
1. $-3, 5$ 2. 0 & -7 3. $-^3/_2$, $-^1/_3$
4. 1, -7 5. 0, 2 6. $-^1/_2$, -4
7. 3.41, 0.58 8. 3.41, -4.41 9. -0.54 & 1.87
10. 2.5, -1 11. 3.62, 1.38 12. 3.58, 0.42
13. $-3, 2$ 14. 7, -10

Section 6: The discriminant — p 39

D6.1: Meet the discriminant
1. No solution because you cannot find the square root of a negative number.
2. $b^2 - 4ac = 0 \Rightarrow x = -^b/_{2a}$ (only one solution) 3. $> = <$

D6.2: Using the discriminant
1. 2 2. 0 3. 2 4. 1
5. 0 6. 2 7. 2 different rational roots

D6.3: Further discriminant problems
1. $-8 < k < 62$. 4. 5 3. $p \le ^4/_3$

E6.4: Inequalities and the discriminant
1. $1 < a < 4$ 2. $k \le -2 \, \& \, k \ge 3$
3. "$b^2 - 4ac$" = ... = $4(q^2 + r^2) \ge 0$ for all q, r so it has real roots

Section 7: Quadratic equations in disguise   p 41

D7.1: Rearrange and solve
1. $-3, 5$ 2. $2, -7$ 3. $6, -4$ 4. $1, -4$
5. $1.83, -3.83$ 6. $4, -3$ 7. $1. 7$ 8. $-1, -3$

D7.2: Quadratics in disguise
1. $6.7, 0.3$ 2. $3.56, -0.56$ 3. $-1/2, 3/5$
4. $0.46, -1.46$ 5. $-1/2, 2$ 6. $4, 3/5$
7. $1, -13/7$ 8. $0, 3.6$

Section 8: Quadratics of functions of x p 42

D8.1 : Quadratics as functions of x
1. $\pm\sqrt{2}$ 2. $1, -2$ 3. $\pm 2/3, \pm 1/\sqrt{2}$ 4. $0, 2$
5. $4/3, 5/4$ 6. $30°, 90°$ 7. $1, 9$ 8. $\pm 1/\sqrt{5}, \pm 2/\sqrt{5}$
9. $(7x + 1)(5x - 3)$; $1/49$, $9/25$ 10. $2/3$, $-4/5$; $\pm\sqrt{(2/3)}$
11. 0.728 & -1.114 ; $t = 0.386$ & -1.5

Unit 3: Coordinate Geometry

Section 1: Properties of lines and points p 45

D1.1: Distance and midpoint formulae
1. (a) $\sqrt{29}$ (b) $\sqrt{17}$ (c) 6 (d) 5 (e) 4 (f) $\sqrt{2}a$
2. (a) $(2, 4.5)$ (b) $(2.5, -3)$ (c) $(0,5)$ (d) $(-2.5, 0)$
   (e) $(-1, 2)$ (f) $(1/2 a, 1/2 a)$
3. (a) NOT right angled   (b) right angled at B
5. You need to show that two sides are equal and that
   the third side is a different length.
6. $(-3, -1)$ 7. (b) $(-3.5, -0.5)$; 17.5 sq units

D1.2: Gradients of line segments
1. (a) $r = 6, t = 4$ (b) $2/3$ 3. (a) $5/2$ (b) 4 (c) $4/3$
4. (a) denominator = 0 and you cannot divide by zero
   (b) infinite ; The x-coordinates are the same.
5. (a) $1, -1$ (b) $1/5$, -5 (c) $-4/3$, $3/4$ 6. All three pairs

D1.3: Gradients and angles
1. 1 2. -1 3. ∞

E1.4: Altogether now
1. $2, -1/2, 2/11$; right angled at B   2. 13
3. (a) Yes (b) No (c) Yes   4. $\pm\sqrt{(5/2)}$ 5. $6b = 4a + 13$
6. 1 7. 5 ; $\sqrt{-4/3}$

Section 2: $y = mx + c$ p 48

D2.1: The standard equation of a straight line
1.

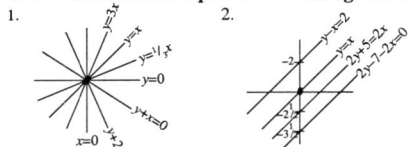

2.

3. (a) $5/2$ (b) $1/3$ (c) -3 (d) -3 (e) $4/7$ (f) $7/4$ (g) $3/2$ (h) a/b

D2.2: Is it a straight line or not ?
1. A, C, E, G, H   2. (a) $y = -7x + 5$
(b) $y = 5/3 x + 1/3$ (c) $y = -3/2 x + 5/2$ (d) $y = 2x + 8$

D2.3: Parallel and perpendicular lines
1. //el   2. //el   3. $|^r$ 4. Neither
5. //el   6. $|^r$

Section 3:Equations of straight lines   p 50

D3.1: Straight line equations
1. (a) length of side is difference in y-coords
   (b) $x - 3$ (c) $\dfrac{y - 4}{x - 3}$ 3. $y = -x + 10$

D3.2: A formula for equations of straight lines
1. $y = 2x + 3$ 2. $3x - 2y + 4 = 0$
3. (a) $y = -5x$ (b) $3y = x - 7$
4. (a) $y = 5x - 1$ (b) $2y = -3x - 1$ (c) $7y = x + 25$
6. $8x - 7y + 25 = 0$ 7. $y = 3x - 8$ 8. $2y = x - 1$
9. $y + 3x + 2 = 0$ 10. $y = -x + 8$

D3.3: Setting out problems
1. $y = x$ 2. $y + 6x = 1$; $6y = x + 9$; $(-3/37 , 55/37)$
3. $2y + 3x = 4$; $(22/13 , -7/13)$
4. (a) $3/2$ & 2 (b) $y = 2x$ (c) $2y = 3x + 1$ (d) $(1,2)$
5. (a) $y = 2x + 20$ (b) $2y = -x - 5$ (c) $(-9,2)$
6. (a) $(-6,-3)$ (b) $9y = 8x + 21$

E3.4: Line challenges
1. B is $(29/8 , 13/8)$ D is $(43/8 , 51/8)$ 2. $2y = x + 6$; $-3/4$
3. $3y + 4x = 16$; $(16, -16)$ 4. 6

Section 4: Sketching graphs   p 54

D4.1: Graphs of $y = kx^n$
1.   2.   3.

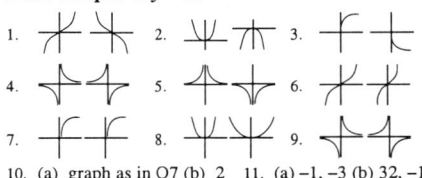

4.   5.   6.

7.   8.   9.

10. (a) graph as in Q7 (b) 2   11. (a) $-1, -3$ (b) $32, -1$

D4.2: Intersecting lines and curves
1. (a) $x = 1/2$, $y = 4$ and $x = -2$, $y = -1$
   (b) $x = -1$, $y = -2$ and $x = 4$, $y = 1/2$
2. $(1,2)$ $(3,6)$ 3. Just one point of intersection
4. 2 points of intersection, so not a tangent. $(0,-6)$ $(3,0)$
5. Tangent at $(1,3)$ 6. $(4,2)$

D4.3: Factorisable quadratics
1.   2.   3.

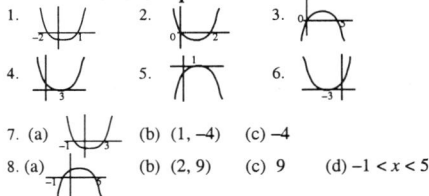

4.   5.   6.

7. (a)   (b) $(1, -4)$ (c) -4
8. (a)   (b) $(2, 9)$ (c) 9 (d) $-1 < x < 5$

D4.4: Factorisable cubics
1. (a) $-4, 0, 3$ (b)   (c) $-4 < x < 0, x > 3$
2. (a)   (b) 2 (c) $x < 0$

E4.5: Intersecting graphs
1. (a) A(0,5) B(3,8) C(-1,0) D(5,0)   (b) $0 < x < 3$
   (c) $x < 0$ & $x > 3$
2. (a) & (b)   (c) $0, 3$ (d) $0 < x < 3$
3. (a) &(c)   (b) $x \le -4$ & $1 \le x \le 3$
   (d) $x \ge -4$

Section 5: Related functions　　　　p 58

D5.1: Graphs of some related functions

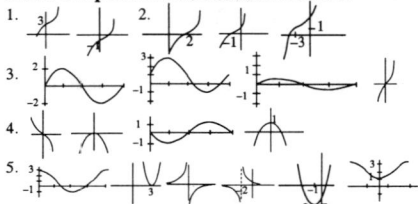

1.
2.
3.
4.
5.

D5.2: A systematic look at graph transformations

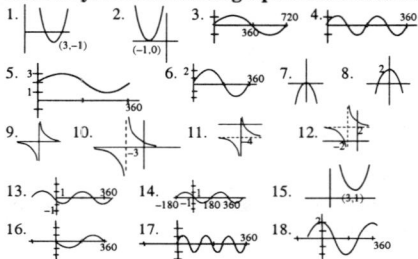

1.
2.
3.
4.
5.
6.
7.
8.
9.
10.
11.
12.
13.
14.
15.
16.
17.
18.

Unit 4: Surds, powers and...

Section 1: Working with surds　　　p 62

D1.1: Basic simplification

1. $8\sqrt{3}$　2. $5\sqrt{5}$　3. $3\sqrt{3}$　4. 3　5. $2+\sqrt{2}$
6. $\sqrt{6}$　7. $\sqrt{5}$　8. 5　9. $4\sqrt{5}$　10. $15\sqrt{6}$
11. $2\sqrt{13}$　12. $2+2\sqrt{6}$　13. $3\sqrt{2}+3\sqrt{3}$　14. not poss.
15. $2\sqrt{2}+6$　16. $6+2\sqrt{6}$　17. $2\sqrt{2}$　18. $10+5\sqrt{5}$
19. $^2/_3\sqrt{5}$　20. 6

D1.2: Brackets and surds

1. 1　2. $5-3\sqrt{3}$　3. $8+3\sqrt{5}$　4. $6+3\sqrt{3}-2\sqrt{2}-\sqrt{6}$
5. $3-2\sqrt{2}$　6. $4+2\sqrt{3}$　7. $x-1$　8. $x-y$

D1.3: Simplest form

1. $4\sqrt{2}$　2. $5\sqrt{2}$　3. $2\sqrt{3}$　4. $3\sqrt{2}$　5. $4\sqrt{3}$
6. $5\sqrt{5}$　7. $10\sqrt{3}$　8. 5　9. $5\sqrt{3}$　10. 7
11. $6\sqrt{2}$　12. $2\sqrt{5}$　13. $\sqrt{3}$　14. $^3/_7$　15. 2　16. $9\sqrt{3}$
17. $10\sqrt{2}$　18. $9-\sqrt{3}$　19. 15　20. $4-3\sqrt{2}$　21. 3　22. $6\sqrt{2}$

D1.4: Rationalising the denominator

1. $^1/_2\sqrt{2}$　2. $^1/_5\sqrt{5}$　3. $^3/_7\sqrt{7}$　4. $^5/_3\sqrt{3}$　5. $^1/_2\sqrt{3}$
6. $^1/_2\sqrt{2}$　7. $^1/_2\sqrt{2}$　8. $^1/_4\sqrt{2}$　9. $^3/_{25}\sqrt{5}$　10. $^2/_5$

D1.5: More complex rationalising

1. $^1/_4(\sqrt{5}-1)$　2. $^1/_2(\sqrt{3}+1)$　3. $2-\sqrt{3}$
4. $5-2\sqrt{5}$　5. $^1/_3(4\sqrt{3}+6)$　6. $6+3\sqrt{3}$
7. $^1/_{10}(2\sqrt{3}-\sqrt{2})$　8. $-^1/_3(2\sqrt{7}+7)$　9. $7+4\sqrt{3}$
10. $^1/_7(5-3\sqrt{2})$　11. $2-\sqrt{3}$　12. $\sqrt{5}-2$

E1.6: Surd challenges

1. $2\sqrt{2}$　2. $\dfrac{-4}{x-4}$ or $\dfrac{4}{4-x}$　3. $\dfrac{x-\sqrt{x}}{x-1}$　4. $\sqrt{x}-\sqrt{y}$
5. $\dfrac{x+2\sqrt{x}}{x}$　6. $x-\dfrac{1}{x}$　7. $\dfrac{3}{1-x}$

Section 2: Positive powers　　　p 65

D2.1 : Basic Rules

1. 5^8　2. 3^{17}　3. 4^2　4. 10^9　5. 3^3
6. 4^6　7. 3^7　8. 5^9　9. 2^9　10. 3^{14}

11. 5^{12}　12. 7^8　13. 5^6　14. 10^{20}　15. 3^{14}
16. 5^{11}　17. 4^{16}　18. 3^7　19. 4^{14}　20. 5^6
21. 3^2　22. 5^2　23. 6^5　24. 4^4　25. 3^{14}

P2.2 : Basic practice

Batch A

1. 5^5　2. 3^{21}　3. 4^2　4. 3^7
5. 4^{18}　6. 4^8　7. 2^3　8. 6^2
9. 3^5　10. 3^{14}　11. 6^3　12. 2^2
13. 3^3　14. 5^4　15. 6^3

Batch B

1. 6^1　2. 3^{12}　3. 2^7　4. 5^2
5. 6^{10}　6. 3^{15}　7. 2^5　8. 3^8
9. 8^3　10. 10^1　11. 2^6　12. 3^8
13. 2^3　14. 5^{10}　15. 3^9

D2.3 : Powers and algebra

1. n^5　2. x^4　3. m^5　4. v^6　5. t^6
6. c^{-2}　7. $9n^2$　8. $125p^6$　9. x^6　10. $8x^6$
11. $6p^3q^2$　12. $20m^3n^2$　13. $15p^4q^3r^2$　14. $36u^2v^6$
15. $24m^3n^6$　16. $9x^4y^6z^2$

P2.4 : Powers and algebra practice

1. e^6　2. k^2　3. a^8　4. h^5　5. u
6. $9x^2$　7. $15x^2y^3$　8. $12a^3b^5$　9. $45p^4q^2$
10. m^7　11. $6x^2y^3z$　12. $8a^3b^2d^4$

D2.5: Simplifying by cancelling

1. $2^3\times3$　2. $6^2\times3^2$　3. $\dfrac{8^2\times5^2}{3}$　4. $\dfrac{8}{3^3}$
5. $7^2\times5^2$　6. $\dfrac{4^2}{7^2}$　7. $10^2\times8^3$　8. $\dfrac{2^3\times5^2}{3^2}$
9. $3y^3z$　10. $10db$　11. $\dfrac{2ab^3}{c}$　12. $4p^3r$
13. $\dfrac{3m^2r}{n}$　14. $\dfrac{r^2}{3p}$　15. $\dfrac{4p}{qr}$　16. $\dfrac{px}{4}$

Section 3: Negative powers and roots　　p 68

D3.1: Negative and zero powers

1. $^1/_9$　2. $^1/_{10}$　3. $^1/_5$　4. $^1/_{64}$　5. 1
6. 1　7. $^1/_{57}$　8. $^1/_{36}$　9. $^1/_{125}$　10. $^1/_{10000}$
11. 2^2　12. 3^6　13. 5^1　14. 3^{-1}　15. 4^{-6}
16. 2^{-2}　17. 3^4　18. 2^6　19. 16　20. $^1/_3$
21. 1　22. 5　23. 64　24. 1　25. $^1/_{64}$
26. 64

P3.2 : Power practice

Batch A

1. 5^2 or 25　2. 3^8　3. x　4. 1　5. n^{-1}
6. 3^4 or 81　7. t^2　8. $9n^2$　9. $\dfrac{1}{2p^2}$ or $\dfrac{1}{2}p^{-2}$
10. $81p^{-4}$　11. $6b^5c^2$　12. m^2　13. $10y^4$
14. $9m^{-4}n^6$　15. $2q^{-1}$

Batch B

1. m^2　2. 3^6　3. 6　4. 8^2　5. 2^{-6}
6. 7^{-3}　7. 3^{10}　8. 6^5　9. $\dfrac{1}{9}m^2$
10. $10p^{-1}$ or $\dfrac{10}{p}$　11. 2^{-1} or $\dfrac{1}{2}$　12. a^2
13. a^3b^{-2}　14. pq^2　15. $3mn^4$

Batch C

1. 1　2. $8s^8$　3. 1　4. c^5　5. $4vw^2$
6. $4n^{-2}$　7. $^1/_6n^3$　8. $25p^4q^{-6}$　9. $25v^2$
10. $^1/_{16}m^{-2}$　11. $\dfrac{q^6}{5p^4}$ or $\dfrac{1}{5}p^{-4}q^6$　12. $p^{-3}q^3r^{-2}$

Section 4: A very important technique   p 69

D4.1 : Writing expressions as sums of powers of x

1. x^{-1} 2. x^{-2} 3. $x^{-1/2}$ 4. $x^{3/2}$ 5. $x^{-1/2}$
6. $x^{-3/2}$ 7. $x^{-1/2}$ 8. $x^{-1/3}$ 9. $x^{2/3}$ 10. $x^{3/2}$
11. $x^{5/2}$ 12. $x^{3/2}$ 13. $x^2 + 3x + 2$ 14. $x^3 - 3x$
15. $x^{3/2} + x^{1/2}$ 16. $x + 3x^{1/2}$ 17. $2x^{3/2} - x^{1/2}$
18. $3x^{5/2} - x^2$ 19. $x + 5$ 20. $x^{-1} + 5x^{-2}$
21. $x^{3/2} - 3x^{1/2}$ 22. $x^{-1/2} + 2 + x^{-1}$
23. $3x^{-1/2} - x^{-1/2} - 4x^{-1}$ 24. $5 + 2x - 2x^{-1/2}$
25. $3 - x^{-1/2}$ 26. $x^{2/3} - 3x^{3/2} + 2x^{-1}$
27. $1 - 2x^{-1/2} + x^{-1} - 2x^{-3/2}$

Section 5: More complex techniques ...   p 71

D5.1 : Evaluating complex powers by simplifying

1. 9 2. $10/3$ 3. $49/100$ 4. $16/25$ 5. 3
6. $1/3$ 7. -1 8. 1 9. $6/5$ 10. 6
11. $1/4$ 12. $5/3$

D5.2 : Evaluating $a^{m/n}$

1. 4 2. 27 3. 8 4. 125 5. 625
6. 1000007. 9 8. $1/243$ 9. 8 10. $729/1000$
11. $4/9$ 12. $27/8$ 13. $9/25$

D5.3 : Solving equations

1. 4 2. -2 3. 0 4. $1/2$ 5. $1/2$
6. -1 7. 3 8. 0 9. 27 10. 3
11. 3 12. 3 13. 3 14. 4 15. 5
16. 3 17. 2 18. 3 19. 2 20. -2

Section 6: Simultaneous equations   p 73

D6.1 : Basic methods for solving ...

1. $x = 3, y = 2$ 2. $m = 1, p = 3$ 3. $x = 5, y = -2$
4. $m = 2, n = 1$ 5. $p = 1, q = 2$ 6. $x = -2, y = 1$
7. $c = -1, d = 2$ 8. (a) $x = 3, y = 0$ & $x = 0, y = 3$
(b) $x = 1\frac{1}{2}, y = 1\frac{1}{2}$ (c) $x = 3, y = 0$ & $x = 1, y = 0$

D6.2 : When one equation is not linear

1. 3, 9 & -2, 4 2. 1, 1 & -3, 9 3. 4, 2 & -4, -2
4. 1, 4 & -2, -2 5. 1, 2 & 4, -4 6. 0, $-1/2$ & -1, -1
7. -1, 3 & 2, -3 8. 1, $1/5$ & $1/5$, $-7/10$

D6.3 : Simultaneous quadratic equations

1. $x = 2$ & $y = 11$ 2. (1,6) & (-4,-9)
3. $x = 3.44$ & $y = 30.03$, $x = -0.77$ & $y = -2.77$

E6.4 : Simultaneous equation challenges

1. -2, 1 & 3, -1 2. (5,-5) & (0,-10) 3. -2, 4, 3
4. 1, 2, 1 5. $2/3(1 - \sqrt{13})$; 3.07, 37.20 & -1.74, 0.35

Section 7: Circular measures   p 76

D7.1 : Radians and degrees

1. (a) $60°$ (b) $45°$ (c) $18°$ (d) $360°$ (e) $22.5°$
(f) $67.5°$ (g) $40°$

2. (a) $\pi/10$ (b) $\pi/2$ (c) $\pi/3$ (d) $\pi/6$ (e) $3\pi/2$ (f) 4π
3. (a) $2\pi/5$ (b) $3\pi/10$ (c) $9\pi/10$ (d) $4\pi/3$ (e) $\pi/12$ (f) $7\pi/36$

4. (a) $115°$ (b) $69°$ (c) $46°$

5. (a) 0.5 (b) 0.924 (c) 0.901 (d) 0.1
(e) 0.5 (f) 0.766 (g) 0.343

D7.2: Arcs and sectors

1. (a) $6/5 \pi$ cm (b) 2π cm (c) 2 cm
(d) 7.5 cm (e) 16π cm
2. (a) $18/5 \pi$ cm^2 (b) 4π cm^2 (c) 10 cm^2
(d) 56.25 cm^2 (e) 160π cm^2 3. 1.25^c 4. 5.2 cm^2

D7.3: Segments of circles

1. (a) 10.27 cm^2 (b) 22.11 cm^2
2. 20 cm^2 3. 5.80 cm^2 and 195.26 cm^2

E7.4: Circular challenges

1. 2.86^c 2. $35/4 \pi$ cm^2 3. 5π cm 4. 2.715 cm^3

Unit 5: Differential calculus

Section 1: Gradients of lines and curves p 81

D1.1: Gradients of straight lines

1. $1/2$ 2. $13/6$ 3. $-2/5$ 4. $4/h$
5. $(x^2 + x)/(x^2 - x)$ 6. $[(x+h)^2 - (x + h)]/(x^2 - x)$

D1.2: Limits of numerical sequences

1. $1/3$ 2. 0 3. 2 4. 5.2 5. 0

D1.3: Gradients of curves

Task 1:

PR	0.1	0.01	0.001	0.0001	0.00001
OT	2.1	2.01	2.001	2.0001	2.00001
TQ	4.41	4.0401	4.004001	4.00040001	4.0000400001
QR	0.41	0.0401	0.004001	0.00040001	0.0000400001
QR	4.1	4.01	4.001	4.0001	4.00001
PR					

grad at P = lim [grad PQ] = **4**
Q−>P

Task 2:

PR	0.1	0.01	0.001	0.0001	0.00001
OT	3.1	3.01	3.001	3.0001	3.00001
TQ	9.61	9.0601	9.006001	9.00060001	9.0000600001
QR	0.61	0.06 01	0.006001	0.00060001	0.0000600001
QR	6.1	6.01	6.001	6.0001	6.00001
PR					

grad at P = lim [grad PQ] = **6**
Q−>P

Task 3:

PR	0.1	0.01	0.001	0.0001	0.00001
OT	1.1	1.01	1.001	1.0001	1.00001
TQ	3.63	3.0603	3.006003	3.00060003	3.0000600003
QR	0.63	0.06 03	0.006003	0.00060003	0.0000600003
QR	6.3	6.03	6.003	6.0003	6.00003
PR					

grad at P = lim [grad PQ] = **6**
Q−>P

D1.4: Gradient functions

1. $6x$ 2. $3x^2$ 3. $4x^3$

Section 2: Deriving gradient formulae p 84

D2.1: Gradients at a point from first principles

1. If $y = 3x^2$
then $y + \delta y = 3(x + \delta x)^2$
$\Rightarrow$ $\delta y = 3(x + \delta x)^2 - 3x^2$
        $= 3x^2 + 6x\delta x + 3(\delta x)^2 - 3x^2$
        $= 6x\delta x + 3(\delta x)^2$
Hence $\dfrac{\delta y}{\delta x} = 6x + 3\delta x$

Gradient $= \lim_{\delta x \to 0} \dfrac{\delta y}{\delta x} = \lim_{\delta x \to 0} (6x + 3\delta x)$

$\Rightarrow$ Gradient $= 6x$

D2.2: Gradient of x^n

1. (a) $7x^6$ (b) $12x^{11}$ (c) $35x^{34}$ (d) px^{p-1}
2. (a) $20x^3$ (b) $21x^6$ (c) $20x^9$ (d) ktx^{t-1}
3. (a) 5 (b) 7 (c) $2x + 2$ (d) $10x + 10$
4. (a) $8x^3 + 5$ (b) $21x^2 - 4$
   (c) $6x^2 + 30x^9$ (d) $15 + 30x^4$
5. (a) nx^{n-1} (b) knx^{n-1} (c) $anx^{n-1} + bmx^{m-1}$
6. (a) $-7x^{-8}$ (b) $7x^{2.5}$ (c) $-4x^{-5}$
   (d) $^1/_2 x^{-3/2}$ (e) $7x^{2/5}$
7. (a) $15x^4 - 16x^7 + 6$ (b) $3.6x^{0.2} - 15x^{-4} + 20x$ (c) $-x^{-2}$

Section 3: Terminology and rules   p 86

D3.1: Terminology
1. $\dfrac{dy}{dx} = 6x + 4$ 2. $\dfrac{dy}{dx} = 5x^4 - 21x^6$ 3. $\dfrac{dy}{dx} = 9x^2 + 4x$
4. $4x^3$ 5. $8x^3 + 18x^5$ 6. $5 + 28x^3$
7. $f'(x) = 4x + 15x^2$ 8. $f'(x) = 6x^5 - 21x^6$
9. $f'(x) = 5 + 18x$

D3.2: Rules for differentiating polynomials
1. $8x + 3$ 2. $-3x^{-2} + 7.5x^{0.5}$
3. $-4x^{-3} + 26.6x^{2.8}$ 4. $^1/_2 x^{-1/2}$
5. $-x^{-4/3} + ^2/_3 x^{-2/3}$ 6. $3.6x^{-2.2} - 2x^{-3/2}$
7. $5 - 2x^{-2}$ 8. $^3/_4 x^{-3/4} - 15x^{-4}$
9. $2 + 6x^{-3}$ 10. $6t$
11. $-4t^{-3} + ^3/_4 t^{-3/4}$ 12. $-12t^{-4} - 6t^{1/2}$

D3.3 : Differentiating powers of x
1. $-x^{-2}$ 2. $12x^3 + 2x^{-3}$ 3. $^1/_2 x^{-1/2}$
4. $^3/_2 x^{1/2}$ 5. $2x + 1$ 6. $2x - 3$
7. $^3/_2 x^{1/2} - x^{-1/2}$ 8. $18x - 6$ 9. $2x - 4x^{-2}$
10. $-x^{-2} + 14x^{-3} - 3x^{-4}$ 11. $^{-1}/_2 x^{-3/2}$
12. $^1/_2 x^{-1/2} + ^3/_2 x^{-3/2}$ 13. $3 + 3x^{-2}$
14. $x^{-2} + 6x^{-3}$ 15. $-^1/_2 x^{-3/2}$ 16. $x^{3/2} + x^{1/2}$
17. $10x - ^5/_2 x^{3/2}$ 18. $^9/_2 x^{1/2} - 1$ 19. $5 - ^3/_2 x^{1/2} - ^1/_2 x^{-1/2}$
20. $^3/_2 x^{1/2} - ^3/_2 x^{-1/2}$ 21. $-^1/_2 x^{-3/2} - x^{-1/2} + 7x^{-2}$
22. $-x^{-11/2} - ^5/_2 x^{-3/2} - ^9/_2 x^{-5/2}$ 23. $f(x) \neq 2x^{-1}$ $f(x) = ^1/_2 x^{-1}$
23. He said that $^1/_2 x = 2x^{-1}$, but it should have been $^1/_2 x^{-1}$

Section 4: From first principles   p 89

D4.1: Differentiation from first principles
1.
Gradient of chord	= $\dfrac{2(x + h)^2 - 2x^2}{h}$
	= $\dfrac{2x^2 + 4xh + 2h^2 - 2x^2}{h}$
	= $\dfrac{4xh + 2h^2}{h} = 4x + 2h$
Gradient of curve	= $\lim\limits_{h \to 0}$ (gradient of chord) = $\boxed{4x}$

2.
Gradient of chord	= $\dfrac{(x + h)^2 + 1 - (x^2 + 1)}{h}$
	= $\dfrac{x^2 + 2xh + h^2 + 1 - x^2 - 1}{h}$
	= $\dfrac{2xh + h^2}{h} = 2x + h$
Gradient of curve	= $\lim\limits_{h \to 0}$ (gradient of chord) = $\boxed{2x}$

3.
Gradient of chord	= $\dfrac{4(x + h) - 1 - (4x - 1)}{h}$
	= $\dfrac{4x + 4h - 1 - 4x + 1}{h}$
	= $\dfrac{4h}{h} = 4$
Gradient of curve	= $\lim\limits_{h \to 0}$ (gradient of chord) = $\boxed{4}$

4.
Gradient of chord	= $\dfrac{\frac{1}{x + h} - \frac{1}{x}}{h}$
	= $\dfrac{\frac{x - (x + h)}{x(x + h)}}{h}$
	= $\dfrac{\frac{-h}{x(x + h)}}{h} = \dfrac{-1}{x(x + h)}$
Gradient of curve	= $\lim\limits_{h \to 0}$ (gradient of chord) = $\boxed{\dfrac{-1}{x^2}}$

5.
Gradient of chord	= $\dfrac{6(x + h) - (x + h)^2 - (6x - x^2)}{h}$
	= $\dfrac{6x + 6h - x^2 - 2xh - h^2 - 6x + x^2}{h}$
	= $\dfrac{6h - 2xh - h^2}{h} = 6 - 2x - h$
Gradient of curve	= $\lim\limits_{h \to 0}$ (gradient of chord) = $\boxed{6 - 2x}$

6.
Gradient of chord	= $\dfrac{3(r + h)^2 + 2(r + h) - (3r^2 + 2r)}{h}$
	= $\dfrac{3r^2 + 6rh + 3h^2 + 2r + 2h - 3r^2 - 2r}{h}$
	= $\dfrac{6rh + 3h^2 + 2h}{h} = 6r + 3h + 2$
Gradient of curve	= $\lim\limits_{h \to 0}$ (gradient of chord) = $\boxed{6r + 2}$

Section 5: Gradients, tangents & normals p 90

D5.1: Calculating gradients
1. 5 2. 48 3. $^1/_{2\sqrt{3}}$ 4. $^{-1}/_{16}$
5. -5 6. 4 7. $(2,6)$ 8. $(1,2)$ & $(-1,8)$
9. $(3,5)$ 10. $(^1/_3, ^4/_{27})$ & $(-1,0)$ 11. $(1,1)$
12. $(2, 3.5)$ 13. 0 & 6 14. $(4, -23^2/_3)$ & $(-3, 26^1/_2)$

D5.2: Tangents and normals
1. $y = 12x - 12$ 2. $y = 5x + 1$ 3. $y + x + 2 = 0$
4. $y = 4x - 4$ 5. $y = 20x - 35$ 7. $x + 5y - 5 = 0$

D5.3: Setting out more complex problems
1. $y = 3x - 2$ 2. $(3,9)$, $y = 6x - 9$ 3. $2y = x + 5$
4. $y = -10x + 20$; $(^4/_3, ^{20}/_3)$ 5. $(5,3)$

E5.4: Differentiation challenges
1. $(-4, -^1/_2)$ 2. $(0,7)$ 3. $3y + x = 2$; $3y = x + 1$; $(^1/_2, ^1/_2)$
4. $(-1, ^{71}/_4)$ & $-^1/_{27}$ 5. $k = ^{55}/_{27}$ & $-^1/_{27}$ 6. $PT = \sqrt{272}$, $PN = \sqrt{17}$

Section 6: Stationary values and ...   p 93

D6.1: Stationary values
1. (a) A to B and C to D   (b) B to C   (c) at B and at C
2. $x = 0$ 3. $x = 3$ 4. $x = \pm 2$ 5. -2.5 6. ± 2
7. $^{11}/_9$ & $^{43}/_9$

D6.2: Stationary values and turning points
1. Max at $(^3/_2, ^9/_4)$ 2. Min at $(2,1)$
3. P of I at $(0,0)$ 4. Min at $(0,0)$
5. P of I at $(0,5)$ 6. Min at $(-^1/_4, -^9/_8)$

D6.3: Maximum and minimum values of functions
1. 12 2. $^9/_8$ 3. 0 4. 1

E6.4: Max-min challenges
1. (i) 5.6 cm^{-1} (ii) 170 cm   2. (b) $x = 0, \pm\sqrt{8}$ (c) 3

Section 7: The second derivative p 97

D7.1: Meet the second derivative
1. 328   2. 6   3. −24   4. 594   5. 1.5

D7.2: The second derivative test
1. Max at (1,1), Min at (2,0)   2. P of I at (2,−3)
3. Max at (−1,−1) Min at (1,3)

D7.3: Problem solving with calculus
1. 18, 8; $^3/_4$ 2. $(8t − 4)$m/s^2 ; 0.5 s ; 0
3. 2.2 m/s, −7.6 m/s ; body's direction has been reversed
4. $^5/_2$; $^{-75}/_4$

E7.4: Challenging problems
1. (ii) $x = 3$, $h = 1.5$ 2. $[^{100}/_9$, $^{-500}/_{27}]$
3. (a) $2rh + ^1/_2\pi r^2 = 500$ (b) (i) 11.8 (ii) $^{1000}/_3$; min
4. (c) 1200 (d) $\dfrac{d^2S}{dt^2} > 0$ 5. $\sqrt[3]{(^{400}/_\pi)}$
6. 4.5 cm by 9 cm by 6 cm

Unit 6: Completing the Square

Section 1: Completed square form   p 103

D1.1: The basic technique
1. $(x + 3)^2 = (x + 3)(x + 3) = x^2 + 6x + 9$
2. $x^2 + 8x + 16$ 3. $x^2 − 2x + 1$ 4. $x^2 + 10x + 25$
5. $x^2 − 6x + 9$ 6. $(x + 3)^2$ 7. $(x +10)^2$
8. $(x − 6)^2$ 9. $(x − 9)^2$ 10. $... + 49 = (x +7)^2$
11. $... + 400 = (x − 20)^2$ 12. $... + 121 = (x − 11)^2$
13. $... + 144 = (x + 12)^2$ 14. $(x − 4)^2 − 16$
15. $(x − 5)^2 − 25$ 16. $(x − 1)^2 − 1$ 17. $(x + 15)^2 − 225$
18. $(x − 25)^2 − 625$ 19. $(x − 2)^2 − 1$ 20. $(x + 6)^2 − 44$
21. $(x − 7)^2 + 1$ 22. $(x − 9)^2 − 67$ 23. $(x − 10)^2 − 85$
24. $(x − 3)^2 − 8$

D1.2: When the coefficient of x is odd
1. $(x − ^5/_2)^2 − ^{25}/_4$ 2. $(x − ^9/_2)^2 − ^{81}/_4$ 3. $(x + ^{17}/_2)^2 − ^{289}/_4$
4. $(x − ^{11}/_2)^2 − ^{93}/_4$ 5. $(x + ^{15}/_2)^2 − ^{201}/_4$ 6. $(x − ^7/_2)^2 + ^3/_4$
7. $(x − ^1/_2)^2 + ^{19}/_4$ 8. $(x + ^{21}/_2)^2 − ^{453}/_4$ 9. $(x − ^3/_2)^2 + ^{15}/_4$

D1.3: When the coefficient of x^2 is not 1
1. $2(x − 2)^2 − 11$ 2. $3(x − ^9/_2)^2 − ^{243}/_4$
3. $2(x + 4)^2 − 29$ 4. $6(x − ^3/_2)^2 − 14$
5. $2(x + ^{11}/_2)^2 − 29$ 6. $5(x + 5)^2 − 121$
7. $3(x + ^{11}/_2)^2 − ^{217}/_{12}$ 8. $−2(x + 3)^2 − 27$
9. $−3(x − ^7/_6)^2 + ^{61}/_{12}$

Section 2: Maximum & minimum values p105

D2.1: Maximum and minimum values
1. $x = 8$, min value $= −3$ 2. $x = −1$, min value $= 5$
3. $x = 15$, min value $= 0$ 4. $x = 2$, max value $= 10$
5. $x = 1$, max value $= 5$ 6. $x = −2$, max value $= −2$

D2.2: Sketching quadratic curves
1. 2. 3.
4. $y = (x − 2)^2$ 5. $y = (x − 4)^2 − 3$ 6. $y = (x − ^5/_2)^2 + ^{15}/_4$
7. $y = (x + 6)^2 − 9$ 8. $y = 2(x − 5)^2 + 10$ 9. $y = 3(x + 1)^2 − 8$
10. $y = −(x − 2)^2 + 1$ 11. $y = −2(x − 2)^2 + 11$

Section 3: Solving quadratic equations p 106

D3.1: Solving equations in completed square form
1. 5,1   2. $−5 ± \sqrt{3}$ 3. 3.5, −0.5
4. 3.45, −1.45   5. −12.24, 0.24 6. −1.76, −6.24

D3.2: More complex equations
1. 3.68, −0.68   2. 1.9, 1.23   3. 0.94, −2.34
4. 1, −4.5   5. 1.3, −0.88   6. 0.6, 0.42

E3.4: Completed square challenges
1. (i) $A(p, p − p^2)$; $0 < p < 1$ (ii)$p = ^1/_2(\sqrt{5} − 1)$
2. $AB^2 = 2(p − 3)^2 + 2$ (i) $\sqrt{2}$ (ii) 3
   Simultaneous equations $\Rightarrow (x − 5)^2 = 0$
   $\Rightarrow$ only one point of intersection

Section 4: More quadratic inequalities p 108

D4.1: Simple quadratic inequalities
1. no solution   2. $x < −2$ & $x > 2$ 3. $−2 < x < 2$
4. all x 5. $x < −3$ & $x > 3$ 6. $−7 < x < 7$
7. no solution   8. $x < −\sqrt{2}$ & $x > \sqrt{2}$ 9. all x
10. $−9 < x < 1$ 11. no solution   12. $x < −2$ & $x > 16$
13. $x − 5 < −\sqrt{2}$ & $x − 5 > \sqrt{2}$
   $\Rightarrow x < 5 − \sqrt{2}$ & $x > 5 + \sqrt{2}$
14. $3 − \sqrt{5} < x < 3 + \sqrt{5}$ 15. −2.873 < x < 4.873
16. all x 17. no solution   18. $1 < x < 11$
19. $1.528 < x < 10.472$

D2 : But what if the quadratic does not factorise?
1. true for all x 2. true for no x 3. true for $x=2$
4. true for all x 5. no solution
6. $x > 2 + \sqrt[1]{2}$ & $x < 2 − \sqrt[1]{2}$ 7. $−1 < x < −^5/_2$
8. $−^5/_2 \le x \le −1$ 9. $−3 − \sqrt{(^2/_3)} \le x \le \sqrt{(^2/_3)} − 3$
10. $^1/_2 − ^3/\sqrt{20} < x < ^1/_2 + ^3/\sqrt{20}$

Unit 7: Integral calculus

Section 1: Reverse differentiation   p 112

D1.1: Differentiation in reverse
1. $2x$ 5. $3x^2$ 9. $4x^3$ 13. x^7
2. $2x^2$ 6. $4x^3$ 10. $5x^4$ 14. $^1/_7x^7$
3. $5x^2$ 7. $5x^3$ 11. $^1/_4x^4$ 15. $^1/_{10}x^{10}$
4. $^1/_2 x^2$ 8. $^1/_3x^3$ 12. $^5/_4x^4$ 16. $^1/_{13}x^{13}$
17. $y = x^9$ 18. $y = ^1/_9x^9$ 19. $y = ^5/_9x^9$ 20. $y = ^1/_{18}x^9$
21. $y = 3x^2$ 22. $y = ^1/_2x^2$ 23. $y = ^1/_4x^2$ 24. $y = ^3/_8x^2$
25. $y = ^3/_{11}x^{11}$ 26. $y = ^5/_7x^7$ 27. $y = x^7$ 28. $y = ^1/_6x^6$
29. $y = ^1/_{n+1}x^{n+1}$ 30. $y = ^a/_{p+1}x^{p+1}$ 31. $y = 3x$ 32. $y = kx$

D.1.2: Applications of reverse differentiation
1. $y = 4x − x^3 + 2$ 2. $y = ^5/_4x^4 − ^9/_4$ 3. $p = 7t − t^3 + 4$
4. $s = 10t^2 − t^3$ 5. 26.5 cm^2

Section 2: Integration   p 114

D2.1: Integrating powers of x
1. $^1/_5x^5 + c$ 2. $^1/_{13}x^{13} + c$ 3. $−^1/_3x^{−3} + c$
4. $^2/_7x^{7/2} + c$ 5. $x^4 − ^1/_3x^3 + c$ 6. $4x + x^{−1} + c$
7. $^5/_4x^4 − x^2 + c$ 8. $^4/_5x^{5/2} + ^2/_5x^{−5/2} + c$
9. $x^4 − x^{−1} − 3x + c$ 10. $5x − ^2/_7x^{7/2} + c$
11. $−1/2x^2 + c$ 12. $^3/_4x^{4/3} + c$ 13. $−2/x + c$
14. $−3/(7x^7) + c$ 15. $−1/(9x^3) + c$ 16. $−1/x^3 + c$
17. $^2/_3x^{3/2} + c$ 18. $2\sqrt{x} + c$ 19. $^2/_3x^{1/2} + c$
20. $6x^{1/2} + c$ 21. $^5/_3x^3 + 1/x + 2x^2 + c$
22. $−1/x^3 + 1/2x^2 − ^1/_4x^4 + c$ 23. $^2/_3x^{3/2} − ^2/_5x^{5/2} + c$

D2.2: Integrating products and quotients ...

1. $x^3 + x^2 - x + c$
2. $^1/_6x^6 - ^3/_5x^5 + c$
3. $^1/_3x^3 + 1/x + c$
4. $^1/_3x^3 + 5x^2 + 25x + c$
5. $^1/_3x^3 + 2x - 1/x + c$
6. $^1/_6x^3 + ^3/_2x - 1/2x + c$
7. $^1/_3x^4 - ^9/_2x^2 + c$
8. $-1/x + 5/2x^2 + 14/3x^3 + c$
9. $^2/_5x^{5/2} + 2x^{3/2} - 2x^{1/2} + c$
10. $^1/_2x^2 + 4x^{1/2} - 1/x + c$
11. $^2/_7x^{7/2} + ^8/_5x^{5/2} - ^{10}/_3x^{3/2} + c$
12. $2x^{3/2} + 4x^{1/2} + 10/x^{1/2} + c$

P2.3: Miscellaneous Practice Exercise

1. $^1/_4x^4 - x^3 + c$
2. $^1/_5x^5 - 5/2x^2 - 10x + c$
3. $^1/_2x^2 + ^2/_3x^{3/2} + 2x^{1/2} + c$
4. $x^3 + 5x^2 - 8x + c$
5. $3x^3 + 18x - 9/x + c$
6. $^2/_3x^{3/2} + 2x^{1/2} + 12/x^{1/2} + c$
7. $x^4 + ^{20}/_3x^3 + ^{25}/_2x^2 + c$
8. $6x^{3/2} + 6x + 2x^{1/2} + c$
9. $^5/_3x^3 - 1/x^3 - 12/x^{1/3} + c$

Section 3: Definite integrals   p 116

D3.1: Definite integrals

1. $^1/_5$
2. $443^1/_3$
3. 42
4. $-^3/_8$
5. 0
6. $8^2/_3$
7. $^5/_6$
8. $10^1/_2$
9. $^{-13}/_{12}$
10. $21^1/_3$
11. $27^3/_4$

Section 4: Areas under curves   p 117

D4.1: Area under a curve

1. 18
2. 80
3. $^4/_3$
4. $2^2/_3$
5. $^4/_3$
6. $^8/_3(3\sqrt{3} - 1)$
7. (a) $(2,0)$ (b) $^4/_3$
8. $20^5/_6$

D4.2: The sign of the area

1. (a) $10^2/_3$ (b) $-2^1/_3$ (c) $8^1/_3$
   (d) $A_1 = \int_{-4}^{0} (4x - x^2)dx$ (e) $A_2 = -\int_{4}^{5} (4x - x^2)dx$
2. $^1/_2 < x < 4$; $14^7/_{24}$
3. $3^1/_{12}$
4. (a) $13^1/_6$ (b) $\int_{0}^{5} (3x - x^2)dx = A_1 - A_2$ not $A_1 + A_2$
5. $41^1/_3$

D4.3: Areas between curves and lines

1. (a) $(1,1)$
2. $^4/_{15}$
3. $10^2/_3$
4. $^{16\sqrt{2}}/_{15}$

D4.4: Area between a curve and the y-axis

1. Step 1: $x = ^1/_{\sqrt{3}}\sqrt{y}$
2. $^{14\sqrt{2}}/_3$

E4.5: Miscellaneous areas

1. (a) $y = 6x + 15$ (b) 4
2. $2^{13}/_{24}$
3. $32^3/_4$

Section 5: Improper integrals   p 121

D5.1: Introducing improper integrals

1. 2
2. does not exist
3. $^1/_2$
4. does not exist
5. does not exist

Unit 8: Trigonometry

Section 1: Sin, cos, tan for angles ...   p 124

D1.1: Values for sin and cos without a calculator

1. $-0.93, 0.34$
2. $-0.87, -0.5$
3. $0.5, -0.87$
4. $-0.64, -0.77$
5. $0.93, -0.34$
6. $-0.77, 0.64$
7. $-0.17, -0.98$
8. $0.5, -0.87$
9. $-0.93, 0.34$
10. $-1, 0, 0$
11. $\tan 330° = \sin 330° \div \cos 330°$

D1.2: Calculating angles

1. $60°, 300°$
2. $35°, 215°$
3. $72°, 108°$
4. $66°, 294°$
5. $15°, 165°$
6. $40°, 320°$
7. $70°, 250°$
8. $23°, 157°$
9. $60°, 300°, 420°, 660°$
10. $85°, -95°$
11. $\pm66°, \pm294°$
12. $32°, 148°, -212°, -328°$
13. $120°, 240°$
14. $135°, 315°$
15. $55°, 125°$
16. $78°, 282°$
17. $240°, 300°$
18. $135°, 225°$
19. $125°, 305°$
20. $255°, 285°$

Section 2: Graphs of sinx, cosx & tanx   p 127

D2.1: Graphs of sinx, cosx and tanx

1. (a) $A(-180,0) B(360,0)$ $C(90, 1) D(270,-1) E(-90,-1)$

(b) 1 (c) -1
2. (a) $P(270,0) Q(450,0) R(-90,0) S(0,1) T(180,-1)(360,0)$
   (b) 1 (c) -1
3. (a) $(0,0)$ $(180,0)$ $(360,0)$ (b) $(540,0)$
4. $360°$
5. $360°$
6. (a) The graph of $y = 2\sin x$ is the graph of $y = \sin x$ stretched by a factor of 2 parallel to the y-axis.
   (b) 2 (c) -2 (d) $360°$
7. (a) The graph of $y = 1 + ^1/_2\cos x$ is the graph of $y = \cos x$ stretched by a factor of $^1/_2$ parallel to the y-axis and moved 1 unit in the +ve y-direction
   (b) 1.5 (c) 0.5

D2.2: Using graphs to solve trig equations

1. $30°, 150°$
2. $-150°, -30°, 210°, 330°$
3. $\pm60°, 300°$
4. $\pm120°, 240°$
5. $45°, 135°$
6. $-135°, -45°, 225°, 315°$
7. $\pm45°, 315°$
8. $\pm135°, 225°$
9. $15°, 165°$
10. $45°, 215°$
11. $\pm50°, 310°$
12. $10°, 170°$
13. $130°, 310°$
14. $-160°, -20°, 200°, 340°$
15. $148°, 328°$
16. $\pm25°, 335°$
17. $\pm160°, 200°$
18. $-115°, -65°, 245°, 295°$
19. (a) 2.5 (b) 3.5
(c) $(270,1.5)$ $(-90,1.5)$ (d) $30°, 150°$ (e) $390°$

D2.3: More sin, cos, tan graphs

1. (a) (b) $180°$
2. (a) (b) $720°$
3. (a) (b) $60°$
4.
5.
6.
7. (a) $A(30,0)$ $D(300,0)$ (b) $a = 2$ $b = 60$

Section 3: Equations with complex angles   p130

D3.1: Solving equations with complex angles

1. $30°, 150°, 210°, 330°$
2. $22.5°, 112.5°, 202.5°, 292.5°$
3. (a) Youslas should have found all the possible values of $2x$ in the range $0° \le 2x \le 720°$ Instead, Youslas found one value of $2x$, halved it to give one value of x. Then Youslas invented the other values of x.
   (b) $0° \le 2x \le 720°$ (essential)
   $2x = 45°, 315°, 405°, 675°$
   $\Rightarrow x = 22.5°, 157.5°, 202.5°, 337.5°$
4. $22.85°, 157.15°, 202.85°, 337.15°$
5. $67.5°, 157.5$
6. $10°, 50°, 130°, 170°$
7. $120°, 600°$
8. $135°, 675°$
9. $105°, 345°$
10. $165°, 345°$
11. $67.5°, 112.5°$
12. $10°, 97°, 30°, 217°, 250°, 337°$
13. $55°, 75°, 235°, 255°$

Section 4: Exact trig values   p131

D4.1: Useful values

1. $\sqrt{2}$
2. 0.5
3. $\sqrt{2}$
4. $\sqrt{3}$
5. 0
6. 2
7. 2
8. 1
9. 1.5
10. 2
11. $30°, 150°$
12. $135°, 315°$
13. $45°, 315°$
14. $60°, 120°$
15. $60°, 240°$
16. $45°, 225°$
17. $150°, 330°$
18. $0°$
19. $60°, 180°$
20. $22.5°, 112.5°, 202.5°, 287.5°$

Section 5: Fundamental identities   p132

D5.1: Trigonometric identities

1. $\dfrac{\sin\theta}{\cos\theta} = \dfrac{^o/_h}{^a/_h} = \dfrac{o}{a} = \tan\theta$
2. $\sin^2\theta + \cos^2\theta = (^o/_h)^2 + (^a/_h)^2 = \dfrac{o^2 + a^2}{h^2} = \dfrac{h^2}{h^2} = 1$

D5.2: Simplifying trigonometric expressions
1. $2 - 3\sin^2\theta$ 2. $5\sin\theta - 1 + \sin^2\theta$ 3. 1
4. $2 \div \cos^2\theta$ 5. 1

D5.3: Solving quadratic trig equations
1. 18.4°, 198.4°, 71.6°, 251.6°
2. 30°, 150°, 41.8°, 138.2°
3. 131.8°, 228.2° 66.4°, 293.6°
4. 14.5°, 165.5°, 203.6°, 336.4°

D5.4: Using fundamental identities to solve equations
1. 60°, 180°, 300° 2. 0°, 120°, 240°, 360°
3. 14.5°, 90°, 165.5° 4. 90° 5. 33.7°, 231.7°
6. −31.7°, 58.3°

Section 6: Radians and trig equations p134

D6.1: Working in radians
1. $\frac{\pi}{6}, \frac{11\pi}{6}$ 2. $\frac{\pi}{10}, \frac{9\pi}{10}$ 3. $\frac{\pi}{4}, \frac{5\pi}{4}$
4. $\frac{\pi}{4}, \frac{7\pi}{4}$ 5. $\frac{7\pi}{6}, \frac{11\pi}{6}$ 6. $\frac{\pi}{3}, \frac{4\pi}{3}$
7. $\frac{\pi}{9}, \frac{17\pi}{9}$ 8. $\frac{2\pi}{9}, \frac{11\pi}{9}$ 9. $\frac{\pi}{3}, \frac{4\pi}{3}, \frac{8\pi}{3}, \frac{10\pi}{3}$
10. $\pm\frac{\pi}{6}$ 11. $\frac{\pi}{5}, \frac{4\pi}{5}, \frac{-6\pi}{5}, \frac{-9\pi}{5}$
12. $\frac{5\pi}{6}, \frac{11\pi}{6}, \frac{17\pi}{6}$ 13. $\frac{4\pi}{3}, \frac{5\pi}{3}, \frac{-\pi}{3}, \frac{-2\pi}{3}$
14. $\frac{2\pi}{5}, \frac{7\pi}{5}, \frac{-3\pi}{5}, \frac{-8\pi}{5}$

D6.2: Trig equations with complex angles in radians
1. $\frac{\pi}{6}, \frac{5\pi}{6}, \frac{7\pi}{6}, \frac{11\pi}{6}$ 2. $\frac{\pi}{12}, \frac{\pi}{4}, \frac{3\pi}{4}, \frac{11\pi}{12}, \frac{17\pi}{12}, \frac{19\pi}{12}$
3. $\frac{3\pi}{2}$ 4. $\frac{\pi}{3}, 2\pi, \frac{7\pi}{3}$
5. $\frac{7\pi}{20}, \frac{19\pi}{20}, \frac{27\pi}{20}, \frac{29\pi}{20}, \frac{37\pi}{20}, \frac{39\pi}{20}$ 6. $\frac{\pi}{4}, \frac{3\pi}{4}, \frac{5\pi}{4}, \frac{7\pi}{4}$

Unit 9: Sequences and Series

Section 1: Introducing sequences ... p 137

D1.1: What is a sequence ? What is a series ?
1. (a) 10 (b) 8 (c) 5 + 10 + 15 + 20 + 25 (d) 275 c
2. (a) 1, 3, 6, 10, 15, 21 (b) 1 + 3 + 6 (c) 10 (d) 56

D1.2: Rules for sequences
1. (a) $\wedge\wedge\wedge\wedge$ (b) 7, 11, 15, 19, 23, 27
(c) add 4 to the last number
2. (a) 1, 2, 4, 8, 16 (b) double the last number
3. (a) | 5 | 9 | 13 | 17 | 21 | 25 | (b) ○ +4 to the last number
   | 0 | 4 | 12 | 24 | 40 | 60 | ● 4 x the next Δ number

E1.3: Extending the idea
1. (a) 1, 5, 13, 25, 41, 61, 85
(b) add 4 more than you added last time
2. (a) 1, 5, 12, 22, 35, 51, 70
(b) add 3 more than you added last time
3. (a) 1, 6, 15, 28, 45, 66, 91
(b) add 4 more than you added last time
4. 1, 8, 21, 40, 65, 96 5. 17, 19

Section 2: Generating sequences p 139

D2.1: Using functions to generate sequences
1. 2, 4, 6, 8 2. (a) 21 (b) 51 (c) 401 (d) 301
3. −2, 1, 6, 13 4. 20 & 29 5. 0 & −4
6. 0 & 70 7. 15, 7.5, 5, 3.75, 3
8. 0, 2, 6 & 72 9. −1, 1, −1, 1, ; −1
10. 1, −1, 1, −1, 1; 1 11. −3, 9, −27, 81

D2.2: Finding the general term of a sequence
1. (a) 5,7,9,11,13,15 (b) $u_r = 2r + 3$ (c) 87
2. (a) 1,4,7,10,13,16 (b) $u_r = 3r - 2$ (c) 43
3. (a) 8,13,18,23,28,33 (b) $u_r = 5r + 3$ (c) 103
4. (a) −4,0,4,8,12,16 (b) $u_r = 4r - 8$ (c) 64
5. (a) 1,−1,−3,−5,−7,−9 (b) $u_r = 3 - 2r$ (c) −59
6. (a) 3,9,27,81,243,729 (b) $u_r = 3^r$ (c) 19 683

7. (a) 5,15,45,135,405,1215 (b) $u_r = 5 \times 3^{r-1}$
(c) 820 125
8. (a) 6, 26, 126, 626, 3 126, 15 626 (b) $u_r = 5^r + 1$
(c) 390 626
9. (a) −1, 1, −1, 1, −1, 1 (b) $u_r = (-1)^r$ (c) −1
10. (a) 1,4,9,16,25,36 (b) $u_r = r^2$ (c) 121
11. (a) 3,6,11,18,27,38 (b) $u_r = r^2 + 2$ (c) 146
12. (a) 2,6,12,20,30,42 (b) $u_r = r(r + 1)$ (c) 420
13. (a) 4,16,64,256,1024,4096 (b) $u_r = 4^r$ (c) 65 536
14. (a) 1,4,16,64,256,1024 (b) $u_r = 4^{r-1}$ (c) 262 144
15. (a) 1,2,4,8,16,32 (b) $u_r = 2^{r-1}$ (c) 256

D2.3: nth term challenge
1. (i) 4, 9 (ii) $t_n + t_{n+1} = \ldots = (n + 1)^2 =$ perfect square

Section 3: Arithmetic Progressions p141

D3.1: Arithmetic progressions
1. (a) Y (b) N (c) Y (d) Y (e) N
2 (a) −5, −2, 1, 4 (b) $-5 + (r - 1)\,3$ (c) $-5 + 3r - 3 = 3r - 8$ (d) 22
3. (a) $4r - 1$; 39 (b) $7 - 3r$; −23 4. (a) 2, 5 (b) $5r - 3$ (c) 97
5. 15, 10, 5 6. (a) 27 (b) 11 (c) 36
7. $199ab$ 8. 4,6 9. 3, 24

D3.2: The sum of an A.P. given its first and last term
1. (b) 210 2. 1875 3. 29 ; 1 537 4. 36 ; 4770
5. 10 ; 40 6. 10100 7. 1404 8. 116

D3.3: The sum of an A.P. when the last term is unknown
1. 825 2. 220 3. 430 4. 8 5. 7

D3.4: A mixture of problems
1. (a) 47 (b) 126.9 km 2. (a) 304 ft (b) 1024 ft
3. 15, 23, 31, 39, 47 4. 5
5. (a) 10 years (b) 3 404 pages

D3.5: Sums of natural numbers
1. 5050 2. 3775 4. 11325 5. 4775

E3.6: A.P. Challenges
1. $d = 2, a = 4$; 460 2. −350 3. 179 m
4. (a) £127 056.95 (b) £2 705.70

Section 4: The sigma (Σ) for series p145

D4.1: Meet Σ
1. 3 + 5 + 7 + 9 + 11 + 13 2. 2 − 1 − 4 − 7 − 10 − 13 − 16
3. $43 + 47 + \ldots + (3 + 4n)$ 4. $\frac{8}{1} + \frac{11}{3} + \frac{14}{5} + \frac{17}{7}$
5. 2 + 2 + 2 6. $2 + 0 + 0 + 2 + \ldots + (4n^2 - 2n)$
7. $24 + 27 + \ldots + 45$ 8. 2 + 6 + 12 + 20 + 30 + 42
9. $\frac{1}{4} + \frac{1}{5} + \frac{1}{6}$ 10. $16 + 54 + \ldots + 2n^3$
11. $\frac{3}{4} + \frac{4}{5} + \ldots + \frac{2n}{2n + 1}$ 12. $2 + 3 + 4 + \ldots + n$
13. $\sum_1^{10} 3r$ 14. $\sum_1^{n} \frac{1}{r}$ 15. $\sum_1 (2r-1)^4$ 16. $\sum_1^{15} \frac{2r}{2r + 3}$
17. A : Y B : Y C : N

D4.2: Alternating positive and negative terms
1. 1,2,3,4,5 2. −1,−2,−3,−4,−5 3. −1,1,−1,1,−1
4. 1,−1,1,−1 5. 1,−1,1,−1,1... 6. −1,2,−3,4,−5
7. Alternates −, +, −, +, ... 8. Alternates +, −, +, −, ...

D4.3: Evaluating sums given in Σ form
1. 34 2. 3115 3. 178 4. 1325 5. 3 6. 18

Section 5: Geometric Progressions p147

D5.1: Geometric progressions
1. (a) 32 (b) 512 (c) 2^{r-1} (d) 1.68 x 10⁷ → 1.68×10^7
2. (a) 4 ; 3072 ; $3 \times 4^{n-1}$ (b) $\frac{1}{2}$; 2 ; $64 \times \left(\frac{1}{2}\right)^{n-1} = 2^{7-n}$
(c) 2; 160; $5 \times 2^{n-1}$

3. (a) $\pm12, \pm108$ (b) $\pm27, \pm3$ (c) $20, -40$
4. (a) $20l, 10l, 5l, 2.5l, 1.25l$ (b) $0,10l,15l,17.5l,18.75l$
   (c) (a) is a GP whose common ratio is $\frac{1}{2}$
       (b) is not a GP because there is no common ratio
5. (a) 6   (b) 6   (c) 9

D5.2: The sum of a GP
1. 242   2. 2046   3. 55   4. 1333
5. (a) 24, 12, 6, 3, ; 0.046875 cm   (b) 47.953125 cm
6. 215.3°   7. 2 & 1.5 or –10 &–1.5   8. 6
9. $\frac{3}{2}$ or $-\frac{5}{2}$ 10. (a) £7 346.64   (b) £54.58

D5.3: The sum of an infinite GP
1. (a) $|r| = 0.5$ which is < 1 so series converges   (b)100
2. (a) $\frac{3}{4}$ (b) $\frac{25}{4}$ (c) $\frac{10}{9}$ (d) $\frac{2}{3}$ (e) $1/(1 - x)$
3. (a) $|y| < 1$ (b) $|y| < \frac{1}{2}$(c) $y^2 > 1$ or $y < -1$ & $y > 1$
4. (a) $\frac{2}{3}$ 5. (a) 75.5 curie-hours
   (b) 2170.8 curie-hours (c) 2250 curie-hours
6. (a) $10 \times (\frac{2}{3})^n$ (b) 58.96 m   (c) 60 m
7. (a) $\dfrac{p}{1-p}$ (b) $\dfrac{q}{1-q}$

Section 6: Sums of powers of natural numbers p150
D6.1: Standard formulae
1. 4900   2. 405   3. 715   4. 14175
5. 3630   6. 42075
7. (a) 650 (b) 845 000 (c) 85095 (d) 1 800 000
8. 7500   10. $\frac{1}{2}n(2n + 1)(4n + 1)$

D6.2: Sums of series with rth terms $ar^3 + br^2 + cr + d$
1. $n(n + 2)$ 2. $\frac{1}{2}n(n + 1)(n + 2)$
3. $\frac{1}{6}n(2n^2 - 9n + 13)$ 4. $\frac{1}{3}n(4n^2 + 6n + 5)$
5. $4r; 2n(n + 1)$ 6. $(2r-1)^2 ; \frac{1}{3}n(4n - 1)^2$
7. $(r + 1)(r + 2) ; \frac{1}{3}n(n^2 + 6n + 1)$
8. $\frac{1}{2}n(6n^2 - 3n - 1)$ 9. $27r^3 ; \frac{27}{4}n^2 (n + 1)^2$
10. $16r^2 - 1; \frac{1}{3}n(16n^2 + 24n + 5)$ 11. $3, 7, 11 ; 4r - 1$

Unit 10: Functions

Section 1: Function notation p154
D1.1: Notation and terminology
1. 9 ; $2; 5; t^2 + 5; \sin x + 5$ 2. $24 ; 3 ; -6 ; \frac{24}{x}$
3. $6; 0 ; 10 ; 20 ; 6 - 2x ; 6 - 4x ; 6 - 6x ; 6 - 10t$
4. $0 ; \sqrt{10} ; 2 ; \sqrt{18}$ or $3\sqrt{2}$
5. (a) 0 ; 0   (b) because at least 2 elements in the
   domain have the same image (2 & 5)
6. (a) 6 ; 6 ; 51; 51 (b) {3, 6, 11, 18} (c){2, 3, 6, 11}
   (d) one-one   (e) many–one   (f) many–one
7. (a) one-one   (b) {2, 11, 26}   (c) $t = 5$
8. (a) $0 ; 7 ; -\frac{1}{2} ; 63$ (b) $x = 5$

D1.2: Composite functions (functions of functions)
1. (a) $\cos(3x - 1)$ (b) $3\cos x - 1$ (c) $9x - 4$
2. (a) $x^2 + 1$ (b) $(x + 1)^2$ (c) x^4 (d) $x + 2$
3. (a) $2x - 3$ (b) $2x - 6$ (c) $4x$(d) $x - 6$
   (e) $\sin x - 3$ (f) $\sin (x - 3)$ (g) $\sin 2x - 3$
   (h) $\sin 2(x - 3)$ (or $2x - 6$)   (i) $2 \sin x - 6$
   (j) $2x - 9$ (k) $4x - 6$ (l) $4x - 12$
4. (a) $x^2 + 5$ (b) $(x + 5)^2$ (c) $\cos(\cos x)$
   (d) $x + 10$ (e) $\cos x + 5$ (f) $\cos(x + 5)$
   (g) $\cos^2 x + 5$ (h) $\cos^2(x + 5)$ (i) $(\cos x + 5)^2$
   (j) $\cos^4 x$ (k) $\cos(x + 10)$ (l) $(x + 5)^2 + 5$

D1.3: Combining functions
1. $4x + 3$ 2. $3x^2 + 9x$ 3. x^6 4. $3x + 3$
5. $x^3 + 3$ 6. $x + 6$ 7. $2x - 3$ 8. $\cos x + 3$

9. $3x^4$ 10. $3x^3$ 11. $\cos x + x + 3$
12. $\cos(x + 3)$ 13. $3x^3 + 3$ 14. $3\cos^3 x$ 15. $9\cos x$

Section 2: Inverse functions p 157
D2.1 : Inverse functions
1. (a) $f^{-1}(x) = \frac{x+7}{3}$ (b) $g^{-1}(x) = 4x$ (c) $h^{-1}(x) = \frac{1}{15}x$
   (d) $k^{-1}(x) = \frac{3}{2}x$
2. (a) {2,3,6}   (b)$f^{-1}(x) = x - 3$ (c) {2,3,6} {–1,0,3}
3. (a) {0,–1,8,35} (b) {–1,3,15}   (c) {–1,0,3,6}
   (d) {0,–1,8,35} ; {–1,0,3,6}   (e) $\sqrt{x+1}$

D2.2 : Inverses of more complex functions
1. $f^{-1}(x) = \frac{1}{2}(x - 1)$ 2. $f^{-1}(x) = \frac{1}{3}x + 2$
3. $f^{-1}(x) = \frac{1}{3}(3x + 2)$ 4. $f^{-1}(x) = \frac{1}{3}(3x + 1)$
5. $f^{-1}(x) = 10 - x$ 6. $f^{-1}(x) = \frac{1}{5}(5x - 15)$
7. $f^{-1}(x) = 3 - \frac{1}{2}x$ 8. $f^{-1}(x) = \frac{3x+1}{x-1}$
9. $f^{-1}(x) = \frac{1}{2}(3x - 7)$

D2.3: Inverses of quadratic functions
1. $f^{-1}(x) = \sqrt{[\frac{1}{2}(x - 3)]}$ 2. $f^{-1}(x) = -3 + \sqrt{[x + 12]}$
3. $f^{-1}(x) = 7 + \sqrt{[x + 44]}$ 4. $f^{-1}(x) = -6 + \sqrt{[x + 36]}$
5. $f^{-1}(x) = 5 + \sqrt{[\frac{1}{2}(x + 45)]}$

Section 3: Graphs and functions p 159
D3.1 : Interval notation for continuous functions
1. $[0,\infty[$ 2. $[2,5]$ 3. $]-1,1]$ 4. $]3,21[$
5. $]-\infty,7[$ 6. $]-\infty,-3]$
D3.2 : Representing mappings & functions graphically
1. (a) $x = 0$ (b) -2 (c) $[-2,2]$
2. (a) $x = 1$ (b) $(1,4)$ (c) 4 (d) $[-1,4]$; $[-5,4]$
3. (a) $]-1,3]$ (b) $[-\frac{9}{4},4]$

4. (a)   (b) $[0,9]$ (c) Yes   (d) Yes
5. (a)   (b) $[0,9]$ (c) No   (d) No
6. (a)   (b) $[1,\infty[$ (c) Yes   (d) Yes
7. (a)   (b) $[0,32]$ (c) Yes   (d) Yes
8. (a)   (b) $[-4,32]$ (c) No   (d) No
9. (a)   (b) $[-9,7]$ (c) No   (d) No
10.(a)   (b) $[-8,27]$ (c) Yes   (d) Yes

D3.3 : Graphs of inverse functions
1.   2.   3. $[1,0[$
4. $[0,1]$ 5. $[-1,1]$
6. Yes $[0,\infty[$, $[0,\infty[$ 7. No – not 1–1
8. Yes $[1,10]$ $[0,3]$ 9. Yes $[-1,8]$ $[0,3]$
10. (a) $A(\sqrt6,0)$ $B(2,2)$ (b) $[0,\infty[$ $]-\infty,6]$
(c) $\sqrt{6-x}$ (d) $]-\infty,6]$ $[0,\infty[$(e) $x = 2$ (at B)

E3.4 : Function challenges

1. $(2x + 1)^3$, $2x^3 + 1$, $\cos(2x + 1)$, $2\cos x + 1$, $(2x^3 + 1)^3$, $\frac{x-1}{2}$, $4x + 3$

2. $\dfrac{x-2}{1-x}$ or $\dfrac{2-x}{x-1}$ | 3. (a) A $(-3,0)$ B$(0,-3)$
   (b) $-\mathcal{R}$, $x \neq 1$ (c) $ff(x) = x$
   (d) $f^{-1}(x) = \dfrac{x+3}{x-1}$ (e) domain & range both R, $x \neq 1$

4. (a) x (b) $f'(x) = \dfrac{2x+3}{x-2}$ (c) $2 \pm \sqrt{7}$

5. $a = 3$, $b = 1$
   (ii) vertex is at $(3,1)$
   (iii)
   (iv) 2

6. (i) *see sketch*
   (ii) $f^{-1}(x) = \frac{1}{6}(\frac{1}{x} - 5)$;
   domain $x > 0$ range $f(x) \geq 0$
   (iii) assume it has roots and show that
   this leads to $5 = 11$, which cannot be true $\Rightarrow$ no roots

---

Section 4: Odd and even functions   p 163

D4.1 : Odd and even functions
1. even 2. even 3. even 4. odd 5. odd
6. even 7. odd 8. odd 9. neither 10. neither

D4.2 : Odd, even and periodic functions
1.   2.

Section 5: Locating roots of equations p 164

D5.1 : Location of roots by change of sign
1. $-1, 0$ & $1,2$ 2. $k = -3, 0,2$
3. $f(z) = -1$, $f(3) = 20 \Rightarrow$ change of sign $\Rightarrow$ root in $[2,3]$
   Root = 2.06 to 2d.p. (Working must be shown)
4. 0 & 1

Unit 11: Polynomials

Section 1: Working with polynomials   p 167

D1.1: Working with polynomials – good habits
1. $7x^3 + 3x^2 - 7x + 9$ 2. $2x^4 - 7x^3 + 3x^2 + 2x - 5$
3. $-7x^3 + 3x^2 - 3x - 1$
4. $21x^5 - 35x^4 + 22x^3 + 25x^2 - 33x + 20$
5. $14x^6 + 17x^5 + 10x^4 - 6x^3 + 15x^2$
6. $2x^4 - 7x^3 + 6x^2 - 3x - 1$ 7. $6x^4 - 2x^3 + 12x^2 - 9x + 2$
8. $5x^5 - 8x^3 + 7x^2 + 3x - 7$ 9. $x^6 - 1$ 10. $-14, -20$
11. $-1, 11$ 12. $-11, -35$ 13. $19, 4$

D2 : Division of polynomials
1. 23   2. 103   3. 20   4. 10   5. $3x + 1$; 2
6. $2x^2 + x + 4$; 9 7. $x^2 - 4x + 16$; -48
8. $x^3 - x^2 - x + 4$; -5 9. $x + 3$; 20
10. $\frac{1}{2}x^3 - \frac{5}{4}x^2 - \frac{5}{8}x + \frac{9}{16}$; $\frac{9}{16}$

Section 2: The Factor Theorem   p 170

D2.1 : Meet the Factor Theorem
1. Yes 2. No 3. No 4. Yes 5. Yes 6. No

D2.2 : Factorising using the Factor Theorem
1. $(x - 1)^2(x + 3)$ 2. $(x - 2)(x^2 - 2x + 4)(x + 1)$
3. $(x - 3)(x + 3)(x^2 + x + 1)$ 4. $(x - 1)(x - 2)(x^2 + 4)$
5. $(x + 1)(x - 2)(2x - 1)$ 6. $(x - 1)(3x + 1)(x^2 + 2)$

D2.3 : Using the factor theorem to determine unknown coefficients
1. 2 2. 8 ; $x + 4$ 3. -1 4. 6 ; 3 5. 7 6. $-1,-30$; $x+5$

E2.4: Factor Challenges
1. (a) $x(x + 1)(x - 2)(x - 6)$(b)
(c) $x \leq -1$ & $2 \leq x \leq 6$
2. $p = \pm 3$; $3(x - 1)(x + 1)^2$; $-3(x + 3)(x - 1)^2$

Section 3: Identities   p 172

D3.1 : Polynomial identities
1. $p = -7$, $q = 49$ 2. $u = -5$, $v = 17$
3. (a) $x = 2$ and 3 (b) $a = -2$ $b = -3$

D3.2 : Equating coefficients
1. $A = 2$, $B = 1$ 2. $A = 5$, $B = 1$ 3. $a = 2$, $b = 8$
4. $a = 2$, $b = -3$; $(x^2 - x + 2)(x - 1)(x + 3)$
5. $4(x - 1)(x - 2) - (x - 3)(x - 1) + 2(x - 2)(x - 3)$

D3.3: Perfect squares and cubics
1. $a = -2$, $b = 1$ 2. $a = 5$
3. $(x + 2)(x^2 - 2x + 4)$ 4. $(x + y)(x^2 - xy + y^2)$
5. $A = B = 1$

REVISION

Unit 2: Quadratic Equations and Expression
1. (a) $4x - 10 > 32$ (b) $x(x - 5) < 104$ (c) $10.5 < x < 13$
2. $x(x - 4)(x + 4)$ 3. $(x - 1)(x + 4)$
4. $k > 12$ & $k < -12$ 5. $x > \frac{2}{3}$ & $x < -1$
6. $-3 < a < 3$ 7. (i) 3.7 (ii) 310 months

Unit 3: Coordinate Geometry and Graphs
1. $(8,2)$ 2. (a) $7x + 5y - 18 = 0$ (b) $\frac{162}{35}$
3. $2y = x + 4$ 4. (a) $y = -\frac{3}{4}x + \frac{5}{2}$
5. $n = -1, -3, -5$; -3 6. $(\frac{25}{9}, \frac{5}{3})$; $m = -7$

7. (a) (i)   (ii)
    $-3a$ a $-2a$ $2a$

   (iii)   (b)
   $-a$ $\frac{1}{2}a$ a $-2a$ $-a$ a $2a$

Unit 4: Surds, Powers, Simultaneous Equations, Radians
1. (a) $y = \frac{4}{3}x + \frac{2}{3}$ (b) $x = -\frac{5}{3}$ $y = -\frac{14}{9}$
2. (a) $\frac{1}{49}$ (b) $\frac{1}{2}\sqrt{x}$
3. (i) $x = 3$, $y = 2$ only (ii) line is a tangent to the curve
4. (b) $r = 5$, $A_{max} = 25$

Unit 5: Differential Calculus
1. (a) $6x^2 - 2x + 6$ (b) $(0,-3)$ & $(\frac{1}{5}, -\frac{28}{27})$
2. Min at $(0,0)$, Max at $(4,32)$; $x < 0$, $x > 4$; $y = 12x - 8$
4. (a) $P = 2x + 4y + \pi x$ (b) $A = 4xy + \frac{1}{2}\pi x^2$
   (d) $x = 14$, $y = 7$ (e) 700 m^2

Unit 6: Completing the square
1. (a) $-6 < x < 6$ (b) $y = (x + 4)^2 - 7$
   (c) change of sign $\Rightarrow$ $1.6 < \alpha < 1.7$
2. $AB^3 = 2(p - 3)^2 + 2$ (i) $\sqrt{2}$ (ii) 3
   simultaneous equations $\Rightarrow (x - 5)^2 = 0$
   $\Rightarrow$ only one point of intersection

Unit 7: Integral Calculus
1. (b) P$(-1,5)$ Q$(2,1)$
2. (a) $\frac{3}{2}x^{-1/2} + 2x^{-3/2}$ (b) $2x^{3/2} - 8x^{1/2} + c$
   (c) A = 6, B = -2 3. $2\sqrt{3}$

Unit 8: Trigonometry
1. $12.8°$, $80.5°$, $132.8°$
2. Points of intersection on graph
   $x = 30, 210$; graphs 'squashed' by 10 in x-direction
   20 solutions
3. $15\sin^2\theta + \sin \theta - 2 = 0$; $19.5°$, $160.5°$, $203.6°$, $336.4°$
4. (a) $(340,0)$ (b) $p = \frac{3}{2}$ $q = 10$

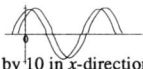

Unit 9: Sequences and Series

1. 4380　　　　　2. (a) 1　(b) 250
3. $N = 38$, $a = 17$
4. (a) $a = 200$, $r = \frac{2}{5}$　(b) $\frac{1000}{3}$　(c) 8.9×10^{-4}

Unit 10: Functions and Numerical Methods

1. (a) $x = 1 \pm \sqrt{6}$　(b) $g(x) \geq 3$
　(c) $fg(x) = \frac{5}{(x^2 + 1)}$;　$0 < fg(x) \leq 5$
　(d) g is many-one ; $g(-1) = g(1)$ etc, so no inverse exists.
2. $a = 2$, $b = -4$　(ii) $[-4, \infty\,[$
　(iii) $f^{-1}(x) = -2 + \sqrt{(x + 4)}$　(iv)

Unit 11: Polynomials and the Factor Theorem

1. (a) Show $f(-3) = 0$　(b) $(x + 3)(2x^2 - x - 5)$
　(c) 1.85, −1.35
2. $x^2 - 2x - 27$; $1 + 2\sqrt{7}$
3. (i) $3a + 2b = -5$　(ii) $a = -\frac{8}{3}$, $b = \frac{3}{2}$ & $a = 1$, $b = -4$
　(iii) −3